S0-BYM-311

is Language

Behavior

is Language

Loving and Living with Individuals on the Spectrum

Carolyn M. Hunsinger

Charleston, SC
www.PalmettoPublishing.com

Behavior is Language

First Edition

Paperback ISBN: 978-1-63837-613-2
eBook ISBN: 978-1-63837-614-9

Table of Contents

Prologue

This manuscript represents my mother's second greatest passion and life's work. I think she would be the first to admit that her greatest passion– and that which, in the end, mattered most– was her work with Hayden. However, I would venture to say that sharing this concept, which she insisted from the beginning should be called *Behavior is Language*, was her second greatest love. She taught it in workshops and seminars, she modeled it in mentoring relationships, she shared it in informal 'gab sessions' and she lived it in every encounter she had with any child she ever encountered, whether 'on the spectrum' or not. I would also venture to say that the living legacy of her work is not only to be found in the person that Hayden has grown to be, but also in all of the numerous children throughout the years who felt validated, 'heard,' supported and loved by their "Grandma Carolyn."

It may be that this manuscript would not be considered commercially viable in its present form by the average publisher. So be it. Some chapters are quite short, some are very long; some seem like an informal conversation between close friends while others are technical almost beyond my comprehension. Stories and anecdotes are woven throughout her teaching in an organic, non-linear narrative that uses remarkable first-hand accounts to illustrate the pillars of my mother's theories. She had her own unique style of writing- and I have chosen to preserve it faithfully for two important reasons.

The first is because I know that she specifically wanted it to be so. In the preface that she wrote, she mentions that both the conversational tone and the non-chronological structure were deliberate on her part. Since this work reflects what I consider to be my mother's great wisdom on the topic I, the posthumous editor, cannot find it in myself to second-guess her choices.

The second reason is, perhaps, more selfish. As I read this manuscript, it is nearly incomprehensible to me that the intelligent, vibrant, passionate author of these words would be gone just two short years after their writing. However, on this topic, the most near and dear to her heart, my mother's voice comes ringing through this narrative so loudly and clearly that it is almost as if she were still here with me in the room. If you are someone who had the opportunity to know her, you may find you have a similar experience. If you did not, by the time you have finished, you will have come as close to knowing her as is possible today. Either way, bringing this manuscript to publication exactly as it was written is a way to hold her close and keep her voice alive.

Especially toward the end, it seemed especially important to my mother that this book be published. While working with Hayden was her great passion, the idea that her key learnings might be lost before they could be passed on was deeply distressing to her. She knew, beyond any shadow of a doubt, that her innovative discoveries and practical applications needed to reach beyond the circle of people she was able to personally touch in her lifetime. While she left us before she could see this dream realized, as her surviving family we have the power to see this project through in her name. *Behavior is Language* is my mother's legacy. May you be blessed by it.

Chelle Hunsinger, 2018

Preface

My grandson, Hayden, is severely autistic. I have been his caretaker for nearly all of his twenty-eight years on this earth, since 1988. Hayden and I began our miraculous journey together through one of the most challenging developmental conditions known to mankind. Now I can say that Hayden truly loves life. But it was far from easy getting there.

Those who have observed the trials and tribulations of our journey have encouraged me to write a book about my views on autism, in particular, how language and behavior figure in to the puzzle that is at the core of this heart-breaking condition. Since I've never written a book before, I've always chuckled at this suggestion. Yet, the idea intrigued me, so I finally decided to give it a go.

The way I work with Hayden is both innovative and effective; it is also respectful of both of us. But the idea of writing about my *methods* felt somehow stilted. So one day, I just sat down and started to write. The result turned out, to my great satisfaction, to be a narrative, a story. It's informal—very much like you and I would converse if we were to sit down for a chat. You would ask me about autism, I would share with you from my heart, soul, and mind on the topic. The narrative is not strictly chronological. Like kids with autism, it has a logic all its own.

Since the premises I work from are so different from the prevailing beliefs about autism, I describe in detail many interactions with Hayden to illustrate the ways he feels, thinks and processes information, and how I use all of this when I work with him.

It's important to note that there was a time when it was assumed that kids with cerebral palsy were as incapacitated in their thought processes and emotional capacities as they were in their physical abilities. But that myth was debunked years ago. As I see it, it's time for the same kind of paradigm shift to occur in our understanding of autism.

Many (perhaps most) individuals with autism are sensitive, intelligent, perceptive, loving human beings—wise beyond their years. Yet, they are imprisoned in bodies that may *appear* normal, but constantly bombard them with frustrating, confusing, inconsistent, unreliable, and conflicting information about themselves and their environment.

Autism also robs some of its victims of the ability to communicate effectively via speech, gestures, and expressions, and also drastically limits their ability to process incoming information in organized, coherent ways.

Moreover, the bodies of those with autism may have internal needs that find fulfillment in behaviors and mannerisms that are considered weird, bizarre, inappropriate, and undesirable by a society that often judges too swiftly, especially when it comes to its developmentally disabled members.

As far as my scholarly credentials go, after graduating from college with a BA in biology with an additional fifth year of education courses, I went on to teach high-school biology and chemistry for four years. My next step was to be graduate school with my eye on a PhD in psychology. But less than a year into my graduate program, I took a leave of absence to care for Hayden. That "leave" has lasted twenty-eight years and counting!

The resources I have drawn upon to write this book are of course all the books on autism I could get my hands on; the assessments and opinions of both traditional physicians and alternative health practitioners; psychotherapists; teachers; community members; trial and error; and an awful lot of prayer, all augmenting my "internship" under Hayden.

So, with no formal degree in autism, but a great degree of understanding and expertise developed along the way, I have been excited to learn that ASD kids do not have to be belligerent, disruptive, or violent, but instead can lead rich, full lives. If this book promotes better understanding and appreciation of autistic children; if it guides parents through the puzzling maze of autism to the beautiful child hidden beneath; if a physician preparing to present a diagnosis of autism to anxious parents can assure them that, first and foremost, their child is a sensitive, intelligent being; if someone, somewhere doing research reads this book and has a vision of a different approach to behavior in autism and children in general, then this book will have accomplished its purpose.

So, I invite you to find a comfortable place to curl up in, a spot where you will be open to looking at autism through the eyes of love, compassion, and wisdom, rather than fear, pity, and objectification. Come with me on an incredible journey: a kinder, gentler journey into autism...

Carolyn Hunsinger, 2016

Part I
Months Six, Nine, Eleven

If I were pressed to pinpoint one specific day on which I knew for certain that there was something amiss with Hayden, I couldn't do it. But I *could* estimate that it was sometime between his six-month and nine-month checkups. It was a very elusive thing, the vague intuition that played hide-and-seek with me for weeks, which finally compelled me to dig out my college text and study the section on child development.

I had already started babysitting for my grandson quite regularly and had been told that developmentally he was *supposedly* right on target. The paperwork from his six-month checkup described him as "normal." And yet, a nagging fear continued to pull at me. And so, in the weeks and months that followed, what started as a small voice in my head became a full-on megaphone reality, as appointments with doctors led to tests, which yielded more evaluations, all of which culminated in **The Conference**.

The result of this nine-month meeting: a diagnosis for Hayden of Pervasive Developmental Disorder (PDD). What in the world was PDD? I never got a definitive answer and

1

now I know why. PDD really stands for "Physicians Didn't Decide."

The insidious fear that had stalked me so stealthily earlier on, now boldly haunted me day-in and day-out. What was it? Fear of the unknown? Of the future? Of a life that felt out of control? All of the above, I concluded.

At the time I took Hayden on, I was a graduate student, doing well and loving it, with the letters 'P', 'h' and 'D' floating around in my head. But caring for a baby was definitely not in my plans. This I felt deeply, despite the fact that so many friends and family members noticed how different Hayden was around me. He seemed more alive and willing to try things, or at least it seemed so for a while.

Not long after, though, at eleven months old, Hayden was diagnosed with Pervasive Regressive Disorder (PRD). I was horrified—he had begun to go backwards. He no longer rolled over or scooted around in his crib; he began to avoid eye contact; and it seemed he refused to hold onto his toys. In fact, he seldom played at all, but instead lay unnaturally still. The only things he excelled at were screaming and just not *being there.*

I talked to Hayden in ways people don't usually talk to babies, especially unresponsive ones. Unaware of it at the time, I had begun to just be *with Hayden. Just there: present, calm, unhurried, devoid of expectations. No demands. No approval. No disapproval. Just lots of intense, unaffected, focused being there. If Hayden screamed, I was with him as he screamed, and acknowledged his screaming, along with his pain, fear, and anger. I fully accepted all of these things as appropriate for him.*

Moreover, if Hayden was just not *there, I was with him in his* not-there-ness *too. My being so present with Hayden was, by almost imperceptibly small increments, laying the foundation for a nearly invisible bridge between* there *and* not there.

2

Over the next several years, this bridge would become solid enough to allow him free access back-and-forth from one to the other, until he became solidly enough rooted in the here that it became where he chose to stay. We never burned that bridge, though. We just moved beyond it. At the time, I had no awareness of what I was doing. I was just being with Hayden, and he was responding positively.

My epiphany at this point came in realizing that although personal contentment would not bestow upon me a doctoral degree, it would surely come with knowing I had done my best for Hayden, even if my best failed in terms of tangible results. I simply could not say "No" to my grandson.

Part II
Eighteen Months

On a September afternoon in 1989, Hayden and I traveled from our small rural town—in the shadow of Mount Rainier—to Children's Hospital in Seattle. Hayden, eighteen months old at the time, lay screaming on the floor of Dr. Alvin's office. He had begun to scream when I laid him on the examining table to undress him; he was still screaming when Dr. Alvin entered to examine him. The doctor looked at Hayden, then at me.

"How do you expect me to examine him when he's screaming like that?"

Aghast, I wondered exactly how he had become a pediatric neurologist when he was unable, or unwilling, to examine a screaming child. I was never able to answer this puzzling question.

What I did know was that he must not have figured out how to properly examine my screaming grandchild. Dr. Alvin went through the motions in a perfunctory way at best, after which he made a hasty retreat back to the safety behind his desk. As he charted his notes, I dressed my still-screaming grandchild, laid him on the floor, and took a seat across the desk to hear the doctor's assessment of Hayden's progress. I was dumbfounded to hear that the doctor thought there had been none.

5

"Keep him in early intervention. His conference will be in a week and they will review his case in three years."

I asked, incredulous, my mind spinning with this news, "What can I do?"

"There is nothing you can do."

I thought to myself, "Wait a minute...there's been no real exam, just a few brief moments in a cold, sterile environment. How could he say there had been no progress? He knew nothing of Hayden. All he had witnessed was the screaming."

It's true. Hayden screamed a lot back then. By the time of the meeting with Dr. Alvin, I had been told on numerous occasions that children like Hayden scream for no reason whatsoever. Despite this, I had become aware, in a fleeting kind of way, that there was something else to the screaming. I asked myself, "What child simply wails for no reason?"

There is no question that Hayden's incessant screaming was difficult for me: it was loud, for one, and terribly piercing. Worst of all, it seemed to emanate from the deepest reaches of an inconsolable soul; the terror in it was palpable.

I had heard lots of babies cry. Was Hayden's scream really so different from the cry of all infants? It seemed so at the time because it made me feel particularly helpless. Perhaps I was hearing in it the universal terror imprinted on every person who walks this earth, the unspeakable fear that makes us doubt that we are loved or loveable. Is this what so unnerved Dr. Alvin?

I believe, in fact, that we all experience this terror throughout our lives when the question of our lovability periodically bubbles up to the surface of our consciousness. We feel terror because we fear the answer will be, "No."

Hayden was still on the floor, in full scream mode, when I sat across the desk from Dr. Alvin. It now appeared that there was not a stitch of compassion for either of us in the doctor's demeanor. And to my amazement, he was also incapable of making eye contact with either of us. He said nothing positive or encouraging, nothing different from nine months ago. I wondered why I was wasting our time with him. Rising, Dr. Alvin looked at my still-screaming grandchild.

"I hope he wouldn't carry on like that all the way home. Haven't you come a long way?"

"We have come a long way, yes, but I don't expect him to scream all the way home. I would like a room where we can be alone and I can settle him down."

"What will you do?"

"I will just help him quiet down."

"Yes, but what will you do?" Dr. Alvin didn't understand. It wasn't a matter of doing something to Hayden, but rather, just being with him in his terror. The doctor said that he would find us a room.

"But first," I said, "I have some questions." In return, he shot me that now-familiar look that says that he was supposed to ask the questions around here. He relented, though, and sat down to listen.

"Hayden has a lot of autistic behaviors..." I began.

I never even got to my questions because Dr. Alvin cut me off immediately.

"Of course. He's autistic," he pronounced.

Dr. Alvin quickly left the room, and I tried to parse what had just happened. I already knew it was autism, so why did his saying the word affect me so? Was it "doctor authority?" Or the ever-present stigma of autism? Or maybe the way he said it? Perhaps it was some of all of these.

My heart had begun to feel heavy with despair when the doctor suddenly returned and briskly announced that he had a room for us. I picked up my toddler—who couldn't sit up by himself yet, let alone toddle—and simply laid him on the floor in the near-empty room. Thankfully, as soon as the doctor left us, so did my feelings of hopelessness and helplessness.

When we were completely alone, I began to talk to Hayden as I stripped him down to his diaper. In no time, his anxiety began to melt away too. The doctor peeked in and saw a quiet, content Hayden.

"Why do you have his clothes off?" The moment Hayden heard Dr. Alvin's voice again, though, his screaming re-commenced.

"Because it's calming for him."

"Well, I don't know what that has to do with it."

I didn't know either. Not then, at least. I just knew by experience that it was true, through the months when he calmed down as soon as I stripped him naked to bathe, change, or clothe him. I also remember distinctly that when Hayden was alone with me in the car, after the harrowing encounter with Dr. Alvin, he didn't make another sound—didn't cry for an instant—all the way home.

AUTISM. Hayden was autistic. My grandson was autistic. The words ricocheted around in my head like bullets in an old Western movie. When I dwelled on it, I felt separate from Hayden. He became a weird, scary, unknown monster, this autistic child. But when I was with him, he was just Hayden, my grandson Hayden, the same lovable little person he had been all along.

As I stood beside his crib that night—the night that followed the harrowing day with Dr. Alvin—and watched Hayden sleep, he looked like any other slumbering toddler. Yet, this beatific scene stood in sharp contrast to another picture of Hayden that was just as real—the propped-up child (he could not sit on his own yet), who made no eye contact, who flapped his hands incessantly, who made—at unpredictable intervals—piercing, other-worldly, sounds.

Part III
The Journey Begins

Chapter 1

Conversations with GOD

It is important to note that though I refer to "GOD"—more in the beginning of this book and less and less as the work progresses—this is not a religious tome. It is, however, a spiritual one. I "speak" to GOD when I'm really stumped about Hayden and what to do for and about him, when I can't seem to get anywhere because of my personal dearth of knowledge about autism, or when the world at large seems clueless about ASD. I could just as easily describe my process of 'learning Hayden' as one in which, especially in the beginning, I often consulted spirit, my inner-most self, my guide within, etc.

But it just so happens that I believe I was given spiritual direction in determining my role in life: to be Hayden's caregiver. Oddly, however, I have not always been properly equipped for the task at hand! On those occasions, I have demanded help from my "boss," GOD:

"You gave me this job, and I've wracked my brain on how to resolve this particular quandary. It's time you help me!"

When I'm at wit's end, I ask such questions in my mind, and most often the answers are delivered to my mind. Often, they come from an internal voice other than my own; sometimes they come as garden-variety epiphanies, as 'ah-ha!' ideas of my own. On rare occasions, I hear a powerful voice within or without.

All I can say is that there are times when it is quite clear that the answers I seek to the questions I ask do not have any part of me as their source, regardless of whether they come to me from within or without. I do not believe, however, that this spiritual element undermines the rational nature of the work I have presented here. Everything makes sense, as you will see, once the groundwork is laid.

As Hayden slept peacefully, I wrestled with my GOD. The plan I had settled on for my life did not include an autistic grandchild, let alone a life of caring for one. I reviewed my plan with my Maker: graduate school followed by a psychotherapy practice. A life of helping other people. And of course, there was the rest of the picture: financial security, weekends off, white wall-to-wall carpet, woolen suits with silk blouses and stylish spiked heels.

GOD was not impressed.

But then, neither was I. As I stood there and watched my stricken angel of a grandchild, I was certain that I could do a far better job running the universe than GOD. In my universe, I would simply not let bad things ever happen to little kids. Period. But in GOD's world, at that very moment, feelings of helplessness, hopelessness and dejectedness welled up in me and coalesced into streams of hot, angry tears that ran down my cheeks, soaking my robe. My grandson was autistic and I could do nothing about it. My greatly anticipated entrance to graduate school now drifted far away into the distant future. And GOD didn't seem to give a hoot! If anything, he seemed to turn a blind eye.

Several anguished hours later, when my tears were spent and my body exhausted, my pity party was, nonetheless, still in full swing. I decided it was time for another conversation with GOD.

"I would make a miracle for Hayden if I could, but I can't," I reasoned. "You could make a miracle for Hayden if you would, but you won't!"

His response was nothing short of life-changing. My world stopped as his booming voice echoed throughout my soul in words that thundered inside me with absolute clarity:

"You think if I zapped Hayden and made him better, it would be a miracle? But I'm God! I can do anything! So that wouldn't be a miracle. The miracle would be if you, who are self-centered, unloving, impatient and full of doubt and fear, move beyond yourself and love when there's no guarantee that love will be returned; when you can work until you're exhausted and keep on working anyway; when you are patient even when you no longer feel patient; when you hold on to your faith when everyone else says there is no hope. Now that would be a miracle. And if Hayden responds, well, that would be a second miracle."

And so, by day's end it became clear that my journey with Hayden was well underway and largely fueled by my sheer stubbornness and will power. That night in Hayden's room I accepted responsibility for my part of the journey–to love and care for him to the best of my ability and to have faith. Ultimately I knew I had no control over how Hayden would respond to my actions, so in a sense, this story is my story, because his journey is my journey. Perhaps someday Hayden will write his own story. Now that would be the third miracle...

Once Hayden's autism was outwardly acknowledged and discussed, I was told that I could not keep up the daily schedule I had implemented for him for even two months without experiencing burnout. Yet, I had already been doing it for a good deal longer than a few months. I believe that my decision to work with Hayden because it was the right thing for me to do regardless of what befell him, took the focus off of whatever progress Hayden did or did not make.

Don't misunderstand. I certainly wished for Hayden to progress, so much so that sometimes my desire for this struck very deep. My heart ached when I compared Hayden to my other grandchildren, grand-niece, and grand-nephew. While I rejoiced in the many accomplishments and the steady normal development of these other little people in my life, I was moved to acknowledge the pangs of jealousy and regret I felt on Hayden's behalf. I could not help but compare. I could not help but notice the discrepancies. It was inevitable that I would feel the pain that came with musing, "What would Hayden be doing if..."

It was as if I had raw, open ulcers on my emotional feet that were incapable of healing unless I continued my Hayden-journey. Every milestone that passed Hayden by, every accomplishment of every normal child I observed—these rubbed raw on my journeying feet. The only way to lessen the pain was to stop trying, stop searching, to end the journey. But I could not, and still to this day cannot.

During Christmastime at the start of the new millennium, I bought a CD featuring Billy Gillman, an exceptional 12-year-old. The CD is both lovely and painful. My then-12-year-old Hayden did not talk; the 12-year-old Billy was able to sing with great beauty, skill, and accomplishment. My 12-year-old could not button his own shirt; this 12-year-old buttoned up a recording contract. Yes, of course it hurt. Pain is a part of life that mostly tells one about oneself. My responsibility was not to avoid pain, but to do everything I could to facilitate improvements in Hayden's skills and capabilities, while being as detached as possible to whether or not they actually did improve.

Had I set myself a task too great to accomplish, indeed, perhaps impossible? Often I was so perplexed, busy, and exhausted that I would mistakenly try to focus on the progress made, just to get some immediate gratification. But progress? With Hayden that has never been—especially in the beginning—an easy thing to grasp. I have always seen it as a slightly shifting goal to simply move towards, like a guiding *constellation on a journey at sea. The stars present themselves in different positions in the sky as the seasons, and one's position on the globe, change. Knowing this, an experienced sailor can always rely on them to dead reckon his course.*

Likewise, with Hayden, we plan as we go, and there isn't a treasure at the end of our path that we're after. It is the path itself that's important. Without fail, every time I think of our life-trek in this way, I experience a success, big or small, with Hayden.

* * *

Before going on a trip, we plan, organize, and prepare. We study maps, decide on routes, figure out the expenses, then create a budget, work up an itinerary, and pack accordingly. And, of course, we have a destination in mind. This journey into autism, however, began with no preparation, no guidebooks, no maps, no supplies, and no destination. The way is often challenging and lonely, there's rarely any respite, obstacles loom around so many corners, and expenses add up exponentially.

Initially, I thought there would be plenty of "white coats," stethoscopes confidently slung around their necks, to consult with, to guide me. But for the vast majority of doctors, their journey into autism consists of only a brief description in a medical text. And since autism can't be heard with a stethoscope, eased by an injection, or corrected with surgery, their journey often leads to a dead end. I learned this one week after Hayden's 18-month conference at Children's Hospital.

All the team members who had evaluated him met with me to discuss their findings, which were as follows: Hayden's social, verbal, intellectual, and gross and fine motor skills were significantly delayed; in addition, he was quite hard of hearing. And he was autistic. Autism is a biochemical brain disorder and there is no cure or treatment. He should continue in early intervention in the school district.

But where was I in all of this? One sentence seemed to satisfy everyone at the conference, save me:

"Carolyn, you must get on with your life."

I felt irreconcilably depressed after this meeting. I knew about the delays (I had lived with them), but the assessment of hearing impairment caught me off-guard. I couldn't accept it because I hadn't experienced it, so I said as much. To this I was told that I wasn't aware that Hayden had any difficulty hearing because I was "too close." When I said that he had no difficulty hearing what he wanted to hear, I was told I was not facing reality. But the reality, as I perceived it, was that Hayden just didn't give a rip about the little beeps in their audiology tests; he was quite adept at tuning out that to which he did not want to pay attention.

Nor did I accept what they had said about his so-called limitations. Someone at that conference said to me,

"You need to understand that these children don't progress much from where they are the day they are diagnosed with autism."

These words became indelibly etched in my mind, and I then realized that the doctors at this conference—the medical pundits whom I had hoped would guide me—were useless. I could not walk down the dead-end path they described to me, despite the fact that at the time Hayden could not yet sit up; we were still, in fact, working on rolling over.

I turned away from these evaluations and started looking for other resources. The books on autism from the library? I ditched them too, because they said even more things I couldn't accept: children with autism have no feelings and cry for no reason, for instance. I knew Hayden had intense feelings and although I often didn't know why he cried, I knew there had to be a reason for him doing so.

For example, it seemed obvious to me that baby animals, with which I had had a lot of experience as a child, cry and fuss when they want something. Why would it be any different for a human baby? It seemed clear to me that when Hayden kicked, arched, and threw his head back, and even bit at things, he was expressing anger.

Soon after receiving the frustrating results of the 18-month conference, an RN friend called and said she had read up on autism. But her take was also that there was nothing to be done for it. She insisted that I needed to accept this and "let those destined for institutions live in institutions." She told me, further, that I needed to do something useful with my life.

In my utter frustration, feeling lonely and unsupported, I was so pleased and, yes, relieved, when I discovered the Autism Society. Without much ado, I put in an excited call to the Washington State chapter president and we had a chat. When she asked me if my grandson was violent, I replied, "No," to which she responded, "Well, he will be." When I said I didn't expect him to be violent, she said, simply, "They all are. HE WILL BE VIOLENT!"

Incredulous, I quickly dismissed what seemed like yet more misinformation that led to another dead end. How solitary I had become through all of this. The doctor and his team, the books, my nurse friend, and the Autism Society—all collectively seemed like my only resources. But what they had to say weighed me down, sunk me in a quagmire of negativity. If these were truly my only resources and I had no faith in them whatsoever, where did that leave me in my quest to understand autism and help my grandson? Alone, is where it left me, and ripe for another conversation with GOD.

"I know nothing about autism, except that I cannot accept what everyone is telling me. So it is just me, and you are going to have to help me. It's just me and you on this one God. Just me and you."

17

My husband (Denny), my therapist, and Hayden's dad were the only people who fully supported me, at least in word, at the beginning of my journey. Yet, even with this I felt alone. It was a very isolated, difficult time for me, especially since it all entailed taking a leave of absence from graduate school. My path was clearly to work with Hayden, and as I saw it, that meant a strict and demanding schedule that started at 6:00 am and ended at 9:00 pm, seven days a week.

The only breaks in this breakneck schedule were my therapy appointments. There was just so much we had to accomplish. But this left me with no free time whatsoever: no social life, no time even for housekeeping. Moreover, there were no stretches during which I could just rest and have someone else take my place working with Hayden.

Today, I feel ashamed about all my whining and complaints of the early days with Hayden, because I have learned things that are not taught in any graduate school program, and I have met many wonderful people. I've also had so many fascinating experiences as well as astonishing spiritual growth. And now I have come to see something truly amazing—that Hayden has been more of a teacher to me than I have been to him.

Throughout our journey, yes, there were countless days filled with the ordinary: diapers, bottles, laundry, meals and bills. Such is life in general for someone caring for a young child. But there was so much more with Hayden, so that I eventually became accustomed to my own new normal. This included dealing with doctors, physical therapists, early intervention programs, and the daily home therapy program I had created for Hayden. None of this latter activity would count as ordinary in any way for a person raising a normal child.

Moreover, there were the memorable days, the days of his firsts: the day when Hayden first held onto a block; first crawled across the room at three years old; the day he took his first step alone at four; when he first climbed into the bathtub "by self," after we had worked on the sequence of steps involved for over two years; the first day of kindergarten in a regular class, with assistance. When Hayden was 11, Poppa (his grandpa, Denny) told him he had brought him a present. Hayden's eyes lit up and he said what sounded very much like "Open!" Another miraculous first—a spoken word!

There were memorable days for me personally as well, spiritually memorable. One in particular comes to mind. I recall crying in frustration at the time because I felt tired, overwhelmed, and depleted, with nothing left to give. It was early morning and I had just gotten up:

"How am I going to make it through this day? GOD, why am I so tired?" I moaned in desperation. I heard a voice behind me, a real voice, not a voice in my mind or my mind's eye, not a voice in a dream. I am certain I was awake.

"You're tired because you're trying to do my job!" it explained. I looked around high and low, but was unable to detect an earthly source for this exclamation.

"What do you mean, trying to do your job?" I addressed this mysterious out-loud voice.

"Well," said the voice, "you're wearing yourself out trying to love Hayden. And you can't. You're so limited. Your job is to be loved. Just be loved, and as my love flows through you, it will be there for Hayden. You don't have to try so hard!"

"But I don't know anything about autism. I'm not a special education teacher. He needs someone who knows what they're doing!"

"He just needs to be loved. That's all," came the voice.

On yet another occasion, I was on my way home late at night with Hayden, after he had received two days of body work in Victoria, British Columbia. We had a 3.5-hour drive before us, plus a 1.5-hour ferry ride, and we were both already completely wrung out. Hayden's response to the situation was to scream uncontrollably. And my response to Hayden's response was, I'm sorry to say, to totally lose it. I yelled at him to be quiet, but he only continued to scream. I felt like I was about to explode!

"Get out of the car," said the unearthly voice.

I obeyed and pulled over, somewhere on Highway 101, somewhere near midnight. I opened my door, got out, locked it behind me, then walked a few feet away and screamed at the top of my lungs.

"Oh, God, I hate him."

The voice was right there with me and said, "Wow, you sure are mad! But I love you." This instantly melted me.

Nevertheless, I was still confused, so responded,

"Me? What? I still don't know what to do! The screaming is so hard to take, so frustrating, so rattling and disturbing."

"Get back in the car and show Hayden the same kind of love when he's being difficult that I show you when you're difficult," came the directive.

Much subdued, I got back in the car. Hayden was still screaming. I drove until I came to a safe place to pull over again, but this time, I climbed into the back seat and apologized to him. I held him close in my arms until he fell asleep...

The lessons I learned in all of these situations so many years ago I have put to use every day since, and will until the day I die, I'm sure.

Chapter 2

Pacing: The Peek and the Mosey

Even though Hayden had made eye contact as an infant, by the time he was close to a year old it was something he actively avoided. This phenomenon is well-documented by those in the know about autism. Although it is considered a significant issue, at the time I could find no information on how to encourage or initiate eye contact. But I knew I needed to, because it was of paramount importance to have eye contact as a starting point for all other kinds of interaction. I also knew, though, that it would not come if forced.

One day I decided to work on this. I laid Haden on the floor, on his back, in his oversized, cotton training pants. Whenever we set out to work on something like this, I made sure Hayden was dressed in cotton, or some other natural fabric such as Huggies, never plastic. Somehow, he always does best in natural fabrics, which I learned early on. I got on my hands and knees over him, moved my head over his, and attempted to catch his eyes, while he turned his head to avoid me. We went back-and-forth, back-and-forth a number of times. When our eyes fleetingly caught, I said in a playful voice, "Peek!" and the volleying continued until I said it again, "Peek!"

The fascinating thing was that once I had elicited three peeks, a subtle, but definite change came over him. He

21

somehow became present, whereas he had not been before. He didn't become receptive to more peeks at that time, however. He just could not fully relate to what was going on yet. He was there, but in a non-engaged way. Nor did more peeks come from him at that time, to covert his mere there-ness to actual presence. As soon as I moved a few feet away from him, he was gone again.

I found out by trial and error that the only way I could get peeks from Hayden again, after I had used up the magic three that he had responded to, was if something occurred that he didn't like. There were a few things on top of that list: my moving away from him spatially, loud noises, bright lights, and getting bumped. Unless he was very stressed and screaming in total overload, I could bring him out with three peeks.

We did lots of peeks in those days, when Hayden was about 18 months old. After a while, he began to smile when we peeked and he was more than just there–he had begun to relate to me, had become engaged. Eventually I could ask for a peek and get it with a smile (did Hayden smile or you here?). Then it became a game for him. I would get him out of his crib, lay him down on the floor and say,

"In a minute I'm going to get a peek from you."

He would laugh and look away and I would start the back-and-forth movement; then he would purposely catch my eye, and laugh. I'd say, "Peek," then I would say, "I got a peek, and in a minute I'm going to get another peek," and get peeks two and three. That's when I knew he was clearly there, present, relating, fully engaged.

Finally, the time came when Hayden really wanted to sustain eye contact. I wanted him to really, really want it and I also wanted a peek to remain totally consistent and safe. Even when he was 18, if he was holding on to any anger, I might say,

"In a minute I'm going to get a peek from you."

He would laugh, avert his eyes momentarily and then search out eye contact.

One morning, when it seemed time to attempt sustained eye contact, after we had done our peeks and were engaged with one another, I said,

"Today we'll do something new. We'll do a "look" instead of a peek." By this time I was almost always breaking the peeks, so I said:

"I'm going to get a look."

I was on hands and knees over him, going back-and-forth to follow his turning head. Then he joined in and we made eye contact.

"Look!" I said, and we held it momentarily before breaking.

He could have held it longer, but I wanted him on the offense, not the defense. A peek was and is, always the same: short eye contact. A look started out as a brief thing, but soon became longer and longer, until I began to get some pretty good eye contact, even without the lead-in peek game.

Eventually, Hayden initiated eye contact with other people familiar to him. The length of his periods of eye contact and the number of people with whom he makes it have gradually increased over the years, and continue to do so. Every once in a while, I am delighted to hear from someone,

"Hayden gave me really good eye contact with me today and he never has before."

It was during the early days of the peek that I learned an important lesson at Hayden's expense. At this time, he readily gave me peeks in response to, "In a minute I'm going to get a peek!" I would engage in our little game during his early morning bottle. By the end of the bottle, he was really present and ready to relate.

One morning I decided that things were moving too slowly (for me) and I asked myself why I was wasting the majority of bottle time just getting eye contact. I thought to myself, "If

I simply held his head still *in order to achieve eye contact quickly, we could then devote all of his bottle time to relating– right?" But when I tried it, he screamed bloody murder!*

Immediately, I released his head and began to search for the problem. I didn't happen to have a mirror handy just then, but if I had, a quick look at my own reflection would have given me my answer. But I wouldn't learn this the easy way!

So I remained blind to the cause of the awful screams, and after I soothed Hayden and got him back to the bottle, I returned to my agenda and told him I wanted a peek. And then I did it again. I held his head to catch his eye. Again, a blood-curdling scream emanated from Hayden, and the saying, Second verse, same as the first, *flashed through my mind.*

I would like to be able to say I caught on after the second time around. But I didn't. Instead, I tried again. But with the third terror-filled scream came the awful sinking awareness that I was the problem: my impatience, my agenda, my need to control were all terribly off course. I soothed Hayden once again, and also this time apologized to him. I promised I would respect his journey, his time frame, and his right to be in control of his own body.

Eventually, on my own earlier journey through life (which I now understand was for me a state of extreme spiritual poverty), I began to learn the importance of a slower pace, a relaxed "mosey," which became my model with Hayden because it seemed to suit him the best. In fact, throughout our autism journey together, Hayden has become my continuing education teacher in this all important issue of pacing, as well as in countless other areas. For example, long ago, we passed over each and every age for all the typical developmental milestones—in the life of a "normal" infant, toddler, school- age child, and so on—and we saw that Hayden pretty much out-and-out failed at each of the developmental deadlines!! At that time, Hayden's educators were constantly telling me the many things he needed to achieve and at what age he needed to achieve them.

I believe these educators were well-meaning and most of their goals for Hayden were correct: he needed to eat solid food, to be in preschool without me, to quit sucking his thumb, and so on. He needed to accomplish these things, yes, just as he needed to learn to make eye contact. But the critical thing I learned was that each of these things needed to happen in his time, on *his* terms, at *his* pace, within the parameters of what his nervous system could handle. We just needed to mosey along together and sooner or later he would make it.

At four Hayden began to tolerate textured foods. During his second year in third grade, he was capable of getting through a full day at school without me and without incident. At 18, he still sucked his thumb, and we are still moseying along on that one, though this behavior is slowly dropping out of his repertoire, at his pace. When he was younger, though, I was adamant that he be allowed unrestricted thumb sucking, because it was clearly something that soothed him, brought him comfort.

It is fascinating to me that this seems to be a problem for some people. Yes, I could have stopped it. My question was and always has been: But why? Does it hurt anyone? No. But it certainly breaks many peoples' rules about the proper place for a young man's thumb! I have come to see that this is not Hayden's problem nor mine, so now, it worries me not. It is true that at one time, I wondered if thumb sucking put Hayden at risk in a physical way. But no physician or dentist has ever said there's the risk of such a problem for Hayden.

Some people think that thumb-sucking is a social issue, but Hayden had many friends at school. One boy from his regular second-grade class summed it up quite well for me on the playground one day, as I pushed Hayden on the swing.

"Everyone likes Hayden."

Back then, teachers told me that new students would look rather questioningly at Hayden at first, but would soon become friends. The kids knew he was different and had been told that he had autism. They noticed that he drooled, stuck out his tongue (and even at times, got it all the way into his nose, to their sheer delight!), sucked his thumb, sometimes didn't respond to them, and needed an adult to help him in the bathroom. Still, they included him in every way they could.

One day, when I had taken the role of Hayden's half-day, third-grade teacher, I observed something in gym class that so warmed my heart. Hayden's schoolmates figured out a way to accommodate him all on their own by modifying a kickball rule. When it was his turn and he executed a good kick, he was expected, just like everyone else, to round the bases. But he was permitted to do this at his own pace. Further, he could not be struck with the ball and called "out" in his transit. Young children often have the capacity to really "get it" and be inclusive when left to their own devices.

With adults, well, it can be another story. I have discovered that adults pretty much "follow the leader"—they react negatively when others around them do so. When Hayden was five, say, I could get by quite easily taking him into the women's room. But I worried about the future, when he would be older and I still had to accompany him into public restrooms. As yet, though, no one has said anything to me, nor have I been given that "put down" look that I've anticipated with such anxiety. I am matter-of-fact and I keep Hayden close. I'm friendly and generous with eye contact to those waiting in line and I have never felt unwelcome. It is true, I have seen 'tween girls point and whisper, but that's just the nature of 'tween girls, isn't it?

You might think that kids would make fun of Hayden because of his appearance and behavior, particularly, his thumb-sucking. He's been called a "baby" for this only one time that I am aware of. On that occasion, he became very quiet, somber, and withdrawn because of the mocking tone of the accuser, and since I had heard it, I knew why. After the incident, I sat down beside him.

"Are you mad?"

He clapped vigorously (which means, Yes!).

"Are you mad about being called a baby because you sucked your thumb?"

He replied by putting his thumb in his mouth and wiggling his pinky finger (which also means, Yes!).

He had definitely experienced that put-down feeling. But he survived because of how I dealt with the situation with a validating technique that I have used with him and other children for years. It is explained in the next chapter.

Chapter 3

The 'Mad, Sad, and I Love You' Songs

A truly stunning breakthrough came one night on a long trip home from a one of my weekly doctor's appointments; Hayden was somewhere between 18 months and two years old. I took Hayden along with me because I had no one to keep an eye on him at home. It was a long ordeal: three hours total driving time there and back, plus the hour-long appointment, plus Hayden's nearly non-stop screaming on the return trip. I tried everything: toys, music, frequent snack breaks, all to no avail. It seemed he was in overload and I just needed to get him home as quickly as possible.

This particular night we had just barely begun our trip home when I heard noises of disgruntlement from the back of the car—"eh, eh, eh"—which always signaled the beginning of screaming episode. I was bone tired, at the end of my rope, and had no patience left for anything or anyone; I knew I was not capable of coping with Hayden's nerve-wracking screams for the next hour-and-a-half.

"I'm sorry, but I cannot handle his screaming for the whole trip home. I just cannot," I told GOD.

As I glanced at Hayden in the back seat via my "Hayden mirror" (which I had fastened to the passenger seat visor and

29

adjusted so that I could easily see what he was up to in the back car seat), these words just came out of my mouth,

"Hayden, are you mad at the car seat?"

His smile was slight, but there was no mistaking that it was a smile. Words continued to pour from my mouth,

"Are you mad because it's too boring to sit in a car seat for so long?"

To my surprise, he started laughing.

"Car seat, you are very, very boring and I am mad at you," I continued.

Then Hayden laughed heartily. And miraculously, there was no more screaming!

This was the spontaneous beginning of a strategy of verbally validating the feelings he had when he was called names, had to be constrained by inanimate objects, was made fun of, etc.

I also started singing what I dubbed, the 'Mad Song.' I sang one to Hayden, in private, at the boy who called him a baby for sucking his thumb. There is a variation of the 'Mad Song' for anything that maddens Hayden. Here's an example of one I still use when Hayden is mad at having to come in from the rain. It is sung—approximately—to the tune of 'The Farmer in the Dell':

You are mad at me. You are mad at me.
I made you come in and you wanted to stay out longer, and play in the rain,
And you are mad at me.
You are mad at me.
You are mad at me.
It feels like if I really loved you,
I would let you do whatever you want and I didn't.
So you got mad.
And you are mad at me.

I love you. I love you.
When you are mad because I won't let you play in the rain, I love you.

Then we moved on to deal with the sadness he often feels after the sting of anger, by singing the 'Sad Song' together (I leave the lyrics to the reader's imagination).

After singing the 'Mad and Sad Songs', I asked Hayden if he was a baby like baby Zayne, his step-brother.

"Look at how big you are! You're not a baby! You're getting to be a big boy. Lots of babies do suck their thumbs, but sucking your thumb doesn't make you a baby. It just makes you an 11-year-old kid who sucks his thumb.

"Most 11-year-olds do not suck their thumbs, but most 11-year-olds do not have autism, which makes your mouth feel yucky. Nor do most 11-year-olds have bodies that are hard to be inside of, like you do. If you need to and want to suck your thumb, you are free to do it. It does not make you a baby.

"I'm sorry for the boy who called you a baby, because I can tell he is very sad inside and feels bad about himself. Otherwise, he wouldn't need to make fun of someone else."

Hayden was content and the thumb came out. He no longer needed it at that moment and he went off to play.

This brings me to my last series of questions regarding thumb sucking. Does it comfort him? Yes! Does it center him? Yes! Does it give him security when his topsy-turvy autistic body betrays him? Yes! On any given day, I would choose a well-behaved 27-year-old who sucks his thumb over a stressed-out 27-year-old who doesn't suck his thumb but acts out in some other way.

When children learn that their feelings can be accepted, and they can be loved and provoke anger at the same time without losing that love, they can then learn how their own behavior might be maddening. And they can then move on to closure because they have been assured of this unconditional love. Thus an example of the 'Mad Song,' sung by me, but this time directed at Hayden:

I am mad at you, I am mad at you,
You got the ketchup out of the refrigerator without asking.
And I am mad at you.
I love you, I love you.
When I am sad or mad or glad,
I love you.

* * *

When Hayden was still a wee one, he awoke from naps screaming. This had become part of his modus operandi. But on my way into his room, I heard the following words very clearly in my mind:

"Hayden needs to learn to reach for you when he's mad." So, I reflected, this is not something that Hayden can just mosey along on. It's a survival skill that he must learn now.

"Okay, then," I had learned to listen with wonder, "Do as directed!"

The post-nap pattern up to that day had been for Hayden to wake up and scream, but not reach for me, and I would then struggle to get him up. But not on this day. When he saw me, the intensity of his screaming diminished considerably. I kissed him and told him I knew he wanted to be picked up and I would pick him up when he reached for me, but he would have to do that first. I reached toward him, but didn't pick him up. Instead, I waited for him to reach back.

But he drew back and screamed even more!

That was the first of many instances of my reaching and his screaming that day. I was with him, sitting by his crib, talking to him, caring for his physical needs, and waiting for *him to reach for me. Sometimes, his chubby little arms would rise up a bit, his tiny hands clenched, his arms waving. But then, he would not fully reach up, would not complete the act of reaching for me.*

I simply persevered and stayed calm, even engaged in some self-soothing of my own. I told him I loved him and I would be there for him, but I couldn't help him if he wouldn't help himself.

"Hayden, I can't do it all. You have to help." I said this over and over again that day, but after listening to me, he resumed a terror-filled scream, one that seemed to come from a far-away place within him that I couldn't reach—the autistic place.

Then, I crossed the room for some reason and glanced back at him. I couldn't believe my eyes because his eyes were following me around the room! So he was not, after all, in that "non-relating" autistic place, because in that place, his eyes do not track at all.

Hayden, I realized, was actually "faking it" when he wouldn't reach out for me! Then I thought that no, he can't do that, he can't fake things. He doesn't have that level of self-awareness. So I walked all around the room again, and he continued to follow me with his eyes. I ran to the phone and called a friend versed in the ways of autistic children.

"Is it is possible for a 20-month-old child to fake an autistic state?"

"Why do you ask?" After I explained what had just happened, my friend said,

"Well, it looks like it is, doesn't it?"

Chapter 4

Wants versus Needs

My heart went out to Hayden and I so wanted to comfort him during these learning episodes. I wanted to hold him, to take away the terror that had gripped him. Everything in me wanted to, but I just knew that there were times, like this should not. Hayden couldn't help me unless he helped himself. I knew we had to stay there, in his room, in the here-and-now, until he reached out, no matter how long it took.

Hayden's dad, followed by his granddad, poked their heads into the room to find out what all the screaming was about.

"How long are you going to let him scream?"

"Until he reaches for me," I responded with confidence.

This scenario repeated itself several times that week. But then, suddenly, it changed. After I entered his room to get him, even if he was screaming uncontrollably, he would reach for me, I would pick him up, and the screaming would stop.

This of course was a major breakthrough for both Hayden and me. It marked the first time I realized that my primary responsibility was not to make Hayden happy, but instead, to meet his needs.

When my daughter was little, I desperately tried to make her happy. I wanted this so badly for her. She was ecstatic when I gave her something she desired. But soon after, she wanted something else. I didn't understand that I couldn't make her happy. Nor did I understand that my intense desire

35

to make her happy was part of a hidden rule I believed in: I will do everything I can do in order to make you happy, and then you will make me happy.

Once Hayden came along, I began to see the error of my ways with my daughter. Children's happiness comes when their needs are met. It cannot be handed to them via some toy. These needs include the right to have their own feelings and physical needs; the right to make their own choices, within reason; and the right to have and express their own feelings and ideas. Children do not need to be responsible for their mom or dad's happiness, unhappiness, or any other state of mind, for that matter. When the needs of children are met, their happiness will come, just as surely as the sun appears at dawn.

My job with Hayden was, and still is, to sort out his wants from his needs. He didn't want to reach for me, but he needed to—for himself. He never wanted to do his daily neuro-developmental work. Sometimes I didn't either! But he needed to. So we did it, and I have never accepted guilt for making him do what he doesn't want to do if he needs to do it. However, I do accept Hayden's anger at me for making him do it.

Generally, I would say that Hayden is now a happy camper. If he is not on some occasion, I know that either his wants or his needs are not being met, and it is my job to figure out the exact cause of his discomfort. It may be a need to have some wants met, but this is certainly not true of all wants. It is a need to have all needs met even though I cannot meet all of Hayden's needs. Because of his autism, he needs nearly constant supervision. Because of his age–27 at the time of this writing–he, developmentally, needs independence. So I acknowledge verbally that it must be boring to always have Grandma or some other adult around, and he laughs and claps, YES!

Hayden was three when he discovered the handles on my chest-of-drawers. He could flap them with the backs of his fingers to make a maddening, clanky sound. He absolutely loved doing this, over and over, again and again–ad infinitum, ad infuriatum! It was a little thing, but it bugged me in a big way. One day, I had just had it with the flapping handles.

"Hayden, stop!" But the voice in my head said, "Why? Why can't he flap the handles? Does it hurt anything?"

For several days, every time Hayden flapped those handles, I grit my teeth and prayed for the grace to keep from yelling at him. Amazingly, it wasn't long before he could handle-flap all day and it didn't bother me a bit.

How often do we parents act out of our own needs or wants and not our child's? Probably way too often, but I'm improving every day. So can you.

* * *

When we're on a journey, we hate detours and being lost, for the journey is only a means to reach a destination. My journey into autism, however, started out as a detour from my life, and since then, there have been many detours and I've been lost so often that I finally understand that this is simply the nature of my life.

I believe it's a myth of our culture that life is about reaching a certain destination. Carlos Castaneda, the sophisticated university student who was taught by the unsophisticated but wise Native American, Don Juan, in *Journey into Ixtlan*,[1] tells us that we must journey to Ixtlan. But Ixtlan isn't real. In Buddhist thought, if we find the Buddha, we are to kill him. This is because the real Buddha is not to be found. Further, Yahweh told Moses, "I am", not, "I will be." And

---

1. Castaneda, Carlos. *Journey to Ixtlan: The Lessons of Don Juan.* , 1972. Print.

Jesus said, "My peace I give," not "I will give." This journey into autism is my life on this day, at this moment. To be fully in this moment is to live life to the fullest.

However, I did have certain lifestyle goals in mind before Hayden came along: recall those spiked heels, white carpet, PhD and the newest model car of my dreams? In short, my aspirations constituted the American dream's version of a successful life. Although I loved kids and had related well to babies and young children as a child myself, even had a distinct knack with them, I specifically did not want to work with children as part of my career.

Yet, Hayden was not just any child. He was my grandson. I would take a detour from my chosen path to care for him, but would return to graduate school as soon as he no longer needed my help 24/7. At one point, years ago, this was my plan.

The first weak link in this strategy became evident the summer Hayden was two-and-a-half. I brought him to daycare several hours a week so he could be around other children. My goal was to get him to learn how to crawl, so I placed him with younger children who were already crawling. I figured he would learn by imitation.

One day I noticed a boy at daycare whom I had never seen before. I could tell that he was delayed—my antennae are always up for special needs kids. I then learned that this child had been in six foster homes in his short 18 months of life. I could only begin to understand how awful life must have been for him.

Later, when I pushed this little boy on a swing, we looked at each other squarely. His eyes asked me,

"Why can't I be loved, too?"

At that moment, with my heart swollen almost beyond capacity, I wanted to take him home. The memory of his eyes pleading, longing for love, is still something I feel.

But I just wasn't set up to do foster care. Besides, I already had a 24/7 child. And anyway, I was going back to graduate school as soon as Hayden no longer required me full-time. Still, the sadness and need in that little boy's eyes...

Later that summer, Denny, Hayden and I went to the 30-year reunion of Denny's high-school class. Not surprisingly, we were the only couple there with a young child. Saturday night the group went to an outside supper and country western concert. Because I thought it would be too long and too stimulating for Hayden, he and I stayed at the house. So, there I was, alone on a Saturday night with a sleeping child in a strange place. I threw a major pity party.

I felt there was no place I belonged, and that made me feel like a misfit, so I turned to my inner voice right there in the middle of my pity party.

"Poor me, I don't belong anywhere," I complained.

"You belong to the human race and the only thing you have to qualify is to accept your humanness. No uniform is necessary. Moreover, every man is your brother, every woman your sister, and every child your grandchild." This was His swift response.

A fulfilling sense of belonging came over me. But then, why did I also experience uneasiness? I knew I cared for Hayden because I wanted my grandchild to have a chance in this tough life. But if all children were my grandchildren, well, it was just not in my plan to somehow care for all of them.

One evening that fall as I was writing, I struggled with the issue of all those other children again. In my mind's eye, I saw myself holding Hayden, but I could also see the outline of the other children off in the shadows. Hayden was taken out of my arms and put with the other children. But then I couldn't distinguish him from the others.

The "voice" said: "Hayden is not your grandson. He is my son."

I said, "Okay, I can buy that."

"My son has special needs. Who will care for my son?" asked the voice.

Growing impatient, I responded, "It doesn't matter what you call him, I have been taking care of him and if you give him back to me, I will continue to take care of him."

God can certainly be exasperating at times!

"But, who will take care of my son?" he repeated.

It seemed God was just being a pain about words, so I said, "You want me to say it? Okay, I'll say it. I will care for your son. Okay?"

Then, Hayden was suddenly back in my arms, but so were all the other children who had previously been lurking in the shadows!

I said, "Oh no! That's not what I meant. That's not at all what I meant!"

All that fall I argued with God. I still had other plans for myself—school, then a practice. I wanted the good life. I had a right to my empty nest. I had a right to not have to deal with drooling and diapers. I had a right to weekends and holidays off, a good income.

But this was clearly not about Hayden. I was wholly willing to care for him. It was about all of those other needy children. By then, people were noticing that Hayden was doing much better than expected and some were suggesting that maybe I should work with other autistic children as well. But I always declined and said that I was going back to school to follow my life's dream. And my dream did not include working with other kids.

When the Reader's Digest next came out, the book section featured, "Nina's Journey."[1] I stayed up late one night to read what turned out to be the harrowing narrative of a young

---

1. Markovna, Nina. *Nina's Journey: A Memoir of Stalin's Russia & the Second World War.* Regnery Gateway, 1989.

girl's life in Nazi Europe. Nina had endured, among other horrors, the destruction of her home. So I said to myself that I had a right to my nice house. When Nina described the conditions of her forced labor, I said to myself that I had a right to my evenings, weekends, and holidays off. When Nina went on to speak of her dearth of warm clothing, I said to myself that I had a right to my wool suits. Reading about Nina's crowded sleeping quarters brought me back to my sense of entitlement regarding my empty nest.

Finally, I addressed GOD. "Okay. It is true that many people didn't have these things during WWII. But that was Europe during WWII. We are no longer in a world war. This is the USA. This is the beginning of the new millennium. Women my age in my country and my culture have pretty homes, blissfully empty nests, and lovely clothes. As a female American woman, I have a right to these things!"

"Yes, you are an American citizen, and yes, these are accepted things in your culture, and you may have them all if you want."

For a moment, I felt relieved. But then he continued,

"If you belong to me, you relinquish your rights as an American citizen or any other nationality, for that matter. You become a member of humanity and all children are your grandchildren! You have no more rights than any other human being."

I knew then that in reality, I was privileged to have the things I had. The saying, "But for the grace of GOD go I," came to mind. It finally hit me that I could have been Nina!

With this, my inner journey came to a standstill. I continued to cling to the things I had wanted, yet I knew in my heart of hearts where GOD was leading me and I tried to ignore it.

But I couldn't ignore it. So there I sat. I had really struggled to get GOD to see it my way, but to no avail. He just wasn't buying it.

Interestingly, I realized I didn't feel guilty for not seeing things the way GOD saw them. I just didn't know how to choose: was it GOD's way or my way? What it all seemed to come down to was a matter of faith and trust. But wow, this was big, that I was having doubts about such major issues. Does God really know what is best for me? Or did I? I was, in truth, smack dab in the middle of a crisis of faith and trust. Yes, this was huge alright. It doesn't get much bigger than this, to my way of thinking!

One day during some quiet time—not long after the full force of this conundrum struck—an image came to mind. I saw myself sitting on a fence. On the right side of the fence there was a well-organized city, with streets, houses, stores, all beautifully laid out. To the left was a jungle, a swirling chaos, teaming with life, rife with complexity and confusion, and with no discernable order. I knew immediately where I wanted to be—in the safe, predictable city. And I knew what I did not want—the crazy, discombobulated jungle!

Since early childhood, I've had difficulty trusting myself to make the right choices. I've struggled with uncertainty, anything new. So nothing whatsoever about a jungle appealed to me. NOTHING!!! I told GOD as clearly as possible and straight from my heart that I wanted the city—the PhD, the structure. I was told I could have it, if that's what I really wanted. Well, I did! Security seemed the most important thing in the world to me. It was simply an indisputable bottom line. Once I admitted this, I began to relax. God had given me permission to have what I want, and that was security.

I looked back at the well-ordered city and realized that it represented the security of someone else making decisions for me, which meant that I had learned to do, be, think and believe what I was told to do, be, think and believe. Now I was being called upon to let go of other peoples' opinions, of texts and experts, and follow my unique way into the unknown, into what was for me an uncharted wilderness. And so, in the end, I said goodbye to the well-ordered city, climbed off the fence, and walked into the jungle.

Epilogue:

Several years ago I told my niece, Dellavon, the story of my journey. She had been to Guatemala with the Peace Corps and informed me that there actually is organization in a jungle, but it is evident only once you enter it and get to know it. Then, she said, it is beautiful to behold. I will always appreciate this insight, because in time I found this to be true of the journey that Hayden and I had embarked upon as well. There is subtle organization, natural cause and effect, and unexpected beauty in this jungle that is autism. It is of the utmost importance that I continually challenge myself to see this.

Thank you, Dellavon!

Chapter 5

How Do You Cope?

See Your Child as a Child

Sometimes on a journey we find ourselves stranded by a flat tire, car trouble under the hood, or even an accident. Or, we may be uncertain about the route to take and could really use some good directions from someone other than our friendly, but clueless, GPS. In short, sometimes we just need assistance.

The same is true for the journey of life. At a gathering of moms with disabled kids, one young mom asked me, "How do you cope?" Her question has inspired this chapter.

When I see my child as a child first and foremost, one who happens to have a disability, my child will see himself as a child, one who happens to have a disability. If I see my child primarily as a disabled child, he will see himself as merely a disabled child.

Hayden leads a full, rich life. He is generally happy, cooperative, and well-behaved. Although there are many things he cannot do, there are also many things he can do. We focus on these.

The local YMCA used to have a special free "disAbility Swim" for families with disabled kids. Hayden wanted to go to that swim until he heard what it was called. Then he didn't want to go. He knows he has autism. He just didn't like that label. Perhaps if the Y had called that free swim time something like "Family Fun in the Pool," Hayden might still be swimming there now, several times a week.

Accept the Totality of your Feelings

All feelings are okay. There are no good, bad, or right feelings. There are just feelings. And a tremendous number of kinds of feelings come up when you have a child with a disability. Work at allowing these feelings to surface, and then work at accepting them. The good news is that they are, in fact, the starting point of your journey. When feels are not honored as valid aspects of ourselves, we may expend precious energy trying to avoid and suppress them, possibly even depleting ourselves before we even get started on our journey.

Feelings are gauges that tell us about our emotional, spiritual selves, just as thermometers, stethoscopes, and EKGs give us information about our physical selves. Unfortunately, in our culture feelings are often not honored. Instead, we hear such false adages as:

- You shouldn't feel that way.
- Big boys don't cry.
- She's too emotional.
- He has an anger problem.

Each one of these phrases is a denial of a feeling, something that is in fact very real. No one should ever deny one's own or another's feelings, regardless of the fact that some of them, like pain and sadness, are just not pleasant to experience. Feelings such as anger and fear are healthy, normal responses to injury and loss. When I accept my feelings of anger and fear and thereby manage my behavior around them, I have an opportunity to grow in compassion towards myself and others. Using my feelings as tools for spiritual growth benefits both me and my child. If I accept my own feelings without censure, it will be easier for me to accept my child's feelings and work through them. Because of life in general, and Hayden's disability in particular, he will face many frustrating situations armed with limited capacity to express his feelings. I want to be able to assist him in alleviating the stress of these limitations, so that his stress doesn't find expression on negative behavior.

Face Your Fears

Franklin D. Roosevelt famously said, "All we have to fear is fear itself." The fear associated with my child's disability is far worse than the disability itself. The debilitating thing about fear is that it can dead-end at helplessness.

In our society, where accomplishment, conformity, appearance, and worldly success are worshipped, parents with disabled children may suddenly be thrown back into their own childhood feelings of not measuring up. This in turn could then leave them to the fear of being unloved. All parents, at least subconsciously, hope and dream that their children will be special and accomplish great and wonderful things. We often also hope that we as parents (or grandparents) will be honored through them. However, when our children's disabilities take them from the victor's podium to the walker, from the head of the class to a seat in the special education class, we ourselves can become vulnerable to the fear of being unloved, because all at once in a rush all their own, our memories of trying to succeed but believing we have not revisit us. These old feelings can easily paralyze us with fear about our children's futures.

Rather than give in to this paralysis, we must continually remind ourselves that everyone has skills of character traits they need or want to improve upon. Some of us have visible disabilities, while others have neuroses, engage in violent behaviors, or act out of extreme selfishness, pride, or narcissism. We all have disabilities, when thought of ways in which we fall short. For our own sanity, as well as that of our children's, it is important to be prepared to remember this as often as possible, to have this at the back of our mind always. In the face this recognition, we must all allow ourselves to love and enjoy the child we have who happens to have a disability.

We must also remember that there have children like our children and my grandchild since there have been children, many millennia before there were cold, clinical names for them, such as Down's Syndrome, cerebral palsy, autism, PDD, birth injured, blind, deaf. Instead of taking our children for what they are—for the imperfect little miracles we are so fortunate to have received—when someone attaches one of these labels to them, it can feel like our heart has been ripped from our chest, as cold shivers run up our spine, and hot tears cascade down our cheeks. These labels themselves hold so much power in our culture that they can makes us feel our children have somehow violated the security of our homes, wiped out our bank accounts, and turned our world topsy-turvy. In reality, our children are like all others, in the important ways, that is. Yet we feel we will never be the same, not after one of these labels has been bestowed on them.

But I promise you, you will begin to see rainbows behind your tears, and eventually, you will laugh again. Further, I'm certain that beauty will spring forth from the ashes and that all the hardship you are now experiencing will nourish the immense spiritual growth that will come to you.

Mourn Your Loss

Mourn the loss of your plans, dreams, and hopes for your children; they will simply need to be refigured. You'll find that in the process of this readjustment, your hopes for your child will become more infused with love and based more on your child's *actual* wants and needs, rather than on you and your wants and needs. But first, you must consciously let your original plans, wishes, hopes, and dreams for your child die and fade away. You can only take up new ones if you mourn the loss of the old and bury them for good. Otherwise they will become weeds in the garden of your heart, strangling your love in the present moment with past expectations.

As most of us know, there are four sages of grief. Denial is the first. Since you've come this far through the telling of my story, you've probably experienced denial. If not, keep reading, remain open, talk to someone who will listen. You'll get there.

Perhaps you've reached the second stage of grief, which is generally thought to be anger (though it is possible to proceed through the stages in any order). You may be angry at everything: your spouse, your child, yourself, the doctors, the hospital, the world, even the universe! It's okay! Your anger is okay! Let yourself really feel it. It can be seen as your inner self-expression of how the world is simply not doing what you want it to do. Experience the anger but don't act on it. This is a choice you have. Think of it as a powerful emotional resource which, once transmuted in a positive way, will nourish your spirit in the form of strength, determination, and creativity.

Perhaps you have been through the anger and now you're filled with the pain of sorrow and loss. Let that pain engulf you too. It's good pain because it's authentic. It contains the seeds of compassion, understanding, contentment and joy.

Having experienced the denial, anger, and pain of grief, in time, acceptance will come, but not only the acceptance that your child is somehow make you realize that your child really is perfect just as he or she is, like all children are.

Make Peace with Your Pain

There will always be pain: the pain of our culture's ignorance and your child's rejection; the pain of developmental milestones unattained while others breeze right through them; the pain of the limitations of traditional medicine, your own ineptness, your family's struggles, your government's disinterest, your school's inexperience, and your child's frustration. Even though the pain is most often unbearable and so debilitating you feel you cannot function because it drains you of every ounce of your strength; it robs you of restorative sleep; it even manages to blacken the entire world, pain is not really the culprit. It is the triad fear-anger-pain that is potentially so obstructive.

However, when you are able to face the fear and anger, let them wash over you, then the pain is simply that—pain. It too will pass, so make your peace with it and let it empower, sustain and teach you. Let yourself really feel it, embrace it for it is your ally. It is the brand seared on your soul that identifies you as a member of the fraternity of the parents (or aunts, uncles, grandparents...) of children with disabilities.

Trust Your Instincts

Doctors know facts about your child's disability; physical therapists are cognizant of developmental sequences and exercises; teachers are qualified instructors; family members can be supportive. Some may be sure they have all the answers. But you are the expert authority on your child. If you're still dealing with the powerful emotions of fear and anger, your knowing this fact about you and your child may be clouded by these very feelings. But, your knowing is still there.

All kinds of people - some with lots of 'life experience,' some with titles and strings of letters behind their names—will give you loads of information, advice, and directives. My advice is to listen to everyone, then ask questions. Explore *their* knowledge. But follow *your* gut. You are the decision maker. Make decisions you are comfortable with, that you can live with. Act on those things with consequences you are most willing and able to accept.

Respect Your Child as a Complete Human Being

Whatever parts may be absent from your child or are deformed or non-functioning; whatever skills may be behind or lacking altogether; whatever behaviors are being expressed; whatever medical equipment is in the way—your child is complete and needs respect as a full person right from the start. Your child is lovable. This may sound simple and redundant, but it's not.

We bring the conditioning of our past into the present. Psychologists say we are only one-tenth consciousness, meaning that we are consciously aware of only one out of ten of the thoughts and motives that determine our choices. The others are unexamined concepts: the results of what we have learned and experienced from our families, friends, church, the media, the educational system, our culture, and what we've read. These unconscious ideas effect our behaviors even though we are unaware of them. In fact, they may act in total opposition to what e consciously want, chose, or believe.

Consciously, for instance, I know that police officers are there to "protect and serve" me. Never have I ever been hurt by a police officer. Furthermore, if my memory serves me, I've only had three traffic citations in my entire life, all dispensed by extremely polite officers. Yet, despite this benign history, at age 73, when I catch sight of a police car, I inevitably experience a moment of panic. In my conscious awareness, everything is okay. That is to say, I have no reason to be anxious to because I have committed no infractions. However, thousands of conscious fears from as far back as my childhood of mean-seeming authority figures send icy tendrils around my heart.

Now that I am aware of the source of this reaction, I can defuse if by letting the conditioned responses of anxiety and fear simply come and go, wash over me. I say to myself, when I see a police car, "Yes, there is a police car and you feel afraid. But you're not doing anything wrong, so you don't need to act on that fear in any way. All is well. You are safe."

Not all the time, but sometimes, I'm able to release the fear and forget the police car altogether. What really amuses me, though, is that I can go through this kind of processing with a particular instance of a particular police car and handle it so well that I actually forget I've seen that particular police car; but then, I experience the same reaction all over again when I see the very same police car only a short time later! Such is the nature of our emotions, to be unpredictable, uncontrollable. Our real choices come in the actions we take.

I believe that most people can relate to the police car phenomenon. And I also believe that we all feel fairly safe talking about the feelings it brings up. But there are some feelings we do not feel safe speaking about with others. For me, they are evoked when I encounter a wheelchair-bound individual. I discovered years ago that upon coming into sight of such individuals, I avoid making eye contact with them.

Until relatively recently, people with disabilities were segregated from the mainstream of society by being institutionalized. Thus they became practically invisible, especially in educational settings. And they were not afforded equal physical access to people, places, and things out in the world at large, something the rest of us take for granted. What I consciously think about people in wheelchairs—that they are people who happen to be in wheelchairs—is contaminated by many years of cultural conditioning. People in wheelchairs, my unconscious says, are different from me, therefore bad.

Further, when I truly examine my unconscious to determine what my gut reaction is to someone whose speech is challenged, or who uses sign language, or even who speaks in a foreign tongue, I realize at least momentarily that I feel superior as a fluent speaker of the English language.

How do we react when we see limb loss, facial scars, or other deformities? In my own case, I take note if someone is wearing hearing aids, though not if they wear glasses. Are we less comfortable with someone in a wheelchair who also has a large cast? A small cast? No cast at all? Do we tend to treat children in wheelchairs, or with braces, or with no hair, the same as we treat other "normal" children? Are we repulsed with someone over two years old who drools? A six-year-old in diapers? Someone who rocks back-and-forth incessantly. Someone who is developmentally disabled? As a recovering perfectionist, I found many reasons to be critical of others, as well as myself, especially when it comes to disabilities and unusual behaviors. But I don't think I'm very different form the rest of the world in this respect. In fact, I know I'm not.

Throughout the history of the human race, people the world over have, time and time again shunned and rejected those different from themselves. In the U.S., at one time thought to be the greatest "melting pot," there is much less melting and a whole lot more pots taken at those "from away" than many of us would like to acknowledge. We routinely categorize and judge our fellow men and women by color, age, employment status, ability, gender, lifestyle, education, religion, accent, ad infinitum. Ad nauseam!

As long as these prejudices remain unconscious, they will keep us from dealing effectively with our autistic child. But the wonderful news is that we can choose to change our actions regarding anything we are consciously aware of. When we recognize and acknowledge that we have learned prejudices about people who are different form ourselves in some way, then, when those feelings and thoughts arise we can tell ourselves, "Oh, that's just my old conditioning speaking." Then we can choose to act in a more loving, inclusive way. Feelings and thoughts, like clouds in the sky, come and go. We are not responsible for them. What we are responsible for is whether and how we act on them—our own behavior.

Years ago I was with a group of elementary-school children and noticed a seven- or eight-year-old who was sucking her thumb. Instantly, I felt critical of the child and her parents. And almost as instantly, I realized that this was a classic case of my early conditioning grabbing hold in my mind. In my childhood, babies were allowed to suck their thumbs up to a certain age, and then it was simply stopped, whatever it took.

The thumb-sucking issue really strikes home for me, since Hayden, at twenty-eight, still sucks his thumb—and with my blessing! Since his kindergarten days, numerous people have pressed me to work on getting Hayden to stop sucking his thumb. But honestly, I've resisted. As far as I'm concerned, he can suck his thumb whenever or wherever he wants to do so. Neuro-developmentally, it's entirely appropriate. So, I am adamant in my decision that no one bug or challenge him or me about this behavior. Yet, every once in a while, I myself have a fleeting thought that he is just too big to suck his thumb. Neuro-typical young men do not suck their thumbs. However, Hayden's body does not function like that of a neuro-typical young man.

* * *

Compassion versus Pity

Two other very important emotions we are programmed early about are pity and compassion. Sometimes, compassion and pity are seen as very similar, but in reality, they are universes apart. To have compassion for another person is to identify with that person—in their human condition: their pain, inadequacies, struggles—and to have the desire to alleviate that person's hardships. If you pity another person, on the other hand, you see yourself as separate from and superior to that person because you don't have the problems they have.

Pity, as I see it, is a kind of put down. If we pity our children, they will come to see themselves as inferior, incapable and inadequate; and, they will see the rest of the world as superior, capable, and adequate. On the other hand, if we have compassion for our children, they will learn to see us as equals. If we see them as capable, adequate, and valuable, they will then see themselves that way as well, especially because we have modeled those traits for them.

The idea that pity is the same as compassion seems so culturally accepted that its poison is camouflaged—but it is

55

still poisonous! Perhaps an illustration would help make this clear. This story, "Everybody Can Do Something," is from the book *Chicken Soup for The Soul*:

Roger Crawford had everything he needed to play tennis—except two hands and a leg. When Roger's parents saw their son for the first time, they saw a baby with a thumb-like projection extending directly out of his right forearm and a thumb and one finger stuck out of his left forearm. He had no palms. The baby's arms and legs were shortened and he had only three toes on his shrunken right foot and a withered left leg, which would later be amputated.

The doctor said that Roger suffered from ectrodactylism, a rare birth defect affecting only one of 90,000 children born in the United States. The doctor informed the Crawfords that Roger would probably never walk or care for himself.

Fortunately Roger's parents didn't believe the doctor.

"My parents always taught me that I was only as handicapped as I wanted to be," said Roger. "They never allowed me to feel sorry for myself or take advantage of people because of my handicap. Once I got in trouble because my school papers were continually late," explained Roger, who had to hold his pencil with both "hands" to write slowly. "I asked Dad to write a note to my teachers, asking for a two-day extension on my assignments. Instead Dad made me start writing my paper two days early!"

Roger's father always encouraged him to get involved in sports, teaching Roger to catch and throw a volleyball and play backyard football after school. At age 12, Roger managed to win a spot on the school football team.

Before every game, Roger would visualize his dream of scoring a touchdown. Then one day he got his chance. The ball landed in his arms and off he ran as fast as he could on his artificial leg towards the goal line, his coach and teammates cheering wildly. But at the 10-yard line, a guy from the other team caught up with Roger, grabbing his left ankle. Roger tried to pull his artificial leg free from the player's grasp, but instead ended up having his leg pulled off.

"I was still standing up," recalls Roger. "I didn't know what else to do so I started hopping towards the goal line. The referee threw his hands up in the air. Touchdown! You know, even better than the six points was the look on the other kid who was holding my artificial leg."

Roger's love of sports grew and so did his self-confidence. But every obstacle gave way to Roger's determination. Eating in the lunchroom with other kids watching him fumble with his food proved very painful to Roger as did repeated failures in typing class. "I learned a very good lesson from typing class. You can't do *everything* — it's better to concentrate on what you can do."

One thing Roger could do was swing a tennis racket. Unfortunately, when he swung it hard, his weak grip usually launched it into space. By luck, Roger stumbled upon an odd looking tennis racket in a sports shop and accidentally wedged his finger between its double-barred handle when he picked it up. The snug fit made it possible for Roger to swing, serve and volley like an able-bodied tennis player. He practiced every day and was soon playing — and losing — matches.

But Roger persisted. He practiced and practiced and played and played. Surgery on the two fingers in his left hand enabled Roger to grip his special racket better, greatly improving his game. Although he had no role models to guide him, Roger became obsessed with tennis and in time he started to win.

Roger went on to play college tennis, finishing his tennis career with 22 wins and 11 losses. He later became the first physically handicapped player to be certified as a teaching professional by the United States Professional Tennis Association. Roger now tours the country, speaking to groups about what it takes to be a winner, no matter who you are.

"The only difference between you and me is that you can see my handicap, but I can't see yours. We *all* have them. When people ask me how I've been able to overcome my physical handicaps, I tell them that I haven't overcome anything. I've simply learned what I can't do — such as play the piano or eat with chopsticks — but more importantly, I've learned what I can do. Then I do it with all my heart and soul."[1]

If Roger's parents had accepted the dire diagnosis and pitied him, it would have been a self-fulfilling prophesy, because they would not have expected him to try, and most likely, he wouldn't have. SO... the prognosis would have become true. It would have been, "Poor Roger, he can't..." And Roger would have believed, "Poor me, I can't..." so he wouldn't have.

Perhaps there are people who felt Roger's parents were harsh; Roger may have felt that way at times as a child. But love and compassion are not ambiguous or subtle emotions.

Love and compassion say: "You are capable, you've got guts, you are invincible. Try and see if you can do it. You may have to work harder than most kids, but you can do it.

Pity says: "You poor thing. I can't imagine life without hands and only one foot, so you're going to have a miserable life. You can't do much, so I'm going to do it for you. Poor you."

When Hayden was two and a half, he began taking a foul-smelling concoction of garlic, herbs, zinc, Metox (an amino acid), and vitamin C to help dispel toxic levels of aluminum, copper, and arsenic in his body. The stuff looked awful, smelled putrid, and tasted just horrible, I must admit. I felt guilty for making him take it and was sure I would throw up if I had to. Still, I struggled to get it into his mouth and swallowed, while he kicked, screamed, and spit.

---

1. From the book Chicken Soup for the Soul by Jack Canfield and Mark Victor Hansen. Copyright 2012 by Chicken Soup for the Soul Publishing, LLC. Published by Backlist, LLC, a unit of Chicken Soup for the Soul Publishing, LLC. Chicken Soup for the Soul is a registered trademark of Chicken Soup for the Soul Publishing, LLC. Reprinted by permission. All rights reserved.

Time, unfortunately, did not improve the situation. In fact, the whole experience of forcing this stuff on Hayden had begun to erode the harmony and mutual respect that had begun to grow in our relationship. But somehow we had to get through three months of this situation—YIKES! Did I need help!

"GOD," I said, "I don't want three months of this battle. What can I do?"

What came back to me was, "There is no reason to pity him—it is his path. Let him walk it." These were his final words on the subject.

However, they made no sense to me. I felt Hayden needed pity for having to ingest such nasty stuff.

And I remember being puzzled when John, my therapist, told me that pity is a form of self-hate. As I mulled it all over for a while, the clouds parted, metaphorically, and I saw clearly that my pity was feeding Hayden's temper tantrums. My attitude was in effect saying to him, "Poor thing! You shouldn't be forced to take this nasty stuff! I'm a bad, mean grandma for making you." I could tell from his behavior that Hayden's reading of my attitude was, "Yes, poor me! I shouldn't be forced to take this! I'm angry! You sure are a bad, mean grandma, and I'm punishing you for making me take this awful stuff."

The truth of the matter was that he was toxic with heavy metals and he needed the medicine. To truly love him was to respect him and his journey and to quit contaminating him with my pity. When it came time for his next dose, I mashed and stirred up the foul concoction and said, as matter-of-factly as I could that it was time for his medicine, but that we needed to talk first.

"I know this is nasty medicine," I said, "and you don't want it, and it seems to you like I'm mean for making you take it. But you need it because you are toxic with heavy metals. I'm sorry, but it's true. You need it. So, you are going to

take it and we are not going to have a fight over it. You're just going to take it." Then I waited with baited breath to see what would happen.

He took it—just like that! Since then, we've never had a problem with him taking his medicine, no matter how repulsive it is. As it turns out, this is the same approach I use with his very limited diet. What I have learned from both situations is that when a child senses we feel pity for or guilt toward them, this elicits an angry, punitive response. When we consistently go to them with decisiveness tempered with equanimity, we're likely to draw forth cooperation.

Take Care of Yourself

There will be more things to do, important things, than you have time and energy to do. Prioritize and compromise. I had always kept a spotless house—that had just always been a priority for me. But once Hayden became such a large part of my life, there wasn't much time for house cleaning. I can deal with dust more than I can with clutter, so I keep the clutter down and let the dust pile up!

Before Hayden, I was very conscious of how I presented myself. I wore lots of makeup, and matched my nail polish to my clothes to my eye shadow. And I managed to walk quite well in my heels. I still like my colors to match when I dress for the day, but I no longer have the time, or more accurately, choose to make the time, to coordinate a wardrobe the way I used to. Now, I generally choose a nice white top then accessorize with my age-old pearls. The rest of my outfit can be any color I want, but is usually the color of blue jeans! Friends tell me I'm well put together so I take their word for it and I'm very satisfied with the fact that it takes almost no time to make myself presentable every morning. Mission accomplished!

I've found that the trick is to consider foregoing things that have taken a lot of time in the past but now I can choose to ignore without feeling deprived. We should try to let these things fall to the wayside and pat ourselves on the back for coming up with hours of time to put towards our children. Hold on, though, we're also looking for more time for self-care! Give yourself mini-breaks. Sit and relax a bit; take time for "you" things. You are important and your needs are legitimate. When you don't have a *lot* of time, take a *bit* of time. I enjoy word puzzles, music, reading, motivational tapes, and occasionally a movie. Respite time is *my* time—no cooking or cleaning! I've actually learned to watch a movie comfortably without first making sure my entire house is clean! Consciously make time for you. If you are stressed, your child will sense that and will take on that stress. Let friends and family help you. Join a support group and meet other people with similar challenges and joys.

Lastly, however you nurture your spirit, keep it up; use your spiritual resources!

Chapter 6

Tacit Rules and Communication

Before we can become licensed to drive a car, we must learn the rules of the road and pass a few tests on them. While the rules of the road restrict how, when, where, and at what speed we can drive, they also help prevent traffic tie-ups, bottle-necks, fender-benders, and more serious collisions, any one of which could potentially place far greater restrictions on our driving and perhaps our lives. Although at times I may feel irritated by some rule or other, in reality I wouldn't want to drive at all if everyone just made up their own rules as they drove along.

If a person were to make and follow his very own rules of the road, we would likely consider that person a sure thing for the reckless driver category. When people make their own personal, unspoken rules intended to govern everyone and everything at all times and all places, there's a good chance they fall somewhere on the autism spectrum. A lot of negative behaviors and tie-ups in family life occur because an autistic family member does not understand—more accurately, is not able to understand—his or her family's rules.

Family members on the spectrum often have in mind their own set of rules for everyone and every situation, and they become extremely confused, frustrated, and angry when their rules are not adopted. Meantime, everyone else in the family is frustrated and confused and possibly angry that the family rules are ignored. Welcome to the world of tacit rules!

Like many kids with autism, Hayden is often frustrated and angry when something changes, not because he can't tolerate change but because it seems to him that one of his rules has been broken. I've found that the key to dealing with Hayden's tacit rules is to identify the one that is at work at any given time, the one he holds to that makes the world seem very much at odds with him. Once this tacit rule is discovered, I can then affect positive change in his world by dismantling it and replacing it with an outwardly acknowledged rule that works for everyone involved.

Deciphering tacit rules is like a game—challenging, even fun, and far more exciting than any TV game show. The concept of tacit rules is a powerful headlamp that lights my way on my journey through autism. I don't remember the very first time I used this light to uncover a tacit rule, but I do remember many, many instances when I've used it. I still do, sometimes on a daily basis.

I should note before going on that kids with autism are not the only people who subscribe to tacit rules. They're a part of everyone's life. For example, a few years ago in early December as Christmas approached, I asked Denny, my husband, if he would go out and buy us a Christmas tree. He came home pleased as punch with the good deal he'd gotten: a Noble Fir for $10.

Well, when I saw that tree my holiday spirit vanished into thin air. For one thing, I have never liked Noble Firs. I like full, fat, round Christmas trees. Nobles are sparse, barren, pathetic looking to me. And they're expensive to boot! A $10 Noble Fir does not look, to me at least, like a classic Christmas tree. But there before me was the official start of my Christmas season: Denny setting up his "good deal" in a tree stand just *like it was a real Christmas tree. Hayden rocked and squealed happily, also just as if it was a real Christmas tree. Then there was me, stewing like the Grinch had just stolen my Christmas, really stewing, so much so that soon Hayden began to grow quiet and somber. Clearly, he had picked up on my seething anger.*

All of a sudden, I realized what was really going on. Yes, I could imagine myself teaching a course on how children with autism create rules about things needing to be the same as they were the first time around or they become angry. I know the phenomenon well. But that Christmas, it was clearly **me** *who had the tacit rule: a Christmas tree must be full, fat, and round. Jeez!*

So, I asked myself, "Is it Christmas?"

"Yes," I answered myself.

"Is this a tree?"

"Yes," was my response this time as well.

So I thought, "Then I can choose to accept this as a Christmas tree." And I did just that, primarily because I had witnessed how dramatically my displeasure affected Hayden. And so, I was reminded that autism isn't all that different from everyday life, when it comes to tacit rules, just more pronounced. It was not the situation I was responding to, but my expectation (rule) that it should be based on past experiences. So it is with our ASD kids.

When Hayden was very young, he screamed, projected his body quite violently backwards, withdrew, refused to look at me, bit, hit, pinched, and scratched me, grabbed my glasses, pulled my hair, poked my eyes, kicked other people and things. Later, he threw toys, and got into things he knew were off limits. All of these behaviors were expressions of anger, frustration, fear, and pain compressed into feelings of rejection and un-lovability. Had I not found appropriate ways to deal with these behaviors, Hayden now at age 27, might have been drugged, labelled as dangerous, and institutionalized.

When Hayden was in his first five years, I could still maintain some measure of control over him with my greater physical size and power. But if that was all I had today, I'd be up a creek without a paddle! The mental strategies children use at two will be the same they use at eight or twelve or even twenty, unless their parents or caregivers model, teach, and insist on something different.

During his preschool and elementary school years Hayden screamed a good deal. But he hasn't done that for many years now. However, he does have quite a repertoire of guttural sounds to choose from when he feels like it. He uses these when he is especially mad.

Hayden may also withhold eye contact, turn his back on me, refuse to respond, withdraw, burp, laugh incessantly, refuse to use the toilet, go to his room and shut the door—to express his frustration, anger, confusion, or to simply protest. And he is not incapable of aggression or violence. In this, he is like most of us when we feel threatened or trapped. But I'm always on the lookout for signs of anger and frustration so that I can deal with them in words, and things don't get out of control.

Anger and frustration will find means of expression; I would far rather it's in words than actions. It may seem like a lot of work to always be on "red alert," and yes, I agree that it is. But if aggression and violence are my child's modus operandi, I'm always going to be on red alert anyway, and frequently beyond, in "potential disaster" mode, where I often found myself when Hayden was younger. I'll take routine "red alert" any day, no matter how much time it takes me to assess what's at the bottom of Hayden's anger.

When Hayden was three, he began using a walker in physical therapy. Laurel, his pediatric physical therapist, introduced therapeutic activities in her sessions in such a way that Hayden would become familiar with them and I could learn how to facilitate them at home. When Laurel felt we were both ready, we'd begin executing a particular activity at home on our own. However, even though Hayden had used the walker independently at PT sessions, he resisted using it at home unless I was very close beside him. My guess at the time was that our home environment was very different: pile carpet at home, smooth carpet at school; novice me at home, competent and professional Laurel at school. And of course, there was Hayden's tacit rule that the walker belonged at school, since that's where he'd always used it before.

The other reason Hayden didn't want the walker at home was that it represented hard work and using it was sometimes even scary for him. We took it home nonetheless. After several days of communicating his displeasure with the walker, he remained adamant about my being right beside him when he used it. This walker issue was clearly something Hayden considered a pesky therapy activity. He just didn't see the value in it because he didn't understand the freedom and mobility he would gain by learning how to walk independently.

When it became obvious that Hayden had no intention of changing his attitude about the walker, I realized it was time for serious strategizing. First, I set him up with the walker at one end of the living room. Then I acknowledged and validated everything I could think of about his not wanting to use the walker at home, especially if I was not right beside him. I also reinforced that I knew he could do a good job with the walker because he had done so at PT repeatedly.

Next, I told Hayden that today he was going to walk from where he was, through the entire living room, kitchen, entry, and playroom, then into the hallway, even if he didn't want to. This was the point at which he began to scream.

"Thank you for letting me know you do not want to use your walker at home by yourself," I acknowledged. "But even

67

if you don't want to, you need to, and you are going to. If you want to scream while you're doing it, that's okay, you can scream. You need to be able to walk while you're mad and screaming, too. So if you want to scream, then we'll practice walking and screaming." Evidently, Hayden did in fact feel he needed to scream, since he walked the entire distance by himself, screaming bloody murder the whole entire way!

Had I understood then what I know now about tacit rules, perhaps I could have eliminated the screaming by dismantling his rule (about having to scream while walking alone at home with the walker) and formulating a new one. Eventually, though, he came to like the freedom he found walking "by self," and he simply released his tacit rule all on his own.

* * *

Hayden came home from the first day of second grade tired and excited. The laughs, claps and hugs I got in response to my questions about how it went indicated to me that it had been a really good day for him. At what I thought was the end of our conversation about the day, I said that he could go to second grade tomorrow too, thinking this would elicit a similar positive response. But instead, he gave me an emphatic "No!" I was totally taken aback, since he had seemed so positive about his first day in second grade. What was going on?

Of course, I wanted nothing but positive experiences for Hayden at school, so I went back over everything that happened with Hayden that day. Basically, I peppered him with questions about every little thing: Did you like your teacher? Did you like the kids? Was it too loud? Too bright? Was there too much going on? His answers seemed to indicate that second grade had been just great! But still, he just didn't want to go back!

In my mind, I asked for help: "GOD, I'm out of options. I need your help here!"

Then I remembered a key fact: Brittany, one of Hayden's special friends, was in the other second-grade classroom. My next question for Hayden broke open the dilemma.

"Are you mad because Brittany is not in your class this year?"

The other-worldly sounds that emanated from Hayden's mouth in response were a signal to me that I had indeed hit the jackpot. I realized that saying no to school was Hayden's way of trying to express his frustration, his sense that something was amiss there. Finally, I had something concrete to work with.

"Are you mad because Brittany's not in your class? Is that why you don't want to go to school again? Is that it?"

Smiles, hugs, squeals, and rocking let me know that was exactly it. He had been heard.

"Maybe," I continued, "you have a rule that Brittany's supposed to be in your class?"

"Absolutely!" was his response.

I then validated him with:

"You have a rule that Brittany is supposed to be in your class at school. That's because in kindergarten Brittany was in your class and in first grade Brittany was in your class too. Now in second grade Brittany is supposed to be in your class. This is a Hayden rule."

As I spoke, he was alert and animated. He looked directly at me. He had been heard, validated, and understood, and he accepted what I said with smiles and claps of agreement.

"Problem is," I continued," you don't make the rules for the school. The school board does. When you were in kindergarten, the school board made the rule that Brittany and Hayden were in Mrs. Coffee's class. When you were in first grade the school board made the rule that you and Brittany were in

Mrs. Clark's class. Now you're in second grade and the school board has made the rule that Brittany is in Mr. Madison's room, and you are in Mrs. Cummins' room. You may not like it, but it's the school board's rule."

Well, more Hayden-style expletives told me he sure didn't like it, not one bit. When I suggested that perhaps he was mad at the school board, he laughed and clapped in agreement.

"Would you like to be really mad at the school board?"

"Absolutely!" he signaled. This was the perfect time to sing a 'Mad Song':

You are mad at the school board;
You are mad at the school board;
The school board made a rule
That Brittany's in Mr. Madison's class and you're in Mrs. Cummins'
class,
And you are mad at the school board.

Hayden was tremendously animated as he laughed and clapped. He looked right at me the entire time, a sign to me that he was exquisitely present. Everything about him told me loud and clear that I was absolutely right-on, so I sang the 'Mad Song' a few more times, exactly the way I had first sung it. Then I decided to change it up a little:

You are mad at the school board;
You are mad at the school board;
Brittany's your friend and you want to be in the same class and
you're not,
So you are mad at the school board.

I wondered at this point if Hayden might also be feeling sad about the whole thing. When I asked him as much, his whole demeanor changed drastically. He grew somber and his *thumb went right into his mouth. When he waved his pinky I had my confirmation: he was not only mad, he was sad as well. Because I knew I had to address this feeling of sadness too, I said,*

"You're feeling sad because you miss your friend Brittany. It's okay to be sad. It doesn't feel good, but it's safe. Would you like to be sad?"

"Yes," he waved his pinky. Time to sing again.

You are feeling sad;
You are feeling sad;
You miss Brittany in you class,
And you are feeling sad.

I sang this a few more times and he became the very picture of sadness as he sat and sucked his thumb. I let a few minutes go by and then asked Hayden if he needed to be sad anymore; he signed that he did not. I commented that he and Brittany did not have the same class, but they did have the same recess and lunch, so he would see Brittany at school after all. He smiled and clapped, so I finished with an 'I Love You Song':

I love you,
I love you,
When you are mad, or sad or glad;
I love you.

"Hayden," I asked, "Do you want to go to second grade tomorrow?" He laughed and he clapped. All was well in his world again.

Hayden's rules and feelings were so intertwined, that I couldn't change one without dealing with the other. I named, acknowledged, validated, expressed, and accepted them as his feelings and rule so that he could release them. With that accomplished, I was able to rewrite the rule that had led to Hayden's original troubled and troublesome reaction in the first place—his not wanting to go to second grade the next day even though his first day had been just fine. That's the beauty of working with tacit rules. You get to change them to better ones!

Maybe you're saying to yourself right about now that this was all just a fluke. Well, I would say to you that maybe it was. But if it was, we must have had a bad case of fluke-infestation back then, because exactly this kind of thing just kept on happening. We need only flash forward to the beginning of third grade to see that this...

Only a few weeks in, Hayden's teaching assistant, Debbie, told me he was behaving badly in music class; she had, in fact, taken him out of every music class since school had started. She reflected that this seemed odd because she was well aware that Hayden loved music and had since Kindergarten. She was mystified as to what had triggered the inappropriate behavior. I asked her what happened just before music, and she drew a blank, at least at first. So I probed deeper.

"Is there anything different about music this year?"

"Nothing...well," she hesitated, "they have a new teacher, Mr. B, but . . ."

I told Debbie I thought I could work out the problem, that I had a hunch. As it turned out, there was nothing wrong with the new teacher. The problem was with one of Hayden's rules. When he came home from school that day, I told him we needed to talk, so he went to our talk chair and I followed.

"Debbie told me you've been misbehaving in music class this year."

He laughed and clapped his agreement; he was very aware of what he had done.

"Since you're a fine boy, but you're misbehaving, there must be a problem with music class," I said.

Hayden clapped loudly. This told me that, yes, there was a problem in music class.

"Behaving badly in music class is not appropriate, but thank you for letting me know you have a problem in music," I said, in accordance with my formula for affirming his feelings. So now it was time to dig deeper.

*"Are you **mad** about something in music?"*

Again, loud clapping ensued. This meant that the specific emotion we were dealing was his being mad, so the very question I asked was an affirmation. Then I asked if he was mad at Debbie and his whole body froze, like a halted movie frame. He signaled with his pinky that he was not mad at Debbie.

"Are you mad at Mr. B?"

*Loud, emphatic clapping, accompanied by many "eh, eh, eh" sounds, told me in no uncertain terms that he was mad at Mr. B. By asking only a few questions, I discovered the reason for Hayden's inappropriate behavior. He had been acting in accordance with one of his own rules, one that told him that Mrs. R taught music: she always had; she was **the** music teacher; so Mr. B just didn't belong there. Hayden had been misbehaving because he was frightened and confused. He had been telling Debbie with his behavior what he could not tell her with words; now he was doing the same thing with me.*

Perhaps you think it's not possible for a severely autistic child to think in this way. However, I am certain that this is the way Hayden thinks. In fact, I suspect that many kids on the autism spectrum think this way too. Let's look even more deeply into Hayden's world.

The world we experience is an interpretation based on the tools we use to examine it. If I use my eyes to look at my finger, I see something quite different from what I see if I use a microscope or a magnifying glass. Things would look totally different still if I were to use an electron microscope.

73

I am aware, further, that the different points of view these various tools afford me co-exist; one does not negate either of the others. It is this that allows me to perceive the world as continuous, connected, inter-related and congruent.

I am also aware of what I call the "mobile effect." If I move any facet of a balanced mobile, the whole thing shifts to compensate and rebalance, much the way my brain works when it lets me see the world as continuous, as illustrated above. This is how a brain *without* autism functions.

But Hayden's brain is an autistic one, which means his sensory systems, interpreting mechanisms, and logic are immature, incomplete. They give him a view of the world that is often inconsistent, therefore unreliable. In fact, he sees his surroundings as divided into little boxes that are separate, disconnected, unrelated. He has no concept of the mobile effect. When one thing changes, his whole world changes and he hasn't a clue why. The sensory world gives him almost no consistency, nothing solid or grounding. This is clearly quite scary for him. It would be for anyone.

An example might help here. Imagine this from the non-autistic point of view: tomorrow the sun rises at 4:00 am and sets at 3:00 pm; the next day it rises at 10:00 am and sets at midnight. Water sometimes flows uphill, sometimes downhill. How would we feel if all of a sudden, this is how the world behaved? We would feel, I believe, just as frightened and upended as Hayden does in his world of disconnected perceptions.

Thomas McKean, an adult with autism, wrote in his insightful book, *Soon Will Come the Light*,[1] that sometimes the keys on his computer feel as hot as fire. What if things felt different at different times—sometimes hot, sometimes

---

1. McKean, Thomas A. *Soon Will Come the Light: a View from inside the Autism Puzzle.* 2nd ed., Future Horizons, 1994.

cool? What if your eyes didn't always focus, or their dominance shifted back and forth: that is, sometimes the right one was dominant, sometimes the left. The autistic person's visual world is often unreliable in precisely this way.

Suppose you could sometimes hear other people's breathing as loud as the ocean's roar? Wouldn't you tune out all sound just to survive? What if you couldn't tell where your body ends and the rest of the world begins? Would you feel safe in crowds, small spaces, unfamiliar places? If the physical world appeared to have no consistency, hence, no security, most likely you would try to find tis security elsewhere and cling fiercely to this "known," as one adrift at sea clings to a life raft because life literally depends on it.

So what about Mrs. R the music teacher. If she had always been Hayden's music teacher before, but this term she's right next door but is not his music teacher, I think you can imagine how unsettled, confused and scared Hayden would be, and that his behavior would reflect that, as in fact it did.

Hayden clapped when I ask if he was mad at Mr. B, so I needed to validate as accurately as I could what he was feeling by asking a few more questions.

"Did it seem like third grade was going along nicely and everything was good, then it was music time, and you love music and you were excited about music class, but when you got there, Mrs. R wasn't there like she was supposed to be? But then you saw her in another room, but in your room some unknown Mr. B was in charge of music. He wasn't supposed to be there, but he was, and he didn't do things right, like Mrs. R did, and you didn't know what happened or what was going on, so you got scared, and then mad, and then you misbehaved?" A mouthful, I know, but it definitely hit the right spot in the autistic brain with which I was working.

While I presented the above explanation to him, Hayden listened attentively and became more and more animated as

I spoke, until he was laughing robustly, squealing, clapping, rocking like there was no tomorrow. Then he hugged me, and hugged me some more. He felt safe. What he was feeling but could not express or understand, had been spoken and affirmed in detail, which made him feel validated. He doesn't understand the world, but I do: I am his liaison to security. Finally, he felt safe because he had been understood. This was my "all clear." Now it was time to dismantle his rule.

"You have a rule that Mrs. R is the music teacher," I said. "But you don't make the rules about teachers, the school board does." I continued, "When you were in kindergarten, the school board made the rule that Mrs. R was the music teacher; when you were in first grade, the school board made the rule that Mrs. R was music teacher; when you were in second grade, the school board made the rule that Mrs. R was music teacher. But now you're in third grade and the school board has made the rule that Mr. B is the music teacher and Mrs. R is the second-grade music teacher."

When I finished, Hayden made his disapproval noises, "Eh, eh, eh!"

"Does this all make you mad at the school board?" I asked.

He clapped his yes, so I asked if he wanted to be mad at the school board; he did. I sang a 'Mad Song' at the school board for making the rule that Mr. B was now music teacher.

Then I asked if he wanted to be mad at Mr. B for being music teacher. The answer was by now obvious, so I sang a 'Mad Song' at Mr. B for being his music teacher this year and at Mrs. R for not being the music teacher this year.

"Even if you're mad, it doesn't change anything," I said. "You do not change the world with your madness. You may keep it, if you want to, or you can be done with it and let it go, if you want to. You are in charge of you. Are you all done talking about music teachers?"

His clapping said that he was, so I sang the 'I Love You Song', and he got down off the talk chair and went off to play.

I had exposed the specific tacit rule Hayden used in this scenario. At the beginning of this process, this rule represented security to him. Then I led him through his feelings, putting into words he could understand the reasoning process he could not perform. Finally, I led him to a higher level of security and closure. Debbie never again reported problems with Hayden in music class.

Behavior is a language to be understood, not a disease to be eradicated. When we listen for the "voice of behavior," it can stop screaming to be heard. In my almost three decades of experience with Hayden, I've discovered that the algorithm I've applied in most cases is a viable, respectful, teachable/learnable, inexpensive, simple (but not easy), effective way to help children with autism and other neurological issues move through their insecurities, fears, and anger to a place of resolution and peace. I've also found it to be effective with infants, toddlers, and older children. Interestingly, after she read an early version of this manuscript, a friend said that applying these concepts helped her care for an elderly relative.

* * *

Acupuncture is among the many complimentary forms of treatment Hayden has undergone. He always felt positive about his sessions, which indicated that they had made him feel better. After about ten treatments with needles placed in his feet, legs and head, however, Dr. T tried some needles in his wrists. This was the first time Hayden was uncooperative when the needles were placed. He acted sullen and unresponsive afterwards.

When Dr. T left the room I asked Hayden if he was mad. He indicated that yes, he was. Then I asked if he was mad at Dr. T, and again, he answered in the affirmative.

"Do you have a rule that Dr. T is supposed to only put needles in your feet, legs and head?" I inquired, and he indicated that he did have such a rule. Next, I asked if he wanted to be mad at Dr. T, and he let me know that he did.

So I figured it was time to sing a 'Mad Song' at Dr. T for putting needles in his wrists when Hayden had a tacit rule that he was not supposed to. I then turned and faced Hayden directly and sang the 'Mad Song' at me for letting Dr. T do this. I watched Hayden's smile form when I thanked him for telling me about his being mad.

Next, I restated his rule, and reminded him that he was not a doctor, nor did he get to decide what the real doctor did. Then I sang the 'I Love You Song' and all was well. Hayden was no longer troubled. But every time after that, when Dr. T placed needles in locations other than his head, feet or legs, Hayden withdrew until we once again dismantled his tacit rule about where the needles should be. Sometimes, this process needs to be undergone several times before it 'takes.'

It would be impossible to list all of Hayden's tacit rules, but there are several more I feel compelled to mention: I'm not supposed to go out without Hayden; he's the only kid who's allowed to play on my bed or I'm allowed to push on the swing; he can play with my hair whenever he wants to; I'm not supposed to go places without him, but he can go places without me; he's the only one who can ride in the front passenger seat when I drive. Furthermore, I'm supposed to let Hayden be the boss and do anything he wants; I'm not supposed to talk on the phone too long; Poppa and I are not supposed to cough or sneeze because it hurts Hayden's ears; Hayden can play with my things; Hayden always gets a bath when the bathtub water is running; I'm supposed to know what he wants; he doesn't have to speak out-loud in English; I'm not supposed to have the hurry-worry blues (i.e., I'm not supposed to be concerned that I haven't accomplished enough or am not on time for something); I'm not supposed to be tired or sick. Basically, the way something is the first time around becomes a rule, or if he particularly likes something a certain way, that can become a rule too.

When Hayden was thirteen, I stumbled upon one of his most deeply held tacit rules. This one in particular revealed a lot about his understanding of the kinds of things we would all consider so obvious that we wouldn't normally consider them at all. It took a long time to dismantle but it was well worth it.

On an otherwise ordinary Sunday afternoon, Hayden's mother Chelle, his sister Chelsea, and two other little girls came to our house unexpectedly. Young children use to love coming over because there were loads of talking, singing, flashing, spinning toddler toys that Hayden adored, along with the inside swing, Tumble Top, Spinner, Cosmic Rocker, a huge therapy ball, bean bags, and all kinds of games. We had converted our living room into a playroom and a brightly colored bedroom for Hayden.

Hayden was not too fond of having other kids here, though, and that included these little Sunday visitors. It was obvious that he felt they invaded his territory, played with his toys too long, made too much noise, interrupted his usual routine, and took my time and attention away from him! This last piece was clearly jealousy on his part.

When all was said and done, though, this time Hayden did pretty well tolerating his surprise visitors, which is to say that he behaved very nicely while they were here. But it was no surprise that after they left he turned away from me and wouldn't respond when I addressed him. The fact that I had not told him that they were coming made the situation difficult for him, despite the fact that I didn't know they were coming either! We sang many Mad Songs aimed at me that began with my not telling him the girls were coming, and went on about my being so busy with them that he felt left out, uncared for and unloved.

We didn't even get through processing it all before it was time for Hayden to go to bed, so at lights out, he turned away from me, which was his way of punishing me for my "transgressions" of the day.

Before I knew it, another Sunday rolled around and I had pretty much forgotten about Hayden's anger of the Sunday before because this turned out to be a busy day too. I was to babysit Hayden's younger siblings while his dad and stepmom packed for a cross-country move to Minnesota.

Hayden genuinely liked Zachary (four), Zayne (two), and Zoe (one), and had always enjoyed their visits. But every other time they had come over, previous to this time, either one or both of their parents accompanied them. So this was a first for Hayden—he was just not accustomed to my having complete responsibility for all of them. His sister Chelsea came over more often and, although he liked her, at times he was puzzled and jealous of the things Chelsea and I did together. He saw a relationship between us that he wanted to be part of, but he hadn't yet been able to figure out how to make that happen.

Even though I explicitly told Hayden I would look after the kids myself this time, because Daddy and Mama Gayla couldn't be there, I'm sure he didn't understand all the ramifications of this because it wasn't in his past experience.

That aside, it started out as a busy, hectic, fun day, though a bit sad for Chelsea, Zachary, and me because we knew it would be a long time before all five kids would be together again. For Hayden, the concept of distance is as obscure as the concept of time. It's a long way to Seattle to see Judy or Bette, and it's a long way to Portland to see Aunt Gerre and Uncle Lowell. But my explanation that Daddy, Mama Gayla, Zachary, Zayne, Zoe and his Great-Grandma Gina were moving a long, long, long, way away—far, far, away—could have been spoken in Swahili, for all the meaning it had for Hayden.

By day's end, it was safe to say that it had been a good one: Grandma Carolyn's house was a fun place, and this day it did not disappoint. Chelsea had a great time helping out with the younger kids, and Hayden had graciously shared his room, his toys and a train movie with the other boys. He also joined in the spirit of the day—or so it seemed—and appeared to even have been successful at sharing me. He played with the other kids some of the time, but every so often shut himself in his room, which was his way of telling me that he needed a break from it all. I knew parts of this day wouldn't be easy for him.

Hayden's usual bath time was after supper, so before our evening meal, I told him that the little ones would have their baths first. I knew their mom was coming soon, which is why I insisted on the order in which everyone would get their baths.

But somehow, I must have been speaking in Swahili again, because as soon as supper was done he went straight to the bathroom and readied himself for his bath. I reminded Hayden of the bathing order and rounded up Zoe. When I returned to the bathroom, Hayden was in the tub, fully dressed! To his way of thinking, bath time was after supper. Supper was done and the water was running, so Hayden got in the tub to take his bath, not letting a simple thing like being fully clothed stand in his way. He could play in his clothes, so why not bathe in them?

Enter me with naked Zoe.

"Oh, Hayden," I said, "You know it's your usual bath time don't you? And I can see you're ready for your bath. Even though you're ready for your bath, and it's your usual bath time, and you want a bath now, Zoe is going to have her bath first, then Zayne, then Zachary, and then Hayden. You'll

have to get out, even if you don't want to." I got absolutely no response from Hayden.

"Hayden, thank you for telling me you want your bath now," I continued. "Maybe you have a rule that says you get to have a bath after supper when water's running in your bathtub."

Hayden did what he always does once he's been understood: he smiled, resumed eye contact, squealed, and rocked, all of which validated that this was indeed the rule to which he was adhering.

"Thank you for letting me know that this is your rule," I validated, "Usually it's my rule too. But today the little kids are here, and my rule is that the little kids do their baths first." To further complicate matters, every time Zachary, the five-year-old, heard me say "little kids," he interjected to remind me that he was not a little kid! So I had to validate for him by responding and saying that yes, he was getting bigger and he was not as little as Zayne and Zoe, though he was littler than Hayden. This seemed to satisfy the little tyke. But it only worked momentarily, until I said "little kids" again! Oh, my word!

In the meantime, Hayden hadn't move an inch. He wasn't disobeying me, though, nor was he acting in a non-compliant, rebellious or obstinate manner. He simply had no comprehension whatsoever of what was happening around him.

You may disagree and even think he simply disobeyed me by getting in the bathtub when he did. And I admit, it sure looked that way. Kids with autism have a reputation for doing this. Thirty years ago I probably would have labeled him not only disobedient and rebellious, but stubborn to boot. I may have also been full of righteous indignation and may have resorted to scolding and punishment as well. Back then, that was the way kids with autism were treated, pretty much across the board.

So, how did I know he was not misbehaving in the bathing incident? Perhaps it was the expression on his face, or maybe his body language at the time (innocence and defiance do not look the same). Or maybe it was the baker's dozen worth of years that had passed, during which I observed him constantly, stuck right by him, prayed for him, came to know him inside and out. I can't say how I knew, just that I know that I knew.

To better understand where Hayden was through this mayhem, think of being told, "Don't see blue today." The (very) old TV's had a button to press that took out certain colors. Our eyes do not. When you see blue, you see blue. It's not an option not to. If you tell a kid like Hayden not to do something he's been programmed to do, it's tantamount to telling someone to not see blue.

So there was Hayden—sitting fully clothed in the bathtub while it filled up with water—doing exactly what he thought he was supposed to do. Again, I validated him by stating that yes, it was his usual bath time, it was his bathtub, the water was running, he wanted a bath, and he was already in the bathtub. But I also emphasized once again that it was not yet his turn to bathe. I followed this by re-stating my rule: little kids go first today, you're the big kid, so the order is Zoe, Zayne, Zachary, then Hayden.

Well, I must have slipped back into Swahili again, because it seemed clear that he could not understand, so would not comply. I shifted gears and moved to a more direct, physical level.

"Hayden," I said, "I know you want a bath now, but it's Zoe's bath time. You need to come out of the tub now."

I took his hand. "Come on, now, stand up. That's right, stand up. Thank you. Good job! Now come on out. Come on, you need to get out. Get out of the bathtub." My hand and voice calmly guided him and out he came.

Though Hayden was confused (think of how you might feel, for example, if the newspaper you were reading suddenly went blank), but I praised him profusely: "Thank you. Thank you!" I said. "You did such a good job, even if you didn't want to. We'll get your wet clothes off and you can play in your room or be mad at me for making you get out of the bathtub." Hayden then went to his room and played, but I knew that in his eyes, I was guilty, and my time of reckoning was just around the corner.

Eventually, all the little ones had their baths and I helped them get back into their clothes. While Hayden was taking his bath, their mom came to pick them up. I had succeeded in getting them ready on time, but there was a price to pay!

Even though Hayden cooperated with me and was present and relating while I shampooed, scrubbed, dried, and combed him then got him into his jammies, I knew he hadn't forgotten what had happened. I knew he would call me on the carpet for all his rules broken that day, and he would do it by acting out. Hayden climbed on my bed and I lay down beside him, as I did nightly, to sing his 'Quiet Song.' Immediately, he turned his face away from me. This was his gesture for a silent scream. It implied that he was mad at me and was punishing me by turning away from me so that I fell unloved like I had made him feel unloved. At that point, I tried conversing with him, but my words brought only silence. I positioned myself on the other side of Hayden, only to have him turn away again.

"You're not wanting to look at me tonight. Maybe you're mad at me?" I conjectured.

Angry sounds from him confirmed that this was the case.

"Are you mad at me because Zoe, Zayne and Zachary had baths tonight in your tub before you?"

Absolutely!!!!!!!

"Do you want to be mad at me?" He most definitely did, so I sang the 'Mad Song' at myself over and over and over again, but the mad in Hayden still didn't seem be over.

We repeated his rule about the bath; we talked about his wanting to punish me; we processed and processed, but still, he wouldn't look at me. I knew there was a missing piece, some anger of his we had yet to address, but I didn't know what it was, so I kept searching.

"Does it seem like I don't love you very much because I let the other kids in the bath first, and if I really, really, really loved you I'd have let you do your bath first?"

A definite yes came from Hayden. Yet, I still I wasn't sure we were over this one. So I affirmed that I loved him even though I let Zoe, Zayne, and Zachary take their baths first. He went silently to sleep, facing as far away from me as he possibly could.

The next morning brought with it more frustration for us both. He wouldn't even give me a hug, which told me loud and clear that he was still mad at me and that there was something we had not yet processed.

"Are you mad at me today?"

His smiling, eye contact, and clapping said, "Yes and NOW I want to talk about it."

"Ah, ha! Now we're making progress!" I thought to myself.

"Are you mad at me for letting the kids into your room to play with your toys?" I asked.

No, he let me know that wasn't it.

"I can tell you're mad at me, but I don't know why. Would you like to be mad at me because I don't know why?"

He indicated he would, so I sang,

> *You are mad at me.*
> *You are mad at me,*
> *I don't know why, but you do and you think I should,*
> *So you are mad at me.*

I followed this with a sort of generalized 'Mad Song' because I knew there was still something he was mad at me for. I just didn't know what. When it came time to get ready for school, we got into that busy routine.

Somehow, I must have missed some sign of this five-year-old's smoldering anger (physically he was 13, but he was developmentally only 5), because Hayden was acting as if I had violated an important tacit rule. My intuition told me all would come to light later in the day. Meantime, I was clueless.

Our getting-ready-for-school routine went smoothly enough. Hayden was cooperative and jovial, but also seemed to be biding his time. After lunch when I picked him up for his acupuncture appointment he greeted me with smiles, hugs, laughter, squeals and rocking. We got into the car, did up our seat belts, and headed to the acupuncturist's office.

We were on the road for fewer than five minutes when Hayden began emitting his disgruntled "eh, eh, eh" sounds, which used to signal that he would soon scream. I suspected they still did and that I was really in for it.

"Sounds like you're mad," I observed.

He clapped, telling me that yes, he was indeed.

"Are you possibly mad at me?"

Piercing, sustained angry sounds poured out their indictment of me.

He was very mad at me! I thought back over what had happened with the kids the day before and even went as far back as the previous Sunday. I conjectured that his anger might have something to do with both weekends. Still, I drew a blank—this was a tough one.

"Are you mad about something having to do with the kids?"

Another long stream of angry sounds emanated from deep inside of Hayden. He wouldn't look at me, and he stopped rocking and laughing. All of this signaled that he was extremely angry, but I still didn't understand exactly why.

I had already processed everything I could think of about the little ones, but had obviously missed something. Whatever it was, he had been mad about it last night, this morning, and now, and possibly even last Sunday night.

"Thank you for telling me that you're very, very mad about something having to do with the little kids, and you think I should know and you're mad at me because I don't."

"Most definitely!" came his assent. Frequently Hayden chose car trips—such as this one on our way home from school—to work on his feelings, so this development was not surprising.

"So you're very mad about something having to do with the little kids who visited and you think I should know what it is?"

"You said it!" he motioned with his pinky finger sign. I could just feel him brooding beside me.

"Are you mad because the kids were at our house yesterday and last week?"

"No," he shook his head. That wasn't it.

"Are you mad because the kids played with your toys and were in your room?"

Not that, either, he indicated. I had decided to double-check the things we had already processed to make sure they had all really been "cleared."

"Are you mad because the kids were too loud?"

A quick glance and smile said to me, "Yes, the kids were too noisy, but that's not what I'm thinking about right now."

"Are you mad about the kids having baths first?" Again, Hayden gave me a quick glance and a smile.

"Are you mad because the kids played and slept on Poppa's and my bed?"

Yet another quick look, plus a smile and a clap, told me I was getting warmer.

"Are you mad because I took care of the kids and you felt left out, unloved, uncared for and unimportant?"

"Yes," he signaled. But once again he indicated that was not what he was mad about right now.

Stumped! That's what I was! But I was also tenacious.

"But you are mad about something to do with little kids?"

Another long, angry burst came from Hayden.

In total desperation, I asked, "GOD, what else can he possibly be mad about that has to do with the kids?"

As I remembered that all I needed to do was ask and I would receive, the answer came, clear as a bell, when my spiritual guide said,

"You carried the little ones but you didn't carry Hayden." As soon as I heard this in my mind's 'ear,' it was as if enough floodlights to fill a whole football field switched on in my brain.

"Of course!" I thought to myself. "How hilarious, and how sad...and how incredible this was! But how it made complete sense! I wondered why on earth I hadn't caught it earlier. Hayden at the time had no sense of logic, no understanding of cause and effect. The fact that he was then almost as big as I was, was irrelevant to him and how he saw the scenarios in which the kids visited: he was not being carried but the other kids were. Hayden was sitting very still while my floodlights beamed brightly.

"Are you mad at me because I carried the little kids and I didn't carry you?" I asked Hayden.

He laughed! He squealed! He rocked back-and-forth with great abandon! And then he made eye contact again, as a long, continuous stream of angry sounds validated that not only was this true, it was intensely true!

I was overcome by the desire to laugh, cry, chide, explain, and defend myself. Yet none of these would have been appropriate. Instead, I contemplated the fact that to Hayden what I had done—or in this case, not done—must have felt like complete and utter rejection.

I sat there in the car and took time to settle down and center myself, to move away from feelings of my own personal 'should haves' towards the peace, love, and understanding that I have always found at my center. I allowed myself to see everything that had happened during the last week from Hayden's perspective.

My memory opened up and set me down in just the right place now...For years, I had carried Hayden, much longer than most kids get carried. Walking didn't work for him even for short distances, until about age six. During the summer when he was eight, I discarded the stroller and we were able to go to parks and zoos without it. When he got tired of walking, he simply looked up at me, like any toddler, to let me know that he wanted to be carried. At the time I said, "Just a little bit. You're too big for me to carry very long," never realizing until now, five years later, that even back then, especially back then, I might as well have been speaking Swahili! Why? Because Hayden had absolutely no comprehension of time that would help him make sense of and feel better about the scenario at hand, where all the little kids had been carried but he had not.

I remembered, further, the last time I had picked Hayden up. He was about ten. We had just finished up one of his neurology appointments and were ready to get in the car and head home. A two-and-a-half-hour drive loomed before us and I was anxious to get going. If we got on the road right away, we might be able to beat Seattle's infamous rush-hour traffic. But Hayden just would not get in the car.

With the patience of Job, I encouraged, then waited; I tried to assist him, then waited some more; I cajoled, then waited again. But fifteen minutes later he was still standing there, outside the car. He seemed to try, or start to try, but just could not get himself into the car. Frustration finally set in for both of us. He obviously could not do this simple thing at that particular time, though he had done it countless times before. I was at a total loss as to why.

Meantime, the interstate grew busier by the moment, and my big-city traffic phobia had begun to grab hold. The clock had ticked off close to half-an-hour and we had made no progress.

I considered going back in to revisit the neurologist; maybe he had missed something in his examination. But in the end, I decided against this. Instead, I just picked Hayden up and put him in the car. By the time we got home, three-plus hours later, I had gotten the message quite unequivocally from the back seat that I was not to pick up Hayden ever again. And he stuck to this, at least for a while.

He seemed fine all the way home but then had a hard time getting out of the car and up our few front porch steps. Why? I didn't know, so I was still concerned about this odd, out-of-the-blue behavior. Should I have taken him back in to the neurologist after all?

But no, there was nothing whatsoever wrong with Hayden's legs, or any other part of him, for that matter. I discovered soon enough my horrifying mistake when I went to toilet him upon returning home. So here's what happened. I had taken Hayden to the bathroom after he had seen the neurologist and before our long ride home. But when I put him back together again, I had neglected to pull up his inner SPIO pants (tight elastic pants he wore back then to help him "find his body," to aid him with proprioception). And there they were, right where I had left them—just above his knees! They of course had prevented him entirely from being able to lift his knees, especially from a standing position!

Not only did Hayden not have the words to let me know I had hobbled him thus, he also had no idea that this was why he couldn't get in the car or up the steps. It just so happened that this was the last time I picked Hayden up.

As the years went by, Hayden gradually let go of the SPIO debacle you-will-not-pick-me-up-under-any-circumstances edict, probably because we worked so hard at expunging his anger about it. In fact, Hayden often came to me after this and looked up with that please-pick-me-up-and-carry-me look when he grew tired of walking. And I refused, because he had grown way too heavy for me. I had come to regard the SPIO incident as an isolated one, a sort of emergency measure just to get Hayden into the car when all else failed. Little did I know that he had grabbed hold of the fact, that fateful weekend years later when all the kids were at my house, that I had carried the little ones but I had not carried him. No wonder he felt rejected and unloved by me that weekend when he witnessed me picking the little ones up right and left. He was very sad indeed, but he had shrouded his sadness in anger.

Once I made the connection about his still active desire to be picked up, all of this flashed like lightening through my mind. I tried to get a sense for how it looked from his side of the fence so I could validate his feelings.

"You're mad at me because I carried the little kids and I didn't carry you. Is that it?"

His behavior told me that this was indeed true.

"Maybe you have a rule that says I'm supposed to carry you whenever you grow tired. But I don't have that rule because you are quite hard for me to pick up now. Remember that I have been saying for a while now that you're just too big for me to carry? I used to carry you so you think I should now. But I don't follow your rule."

As I said the above, he listened intently. When I finished, he laughed, rocked in earnest, clapped, and reached over to touch me.

"Does it make you mad that I won't carry you, when you have a rule that says I'm supposed to? Do you want to be mad

at me because I'm supposed to carry you always and I didn't, in fact, don't anymore?"

He did want to be mad at me for this, so I sang the Mad Song at me because I no longer carried him and I used to, and he had a rule that said I'm supposed to, always. As I sang, he made angry, guttural sounds, using his voice to accentuate just how mad he had been.

"You must be very, very mad at me."

With marked animation, he looked directly into my eyes and laughed, squealed and clapped.

"Maybe you're very, very, very mad at me because I won't carry you anymore, but I did carry the little ones."

Unusually loud, other-worldly noises spewed from Hayden over the next several minutes, proclaiming the intensity of his feelings of rejection, unfairness and alleged against-him-ness that I had displayed, as well as my obvious unloving-ness of him. I had the distinct feeling that he felt that not only did I, for no good reason, refuse to carry him, but I had blatantly and shamelessly carried various other little kids. For Hayden, this felt like betrayal to the nth degree!

The humor that juxtaposed the pathos of this turn of events presented a poignant symbol of human misunderstanding. My five-foot-three, one hundred-and twenty-pound, fifty-eight-year-old body refused to carry his five-foot-one, ninety-pound, thirteen-year-old body, but willingly and freely carried thirteen-month-old Zoe and not-yet-two-year-old Beti. But in reality, this didn't mean that I had rejected Hayden, stopped loving him, or refused to care for him. Yet his feelings of being rejected, unloved and uncared for were as real and devastating to him as they would have been if I had dropped him off on some lonely road and had never come back!

Understanding this duality in perception is important in any relationship, and extremely critical with children who have impaired neurological function. There is no right or wrong viewpoint; nobody's to blame for a misunderstanding. It's simply a misunderstanding.

For example, my perception may be more accurately attuned to the physical laws of the material world, wherein there are limits. Hayden's perception, on the other hand, may be more accurately attuned to the spiritual laws of the non-material world, where there are no such limits. If I need to be right and make him wrong, I must resign myself to negative behavior from Hayden because he's not going to change his perception of his rightness and my wrongness. Indeed, he's not capable of doing this. No amount of logical reasoning is going to change that.

Consequently, it is of the utmost importance to understand that there is no blame in these situations. Hayden's feelings are valid; my position is valid. I am the adult; I am in charge; my attitudes set the tone. I validate his feelings and I validate my position. When I respect both of us, he learns to respect us both, in spite of the fact that we see the world quite differently. Finally, I can slowly replace his rules with my rules, trying to be fair to us both.

Our kids are not the *only* ones who invent tacit rules about how the world should behave, then become righteously indignant when they're not conformed to. Do you ever get impatient, or worse, angry when the car in front of yours moves too slowly or doesn't turn quickly enough for you? Why? Because you have a tacit rule that stipulates that the cars around you are supposed to be going just as fast as you want them to go.

You might disagree and say, "No, I'm just in a hurry," or "They're just moving too slowly!" But if you had no expectations regarding how fast everyone else around you is going, you wouldn't be angry, but would instead accept total responsibility for yourself and getting where you need to be on time. If you're running late, if indeed, you arrive late, you should have left earlier.

The driver in front of you is certainly not responsible for your getting somewhere on time. If you left late and expect to drive sixty mph all the way to arrive at your destination on time, you have clearly invented tacit rules about how everyone around you should drive in order for you to achieve your desired outcome. You feel justified in your anger at that jerk in front of you; your expectations (tacit rules) for other drivers seem logical, reasonable, normal, and appropriate to you.

Understand that ASD children feel exactly the same way about their tacit rules. For Hayden, it seemed entirely reasonable and appropriate for me to carry him. Hadn't I always done so? Didn't he get tired walking? If I loved him wouldn't I take care of him? What does being too big have to do with anything? Tacit rules are written from the Child Position, and thus from a position of powerlessness. Oral or written laws come from the Parent Position, and as such are based on physical, even socio-political, power.

The Adult Position, on the other hand, carries true spiritual power because it is based solely on the Law of Love. When I live from my Adult perspective—my spiritual dimension—I approach interactions with love, and this allows me to access my inner peace and serenity. When I live from that space, my child will have an easier time feeling peaceful and serene as well.

* * *

When we travel our highways we notice many signs that give information, directions and warnings. There are stop, yield, railroad-crossing, speed-limit, and exit signs, along with mile markers, signs telling us how far it is to the nearest services, where to eat, where to get gas, and so on. Without these, we might feel nervous, insecure, lost at times, and generally uneasy. Is this the right road? How close am I to where I'm going? What's the legal speed limit? Is there a bathroom coming up? Where can I get gas and something to eat?

Because we are able to read signs and maps and think and speak logically and sequentially, we can come and go quite readily in our communities and beyond. Living life is like driving on an interstate in the daytime—fairly straight, well-marked, with plenty of maps available. But for an individual with autism, life is more like traveling an unknown, unmarked, one-lane, gutted, gravel road full of S-curves, sharp turns, detours, tunnels, and roadblocks, on a foggy night, no less.

You may disagree. Your life may feel pretty uncertain and difficult; and yes, it may well be. However, if you are among the vast majority of people inhabiting this earth, maintaining an upright position is not a challenge; the information you receive from your eyes, ears, nose, and skin is for the most part consistent from hour-to-hour and day-to-day; you are able to close your eyes and know where your body is; you understand that if you turn on only the hot water in your shower, you'll get burned. You see, I'm not talking about your life that you live with respect to the various activities you engage in, but your life of *being in your body*.

For Hayden, just being in his body is disconcerting. If you don't even feel safe and comfortable in your own body, the whole world is a terrifying place. To help him feel more secure and at ease in his world, I talk, talk, and then talk some more to him. I talk to him all the time about everything. I use words to build a constant, consistent, predictable world for him, one that autism has robbed him of. The information that I impart helps reduce his stress and insecurity and helps eliminate potentially negative, destructive behaviors. I do this to give him security on the road of life.

When Hayden was very young, I talked to him constantly in order to give him a connection to the world outside of his autistic cocoon. In spite of his doctor's insistence that Hayden was quite deaf, I talked to him from the very beginning. I knew he listened and understood everything I said and that it was centering for him. I still talk to him about everything. I tell him exactly what is going to happen—when, where, who, how, and why—a full week before it happens (if I know that far in advance), and every day until it happens, and then even afterwards. I cover feelings, situations, reasons, everything. A number of people have questioned why I talk to him in this way.

"Do you think Hayden *understands* any of what you say?" some ask with an incredulous tone.

"No," I answer, "I don't merely think, I *know* he understands everything I say.

When Hayden was very young, during the scream-a-lot days, I found that his screaming would diminish considerably when I explained exactly what was happening. The light really came on for him in his second year on our first real outing (not counting, that is, medical appointments, family gatherings, or church). My niece, Danita, her children, Hayden, and I went to the Children's Museum in Seattle, an hour-and-a-half drive from home.

Meticulous planning went into this trip. In addition to having on hand the usual diapers, extra clothes, baby food and wipes, I also armed myself with a Plan B: What to do if the museum didn't work for Hayden. Plan B consisted of what to have in the car to entertain him if he became over-stimulated, on the one hand, or totally bored, on the other; if he began to scream for some unknown reason; if his auditory sensitivity somehow made the museum too painful an environment for him.

But none of these things happened. Instead, everything went smoothly and a good time was had by all. Hayden tolerated everything well and had a good time, even at lunch in the Seattle Center Food Circus, a busy, boisterous square with loads of cafes and fast-food joints.

By the time we stopped at Danita's to drop them off on the way home, I was feeling pretty smug. I had pulled it off! I had taken a two-year-old autistic child on an all-day excursion with another family to a large community center without a glitch. Since we'd been to Danita's house many times, I figured we were home free once we arrived there.

Was I in for a surprise! We went into Danita's for a stretch, some gab and a potty break, and Hayden started screaming, the really big kind of screaming. Nothing I did soothed him. He just screamed on-and-on. I thought, "Well it was a long day and he's gone into overload, so he'll probably make a ruckus until we get back home," and braced for a noisy drive home. But to my utter astonishment, when we got back into the car the screaming stopped and Hayden seemed quite content.

Now this was a strange development. When Hayden went into overload in those early days, his screaming didn't end until we had arrived home, he was out of the car, into the house, and finally undressed. But this seemingly premature silence was odd indeed. Whatever had disturbed him at Danita's was over, as was his screaming. I was perplexed, but also elated, because it now seemed I could take him places with ease!

The next time we took a day trip, it was to Point Defiance Zoo in Tacoma; we joined forces with Danita's gang again and had another fun, successful day, until, that is, we unloaded at Danita's house, at which time Hayden began to scream inconsolably. All I could think was that he had gone into sensory overload again, from a long, tiring day. Once again, though, just last time, the screaming stopped when we got back in the car. "Wait, I thought to myself, "Something doesn't make sense here." I couldn't figure it out, but that didn't alter my sense of the overall success of the venture.

Our third outing was to a park nearby. It, too, went smoothly, but only until we unloaded at Danita's. Then the screaming commenced. This altered pattern of Hayden's behavior—screaming after a seemingly successfully outing with Danita and her crew, just until we got in the car and started for home—just didn't add up.

Well, as the saying goes, Third time's a charm. *At least this third time was enough to finally convince me something was consistently happening to cause the screaming, something I wasn't catching on to. So as I drove home from Danita's, I backtracked in my mind, starting from the time we had stepped foot in Danita's house. What had happened? What had been said? Why did he not want to go to Danita's house these three times when many times before we'd gone there and he was fine with it? Nothing came to mind, other than the question, "What's different about these times?" Though I had not asked for any divine inspiration this time, the following mental "conversation" came to mind, nonetheless:*

"Backtrack," came the response.

"But I have," I exclaimed.

"Backtrack some more. Go back to the park."

I pictured us all at the park, where we had played and played, but then got ready to leave. I remembered I had given Hayden the usual warning: "One more time. You can play one more time and then we're going to get in the car and go home."

Uh oh! Go home. GO HOME! That's it! When we left the park, I had said we were going home, but then we went to Danita's instead. I know how Hayden thinks. By not doing

98

what I said I would do, I had confused him. He felt lied to, insecure. He thought he couldn't trust me because I hadn't kept my word. That was why he screamed when we went to Danita's house and stopped when we got back in the car. Finally it all made sense. I was both elated and frightened: elated that he was so aware, but frightened by the awesome responsibility of the effects of my words. Would I always be able to handle Hayden's hyper-awareness? At the moment, however, all I could think was that I must always tell Hayden everything that's going to happen right down to the smallest detail.

As you might imagine, I was excited to embark on another outing to test my new theory. I even rehearsed it: "Hayden, it's time to start going home. But before we go home, we're going to stop at Danita's house to drop off Danita, the boys and their stuff. We'll also change your pants at Danita's before we start for home."

To this day I can't remember what the next outing was, but I've surely not forgotten the fact that after I performed my bit, there had been no screaming when we arrived at Danita's. Amazing, huh?

All those times I had run around doing errands and there had been screaming when we returned to the car—was it because I had said I've got to do this or that and then did these and those instead? I'll never know, but what I do know was that this was a major turning point, the beginning of very carefully planned agendas.

"Hayden, I have some things I need to do. I'm going to get the mail, go to the grocery store, go to Puget Sound Energy and pay the bill, go the bank, and then we'll head back home." Once the errands began, I simply named each task as I was about to do it, then told him the next thing that was coming up.

It was not the running around that Hayden couldn't handle. No, it was, from his perspective, that I had left him unprepared on those early outings. This made him feel insecure; it also made me appear untrustworthy. Amazingly, I found I could do any number of errands without triggering Hayden's screams as long as I told him exactly what I was going to do, that I had just done it, and what came next.

One small problem arose with this strategy, though. It seemed someone had wired my car so that it stopped automatically at every garage sale it came to, which is to say, the problem with the transparency-of-my-itinerary solution was that there was as yet no room for spontaneity in my new way of communicating to Hayden everything about to happen.

But how do you plan to stop at a garage sale, unless, of course, you're just going garage sale-ing?! The way I saw it was that this was part of the fun of stopping at garage sales— the spontaneity factor, the stopping at a whim when you're not just garage sale-ing. I suppose I could have just stopped when I felt like it and put up with the screaming. But my overall goal was to establish consistency and security in Hayden's world by being impeccable in my word.

After several months of disciplined scheduling and minute-to-minute reports to Hayden on the progress of our schedule, we were able to pull off long errand runs with absolutely no screams. Soon, however, along came a Friday when I found myself thinking about garage sales; I had a brainstorm and I tried it out. I recited the day's list of activities and stops to Hayden.

"And maybe sometime today," I added, "we'll stop at a garage sale." Soon thereafter, my trusty vehicle automatically put on the brakes at a particularly promising-looking sale.

"Remember I said sometime today maybe we would stop at a garage sale? Well, now is sometime and we're going to stop at this garage sale."

I held my breath and waited for his reaction. I wondered if he would scream, fuss, land in overload. But, no! It appeared

I could introduce an unknown something into the itinerary and he could handle it. Whoopee! I had done it! I felt so liberated! I had established myself—my word—as his stability and security so deeply that I could add an unknown factor to his world without him feeling threatened. I must say, I felt rather elated. It was just a little change, but no matter. If I could change one little piece, I knew I could eventually change anything little-by-little.

It was in this way that I came to realize that Hayden could in fact handle change. What he couldn't deal with was insecurity, and this fact has never changed. If I could give him an overall sense of security, perhaps he wouldn't need such a rigid environment. Wow. This was big.

Maybe this one little adjustment doesn't seem like much, and in a sense it wasn't much. But the saying, 'A journey of 1,000 miles begins with one step,' came to mind. I now knew that if I proceeded slowly and changed one thing at a time until each new thing became commonplace and secure, the whole world would eventually open up to Hayden. And you know what? It has.

The next summer, when Hayden was three, my family had a reunion some two thousand miles away in southern Texas. I hadn't seen my mother for several years, and Hayden was handling new situations quite well. After much deliberation—I thought, prayed, tried to work out the logistics in my mind—I decided we could do it because I was quite sure it would work out fine.

My decisions about what Hayden can and can't do are made with much deliberation. I consider all the challenges, all the reasons why it might not work. Then I tally up all the potential benefits. I try to decide if the benefits outweigh the challenges and whether I can deal with those challenges. Then I decide. Once I make a decision, however, it's made. If I say no, it won't work, it's really no, and I simply close that door.

For instance, during the summer when Hayden was just over a year old, my family also had a reunion and I decided not to go. I considered it, yes, in minute detail. But the final decision was a no-go and that was that. I didn't think Hayden was up to it yet. But this time the answer was "Yes!"

From then on there was nothing but challenges; I rose to the occasion, however, and figured out how to make it all work. I thought through all the angles and decided Hayden and I would make the eight-hour plane trip to Texas for a ten-day stay. The trip included loads of unfamiliar people, borrowed living quarters, sweltering heat, the two-hour time difference, and a schedule thrown totally askew for a spontaneous trip down to Mexico. But it all came off without any major hitches.

The most inconvenient aspect of the trip was that in true Rain Man fashion, Hayden's body knew what time it really was. His body was still in the Pacific Time zone and it stayed there for the entire trip! This meant that he went to sleep at 9:00 p.m. Pacific Time on the button (which was 11:00 p.m., Texas time), and slept until 6:00 a.m. Pacific Time (8:00 a.m., Texas time). But the only person who cared was me. My time to relax was after 9:00 p.m., when, typically, I didn't need to worry about anyone else's safety, wants, or needs. I missed that. (Do you hear shades of a tacit rule here?)

Overall, though, it was a wonderful trip and we flew home on cloud nine! I remember it felt like I had taken a difficult exam and passed, no, aced–it. I was ecstatic. All that gloom and doom I'd heard about kids with autism—about their negative behavior, not being able to handle change, not being able to go anywhere or do anything–I thought I had proven it all wrong. The success of this trip validated my approach to working with Hayden and my beliefs about autism. No longer did I feel intimidated by or helpless in the face of autism; it had lost its sting for me. I remember at the time thinking that autism was simply irrelevant.

Autism is irrelevant. Only faith, hope and love are relevant. Yes, a lot of hard work is necessary, but when isn't it if something challenging is in the balance? So in a sense, even the hard work became irrelevant, a given.

* * *

It is often assumed that kids with severe delays in physical and language development are also delayed in receptive language and social skills. One day when I went to pick up Hayden from his regular Kindergarten class, his teacher Debbie said,

"Hayden was very autistic today."

"Meaning?" I asked.

"Meaning he behaved very badly, was uncooperative, hit and kicked other students on the playground, threw things and was generally belligerent and uncooperative."

"Oh, was that all?" I thought. "Jeez!"

This was the first time Debbie had reported that Hayden had engaged in negative behavior. Because I believe that behaviors are a special kind of communication, I asked her what had been different, what had happened at school. She couldn't think of anything noteworthy. Then I asked her to think back over the entire morning and tell me exactly when she first noticed anything unusual about what Hayden had been up to. I recalled that he had been fine at home before school and, subsequently, when I left him in the classroom.

After replaying the scene in her mind's eye, Debbie said, "It was when I told him, 'Get your rabbit and we'll go to circle,' that he refused to pick up his rabbit. He threw it to the floor, and then wouldn't go to circle."

The moment Debbie said "rabbit," I flushed all over and a sinking feeling seized my insides. I hadn't understood why at the time, but now I realized I was most likely the cause of Hayden's having acted out.

Let's back up a bit to fully understand what happened, because this one's a doosey! Each week, Hayden's Kindergarten class learned about a single letter of the alphabet. They learned how it sounded, how to recognize it, and how to write it. Then they were taught how to find words beginning with that letter. Finally, each child was invited to bring to class from home one or two items that began with the letter of the week; the idea was to share these with each other in daily circle time so that everyone learned a bunch of new words.

So, at the beginning of each week, I would gather a heap of things that started with that week's letter. Then I would let Hayden pick one item from among them to put in his backpack to bring to school. This week, it so happened, was R-week, but my R-pile was a little sparse. In fact, by Thursday, the only thing left was a soft, cuddly, stuffed rabbit, which Hayden had emphatically rejected each and every previous R-day that week.

Well, that particular morning commenced with the clock suddenly and entirely on its own jumping ahead a good fifteen minutes; it was time to leave, but there was just no way! I was running late, like a train at rush hour. And again, Hayden rejected that lone rabbit. But nothing else was readily available; my house had been stripped of all R-things! Of course, I didn't want Hayden to arrive at circle time empty-handed, so I grabbed the little rabbit anyway as I muttered to myself, "I don't know why he doesn't want this rabbit; it makes for a perfectly good R-word." Hastily, and I must admit, a tad surreptitiously, I stuffed it into Hayden's backpack and we toddled off to school. Little did I know that in so doing I had set into motion a perfect storm, culminating in a hell of a tsunami of tacit rule-ism.

When Debbie, after the fact, said "rabbit," uh-oh, I knew I had goofed big-time. I told her to say no more and that Hayden and I would work on it. Then I took a belligerent Hayden home, and mentioned that when we got there we would need to talk. I, that is, would do damage control. We went straight to the talk chair.

"Debbie said you behaved very badly in school today," I said. He acknowledged that this was true.

"It seems to be because of the rabbit," I continued. He made his typical disgruntled sounds.

"That was my fault. You said you didn't want the rabbit and I put it in your backpack anyway."

Loud angry sounds followed, not at all to my surprise.

"I was a butt-in-ski grandma. I had no right to interfere with your school work and I put that rabbit in your backpack anyway."

Finally, he laughed and clapped in agreement.

"Maybe that made you mad at me."

Again, he clapped.

"Do you want to be mad at me?"

He clapped yes, so I sang a 'Mad Song':

You are mad at me.
You are mad at me.
I put the rabbit in your backpack that you didn't want.
You are mad at me.

After I sang this several times, he laughed and made eye contact freely, so I finished with an 'I Love You' song. I then asked him to forgive me for being a butt-in-ski grandma, which he did. I promised not to interfere in his schoolwork anymore. Still, I had trouble letting go of this R-word thing.

"But I still don't understand why you didn't want the rabbit. 'Rabbit' is a perfectly good R-word," I commented.

Once again, loud, angry sounds emanated from the very depths of the place where Hayden held his frustration about a world he could not express in words. Then he ran off to play, or possibly perseverate, and I was left to further ponder why he had been so adamantly against the rabbit. There were still some stormy, gray clouds on the horizon, it appeared.

"GOD," I asked, drawing from my place of frustration, "Why is he so against the rabbit?"

Though no answer came—which usually meant I was to figure this one out on my own—at least Hayden's belligerence had dissipated and he had more or less returned to his old self. As I saw it, though, those clouds on the horizon hadn't moved an inch.

Later on that afternoon, still puzzled, I sat before that poor rabbit, which had been returned to its home in the living room; I tried to retrace the course of the storm. It didn't take too long: Boom! I realized my mistake: it's a bunny *rabbit, not just a rabbit!*

When Hayden came home from school, I was right at the door, more than excited to test my theory:

"Is this a bunny rabbit?" I asked.

He laughed wildly; he clapped raucously. And then he hugged me like he had never hugged me before, because I had finally seen the light! He hadn't wanted to take a B-thing during R-week; and, he must have felt that even if I was wrong about the whole thing, then Debbie would get it right. But when he got to school and Debbie called it a rabbit too, his whole world turned upside-down and inside-out. No wonder his mind had swirled wildly in confusion and fear. Since he had no idea why, he had lashed out in anger.

When I took Hayden to school the next day, I laid it all out for Debbie and said I didn't expect any further problems—I had figured it all out.

Ah ha! Not so fast! By then she had been able to shed even more light on the incident.

As it turned out, the previous week had been B-week and many of the kids had brought in cute, fuzzy little stuffed bunny rabbits quite similar to the oft-rejected one we had at home. Poor thing. I could swear its ears had begun to hang even lower as Hayden repeatedly snubbed it.

Debbie further reported, though, that Hayden seemed to have been okay with this because he had plenty of perfectly acceptable B-items to choose from to present every day that week, though apparently I had failed to include our infamous little bunny rabbit among them.

Believe it or not, this was Hayden's only major episode of negative behavior in Kindergarten. And in the end, it was all my fault!

* * *

In second grade, Hayden's school staged an earthquake drill that really threw Hayden for a loop. Debbie, who had by then functioned as his trusty teaching assistant, and worked alongside me until I phased myself out at school, felt she had prepped him as well as possible. We both realized, though, that there was no avoiding the element of surprise inherent in a drill of any kind. The school let us know, as caregivers of Hayden, what day the drill would be on, yes, but not what time it was secretly scheduled for. So when Hayden and his classmates were instructed to crouch under their desks, he panicked and sounded his own alarm—a blood-curdling scream of fear and uncertainty, of unbridled angst.

As soon as I mentioned proprioception (the ability to be aware of one's body's physical limits in space—something that many autistic people are unable to sense), Debbie knew precisely what had happened. Cramped in a small space, Hayden was absolutely terrified. If she had been able to put her body around his, thus defining his physical parameters, he'd have been okay. She suggested to the powers that be at school that standing in a doorway was perhaps a more Hayden-feasible alternative for the next drill.

I certainly wouldn't classify Hayden's screaming through this drill, hair-raising as it was, as bad behavior on his part. In reality, the whole thing was a set-up for failure for him, but one, thankfully, that didn't endanger him or anyone else. Debbie and I were able to brainstorm and modify his response to drills in such a way that when they happened again, Hayden felt safer.

But there was a major incident when Hayden was in third grade that required quick thinking and acting on Debbie's part. At the time, Hayden wore a SPIO throughout most of the day. In other words, once he had squeezed his way into it, it gave Hayden a whole lot of invaluable input as to where his body was. Hayden chose to wear it because he was far more comfortable and relaxed with it on than without it. Though he no longer choses to wear it, when he did and summer rolled around, he donned a SPIO I altered by shortening the legs and arms, thus making it a bit cooler. Spring presented its challenges, though, for Hayden and all things SPIO. Some spring days in in the Pacific Northwest, while starting out quite cold, can become warm and sunny once the sun reaches its apex.

On one such day, when Hayden was in his third-grade classroom, for apparently no reason obvious to an uninformed observer, he began to scream. Debbie quickly undressed him because she surmised that overheating was the trigger. Once she had stripped him down to his SPIO, he grew calmer. Next, she took him to the bathroom, removed the SPIO as well, and got him into his regular clothes. Then all was well.

Like many individuals with autism, Hayden does not have a normal awareness of heat or cold. By the time he became *aware that he was overheated, he had already surpassed his trigger point, so he panicked and screamed.*

These were the only major episodes of inappropriate behavior that I can remember from Kindergarten through fifth grade, counting third grade twice, except, that is, for the infamous music teacher situation. All three incidents occurred because Hayden was not able to understand his environment or communicate his questions or needs.

Communication issues are so common with autistic people. But I cannot over-stress my observation that they are most often behind incidents that would otherwise be judged as cases of misbehavior. To judge them thus is not only inaccurate, but does not serve anyone well either. It is by learning the language of the autistic person's behavior that we can come to know, love and understand that person and move with them toward a life of more joy.

* * *

As is true of many children with autism, Hayden was and still is—even as a young adult—fascinated by the feel of hair. He just loves to play with it and makes a beeline to it whenever possible, much the way an infants have an affinity for their mother's hair. So it has always seemed to me to be a safe and harmless way for Hayden to initiate physical contact with me. However, when he began pre-school and initiated contact with his classmates by grabbing their hair, I realized it wasn't as harmless as it at first had seemed!

Hayden's relationship with me was his model for relating, and so he thought that because it was okay to touch my hair, it was okay to play with other people's hair too. We worked really hard at creating rules about playing with hair and learning that there are restrictions. At the beginning of this endeavor, we had only one rule: When I'm ready to go out somewhere, I don't want my hair messed up. To me, this seemed a simple, straightforward, reasonable rule. But when I told Hayden, "I just combed my hair and I don't want it messed up now," it just fell on deaf ears, even though I had known for some time that his hearing was just fine.

My response then was to state my position, remove his hand, and affirm my love for him. But again, he reached for my hair. So again, I calmly re-stated my position, removed his hand, and affirmed my love. Regardless, he reached for my hair yet again! I calmly restated my position, removed his hand, and affirmed my love. But it was clear, nonetheless, that we were on a kind of merry-go-round with this for a while, except it was getting to be anything but merry! In fact, it was a frequent tension-creating situation for several months.

In the midst of this particular learning point, I admit that at times I felt myself grow angry, because it seemed Hayden was outright disobeying me. But I managed to keep my cool and continued to respond calmly to his almost magnetic attraction to hair.

I'll also admit that it wasn't particularly easy to recite our single rule about hair each and every time I got myself ready to go out. Nor was it a piece of cake to witness what appeared to be Hayden's defiance toward and disregard for me in the moment. It seemed he had figured out, somewhere along the way, how to push my buttons, or at least one of them!

One day, as we un-merrily boarded our merry-go-round, I was peeved and sent out a peeved-sounding I-statement to Hayden:

"I don't like my hair messed up when I'm ready to go somewhere."

The look he gave me was so full of innocence and pain that it snapped me right out of my peeved mood. After all, he didn't know what had upset me...But then, how could he *not know? I'd made it plain, or so I thought, on hundreds of occasions!*

Prayer, authentic prayer, is such a wonderful thing. It's always at my fingertips, so why do I wait so long to use it? Now was the time, alright!

"Okay GOD, what's going on?" I asked, peevishly, of course.

"You've been saying you don't want your hair messed up. He doesn't think he's messing it up, that's all," came the simple response.

Well, if this didn't make me feel just like the woman in the story, "The Cookie Thief," from one of the 'Chicken Soup' books! Here's how it goes:

The Cookie Thief
By Valerie Cox

A woman was waiting at an airport one night,
With several long hours before her flight.
She hunted for a book in the airport shops.
Bought a bag of cookies and found a place to drop.

She was engrossed in her book but happened to see,
That the man sitting beside her, as bold as can be.
Grabbed a cookie or two from the bag in-between,
Which she tried to ignore to avoid a scene.

So she munched the cookies and watched the clock,
As the gutsy cookie thief diminished her stock.
She was getting more irritated as the minutes ticked by,
Thinking, "if I wasn't so nice, I would blacken his eye."

With each cookie she took, he took one too.
When only one was left, she wondered what he would do.
With a smile on his face and a nervous laugh,
He took the last cookie and broke it in half.

He offered her half, as he ate the other.
She snatched it from him and thought...oh, brother.
This guy has some nerve and he's also rude.
Why he didn't even show any gratitude!

She had never known when she had been so galled
And sighed with relief when her flight was called.
She gathered her belongings and headed to the gate,
Refusing to look back at that thieving ingrate.

She boarded the plane and sank in her seat,
Then she sought her book, which was almost complete.
As she reached in her bag, she gasped with surprise,
There was her bag of cookies in front of her eyes.

If mine are here, she moaned in despair,
The others were his and he tried to share.
Too late to apologize, she realized with grief,
That she was the rude one, the ingrate, the thief.[1]

I realized that I had grown self-righteously irritated with Hayden during the months when we were working on the hair issue. So after I apologized to him for being so crabby, I asked him if when he played with my hair, he thought he messed it up. His answer was, of course, "No."

Someone once shared with me the observation that when you point a finger at someone else, there are literally three of your fingers pointing right back at you (Point your finger

---

1. From the book A 3rd Helping of Chicken Soup for the Soul by Jack Canfield and Mark Victor Hansen. Copyright 2012 by Chicken Soup for the Soul Publishing, LLC. Published by Backlist, LLC,a unit of Chicken Soup for the Soul Publishing, LLC. Chicken Soup for the Soul is a registered trademark of Chicken Soup for the Soul Publishing, LLC. Reprinted by permission. All rights reserved.

and look at the configuration your fingers automatically take—you'll see just what is meant.) With the hair issue, I had simply seen myself as blameless and put all the blame on Hayden. In reality, this was not a question of blame, not at all. This was instead a clear case of the existence of a cavernous communication gap. I learned from this hair issue not to judge harshly and blame others, but to be more aware of exactly what I mean to say.

Hayden still has an immense attraction to hair; this has not changed. It's a way of "stimming," by which he comforts himself; it is in this sense a cousin to rocking. By now you know that I allow Hayden these self-comfort measures because they are harmless. But I anticipated his playing with other peoples' hair at, say, eighteen, and I realized that I needed to be proactive and put into place a rule about this. So when he was eighteen, what I said to him was exactly what I meant:

"Playing with hair belongs at home. You may play with my hair at home when we watch a movie or when we snuggle."

Hayden has developed so much since then, that in the intervening time, he has learned not to play with anyone else's hair. Once I understood him, he understood me and he has complied with what I considered appropriate behavior ever since.

The takeaway is that we always need to give the autistic people in our lives the benefit of the doubt. What may appear to be misbehavior may be instead our misunderstanding of their behavior, which may in turn stem from our lack of transparency in communicating with *them*.

* * *

Hayden processes things differently from most people. He absolutely loves music, practically any kind of music. He thoroughly enjoys going to concerts, and also is fond of other types

113

of performances, even plays. Because of his desire to go, I take him whenever possible. These outings are, after all, opportunities for him to learn and have fun. When he was twelve-and-a-half years old, we planned an outing to a concert.

"There's a guy, Dax Johnson, who plays the piano, and he'll be giving a concert next week in Tacoma at the Rialto Theater. Your mommy and Chelsea are going," I said, "Would you like to go?"

He laughed; he clapped; he squealed; he showered me with huge hugs. This, of course, was an unconditional "Yes!" But in fact, there were conditions. Yes, conditions, rules, but not unknown, undiscussed edicts about behavior. And I always give Hayden choices when I introduce new rules. This is absolutely key!

"Well, you know," I continued, "there are rules for concerts. It's not appropriate to squeal (just what you would think this would be—loud mouth-play), squish (a term I came up with that means mouth-play with saliva involved), rock a whole bunch, or be loud in any other way at a concert. So if you go, you'll have to choose not to do these things. Do you still want to go?" He indicated that yes, he would still like to go.

I always plan ahead for an outing of any kind, especially a performance. We need to have front-row seats because of Hayden's poor eyesight and his inability to automatically select a visual focus and stick with it. Whatever is directly in front of him is all his autistic brain will allow him to focus on. So it's best if he's not far from the performers and also, if there's nothing between him and the stage, such as a row of audience members' heads.

In addition, because of his deficiencies in proprioception, Hayden fares much better when he isn't hemmed in on all sides by people he doesn't know—being bumped, even lightly touched, by such a person makes him extremely uncomfortable.

I've also found it to be beneficial if, on the day before an outing, we work on the challenges presented by crowds. So we go over how to deal with lots of noise, waiting in line, biding our time before things get started, and the urge to squeal. Practice at sitting quietly for a few hours at once is also paramount.

I've learned through the years that while there is music playing, sitting still without rocking is almost impossible for Hayden. This is because the center for hearing, located in the middle ear, is adjacent to the center for balance, which inhabits the inner ear. This means that when hearing is stimulated, so is movement. But we have worked for years at keeping the rocking to a minimum.

When we arrived at the Rialto on the evening of the Dax Johnson concert, we learned that the performers had been involved in a car accident on the way there, and although no one was injured, the band members were badly shaken and some of their equipment was damaged. So, the concert was canceled.

My nine-year-old granddaughter, Chelsea, was clearly disappointed, but she understood and was able to shift her focus quickly to the very near future and think, "Now what?" But with Hayden, the situation became quite complex.

We began our Plan-B by first acknowledging that we needed one! I took the lead:

"We came to hear Dax Johnson play the piano here in Tacoma at the Rialto Theater. We are here. There is the theater. Your mommy and Chelsea are here just like they said they would be. Even though we're all here at the theater, there's not going to be a concert because Dax Johnson and the people with him had a car accident on the way here. They're okay. They didn't get hurt, but they're pretty upset and some of their stuff got broken. So there's not going to be a concert tonight. It will have to be on a different night."

Immediately, the brilliantly exuberant anticipation drained right out of Hayden's face. He understood that there would be no concert, but from his somber expression, down-turned eyes, and lack of any further response, I could tell he was angry.

"Does it make you mad that there's no concert tonight?" I asked.

His clapping was an immediate affirmation.

"Does that mean that when you go to a concert and they don't have it, you have to be angry?"

Clapping, again.

"Do you need to be mad right now, then?" I asked next.

He clapped yet again.

"Are you mad at Dax Johnson?"

"No," Hayden indicated.

"You're not mad at Dax, but you're still mad. Is that it?"

More clapping.

"Are you mad at Matthew, his producer?"

Hayden was as still as a statue. This meant he was probably not mad at the producer, but considering it. Hayden's stillness is his sign for some degree of ambivalence.

"Then who are you mad at?" Usually I start off by asking if he's mad at me, but I was so obviously not the object of his anger this time. So I continued this line of detective-like questioning that understanding autism had taught me.

"Dax was supposed to play and Dax didn't show up. Are you sure you're not mad at Dax?"

"How about his producer? Are you even a little mad at him now? In the end, he wasn't mad with Dax or his producer.

I finally asked, "It is me? Are you mad at me?" He started clapping and made eye contact with me.

"So you're mad at me because there's no concert tonight?"

He laughed, clapped and squealed—the usual trifecta of affirmation for Hayden.

So, he was mad at me after all. Why me? Then I got it. "I promised you a concert and I'm not taking you to a concert so you're mad at me."

He laughed, clapped, and even squished!

"So that's it," I thought to myself. "You want to be mad at me?" He did indeed, so I sang the Mad Song at me for promising Hayden a concert and not taking him to one.

You are mad at me
You are mad at me.
I promised you a concert tonight,
But I'm not taking you to one.
So, you are mad at me.
You are mad at me.

After I sang this a few times, Hayden came out of the deepest, darkest part of his funk. However, despite the fact that he began to relate and smile again, he was markedly subdued for the rest of the evening. His disappointment was palpable, yet he was not unreachable, nor did he scream or act out.

The next day brought with it a conversation between Hayden and me about how the previous evening had been such a big let-down, so we sang through a 'You Are Disappointed' song several times. Then we hatched our plan to go to the concert when and if Dax came our way again.

Of course, we were both thrilled to hear a few weeks later that Dax, no doubt bummed that he couldn't give his fans a show to remember the first time around, was due for a return engagement in Tacoma just a few months down the line. Hayden and I and the rest of our original gang had a terrifically fun re-do at the Rialto. If at first you don't succeed…

Some may think it inappropriate of me to have accepted Hayden's anger and blame for the Dax evening gone awry, when in fact I believe it was vital that I did, and that I *didn't* attempt to explain everything to him. This is because any further explanation would have been futile.

Hayden lives at the level of feelings. My intention is always to meet him where he is so I can move him into a place closer to reality. Even though they are not usually based on logic, Hayden's feelings are very real. Everyone's feelings are real. So I must begin with them if I hope to move beyond them. Feelings are always the natural starting point in any therapeutic relationship.

Perhaps it helps to think of it this way. Suppose your kids get lost, though you know no wrong-doing has occurred. Of course the first thing to do is discover where they are. Then you must go to them, meet them where they are, literally. This is the only way you can get to the point of bringing them home. There is no way to skip this step of going to where your children are. Even if you know exactly where they are, you must meet them there in order to bring them home.

The same is true of feelings. You must start where your children are, not where you want them to be. Then and only then can you lead them to where you want them to go. Since I knew Hayden's anger at me was just his way of compartmentalizing his disappointment at the canceled concert, it did not touch me personally. It was only relevant to me insofar as it was Hayden's way of communicating his feelings.

One day when he was in grammar school, when Hayden came home, he headed straight to our talk chair, right after his usual bathroom run. I went to him there and sat with him. He rather quickly grew subdued.

"Looks like you need to talk," I offered.

"Yes!" he clapped.

"Did you have a problem at school today?"

He clapped his agreement again.

"I'm sorry you had a problem at school. It must have been a problem with a kid or a teacher. Was it a problem with a

kid?" Hayden took on that eerie, statue-stillness that indicates ambivalence. I concluded it was likely not a schoolmate.

"Did you have a problem with a teacher?" I asked.

He signaled that he did.

"Was it Martha?"

"No," he signaled.

"Was it Melissa?"

"No," again. I was really bringing into play some of my best autism detective work.

"Was it Laura?"

"Nope." She wasn't the culprit either.

"Hmmm..." I mused.

"Was it Michelle?"

"No," was his emphatically negative comeback.

"Was it Mrs. Z?"

"Yes!" he finally clapped.

"You had a problem today with Mrs. Z. Okay. I wonder what kind of problem you had with Mrs. Z. Did it seem to you like Mrs. Z was mean and grouchy today?"

His claps, laughter and squeals indicated I had hit the nail on the head.

"Did Mrs. Z have the hurry-worry blues today?" Right again. Now I was getting somewhere!

"Did it seem like Mrs. Z was a yucky teacher today and you are mad at her?"

Lots of claps and even intense rocks ensued.

"Do you want to be mad at Mrs. Z?" It seemed he did, so we sang the 'Mad Song' at Mrs. Z a couple of times:

You are mad at Mrs. Z
You are mad at Mrs. Z
It seemed to you like Mrs. Z was mean and grouchy today
And you are mad at Mrs. Z

119

While he laughed and clapped, I snuck in a few changes:

You are mad at Mrs. Z.
You are mad at Mrs. Z.
You were having a fun day at school, and then
Mrs. Z seemed mean and grouchy, and she got the hurry-worry blues,
And you felt put down and unappreciated,
And sad and unloved, so you got mad,
And you are mad at Mrs. Z.

Hayden's laughs, claps, rocks back and forth, hugs, squeals—all of it was music to my ears. They were what told me that I was exactly in tune with his feelings and that I had finally met him where he was.

After singing the 'Mad Song' at Mrs. Z a few more times, I asked Hayden if he was all done being mad at her. He was not! So I said,

"Wow, I can tell you're very mad at Mrs. Z. Shall we be mad two more times and then be all done?"

This he agreed to.

So I sang the 'Mad Song' twice again, told Hayden our "two more times" were done, then sang the 'I Love You Song'. When this was all completed, he got down from our talk chair and picked out a video to watch. That's when I knew it was over for good. There was no more sullenness, no pouting, no negative behavior. He had been heard, validated and accepted so was able to move on.

* * *

Hayden's receptive communication skills are excellent. When he was a Kindergartner, he loved to go to church because this was a place where he could experience fully the musicians making their music. It was also easy to claim our front-row seats every time we attended—they came to be known as ours, the way they do at small country churches. This of course made it easy for Hayden to receive the full sensory impact of the drummer and his drumming, along with the many and varied sounds coming from the other instruments too.

During music time at church, he was also entirely free to walk around, rock, twirl and move however he wanted to. He was gloriously free to react to and connect with the music in the moment. This was very precious time indeed, when his vestibular system was unfettered in its response to the extremely rich input. Hayden also knew that he must settle down and sit quietly once the minister took to the pulpit to deliver his wisdom. Out came the picture books, and Hayden's attention shifted his focus to them.

On one otherwise very ordinary Sunday, as Pastor Del began to speak, I casually glanced over at Hayden. To my total dismay I saw that his little face was contorted and tears ran down his puffy cheeks. I knew what all of this signaled: he would soon be wailing. And in fact, as I hurried him out of the church toward the car, the screaming began. I thought perhaps he had a painful ear infection, or possibly even appendicitis. There was just no way to know at the moment.

As quickly as I could, I heated up the car, bundled Hayden up, then grabbed our facilitating board. On it were the letters of the alphabet, the numerals one through ten, and four faces expressing happy, tired, angry, and hurt. Immediately, Hayden hit the angry face, and I breathed a super-sized sigh of relief. Though I had no idea why he was angry yet, anger was something I could process with him. It was a tremendous help to know I didn't have a major medical issue on my hands.

"So you're mad?" I attempted to confirm.

His clapping told me he was, yes! The volume of Hayden's screams then dropped precipitously. Amazing! He had been heard.

"Do you want to work on your madness?" I asked.

He clapped as his screams trailed off and his tears dried.

There were many times when Hayden just didn't want to work on things, but instead wanted to stay with the anger. If this was the case, a rule we had created would come into play: if he wanted to stay mad, he could do so in a designated place and scream to his heart's content. At home that place was his bedroom with the door closed. When we're away from home, the designated "mad place" was in the car, buckled in. No matter where he was, however, he was not permitted to throw things or be destructive in any way. These rules still stand, though for years now he's not engaged in any of this kind of behavior.

To further clarify, when Hayden was young, whenever he indicated that he wanted to stay mad, I would say to him very matter-of-factly,

"Okay, be mad. Be as mad as you can be! Try to be madder than you've ever been before. See if you can change the world by being mad. And while you're at it, enjoy yourself! I'll check on you later."

With this in mind, let's go back to church. This was clearly a time Hayden opted to work on his anger. My next step, then, was to determine the 'who, what, and why' of it all. Very early on, I had learned that it was always best to look at myself— my words and actions—first, because more often than not I am the object of Hayden's anger. This made sense: I was his constant companion, and he mine. But on this particular Sunday, what I might have done to offend him so egregiously was not at all obvious. Consequently, this time I was really in the dark.

My all-around most common offenses according to Hayden, were at the time, and still are: talking on the phone; having the hurry-worry blues; talking on the phone; being mean and grouchy; talking on the phone; not letting him be the boss (not letting him do what he wants to do and making him do what he doesn't want to do); not knowing what he wants to do; being busy with boring grandma business; spending time with other kids; and last but not least, talking on the phone!

But after I reviewed my behavior on the Sunday in question, I was still baffled. I had done none of the above, though Hayden can often identify my transgressions when I cannot.

So I asked him, "Are you mad at me?"

"No," was his answer.

What a shock--it wasn't me! Who could it be then? The only other person he had been with that morning was Poppa.

"Are you mad at Poppa?" I asked.

He emphatically clapped and even screamed his agreement.

"He's mad at Poppa," I thought, "really mad. But why?" Grandma-the-detective started sniffing out the clues. I went over the entire morning several times. But still I drew a blank. The question remained: why was Hayden so mad at Poppa?

Then a crucial thought crossed my mind: the morning scenario had only one variable and that was Del. But was it even possible for Hayden to be mad at something Del said? Hayden wasn't even listening to Del. He was looking at books just as he always did while Del was sermonizing.

But I couldn't shake the thought that Del was the only variable. Still, this couldn't be it. That would be crazy. But I had to check it out since it was my only lead. I thought about what Del had been talking about. Often people say one thing, but their actions say another. This had been Del's topic. He had pointed out that Americans say they're not materialistic, but then act as if they are by acquiring as many things as they possibly can. He had also questioned that dad who says he loves his son but works all the time and is never home for his family.

My mind swirled and my gut grew uneasy as I realized the import of what may have transpired many days in our household. Denny, aka Poppa, works all the time and is never home; but, Hayden hadn't caught on to that, had he? And besides, Hayden wasn't listening to Del...Or was he?

I asked Hayden, "Are you mad at Poppa because he says he loves you but he works all the time and is never home?"

Angry sounds verified that this was the case.

Mind-blowing! I had known for some time that Hayden understood everything said around him, but in church when he was looking so intently at his books?

"Do you want to be mad at Poppa?"

Clapping ensued, so I sang the 'Mad Song' at Poppa a few times while Hayden laughed up a storm.

"Are you all done being mad at Poppa?"

He clapped some more, so to close this episode out, I sang the 'I Love You' song. Then I asked, "Do you want to go back into church now?"

He did, so we did just that.

* * *

Now that Hayden is a young adult, he never chooses the screaming option when he's angry, though he frequently did when he was younger. He used to throw things too—his toys, mostly—around his room. When that happened, I would calmly and firmly say to him, "That is not appropriate, but thank you for letting me know you're very mad." Hayden hasn't thrown things in anger since he was five years old. He's now twenty-seven...

One of the funniest and most revealing incidents about Hayden's screaming occurred when he was six. It was spring and warm enough to get in the pool. Our pool is the largest-size fiberglass stock tank. First it had to be scrubbed, so I started the job by leaning way in with my brush and going at it. Before I knew it, I heard Hayden's "eh, eh, eh" which in that particular context translated as,

"I'm mad that you're taking so long!"

But I also knew these sounds were the precursor to full-blown screaming. So I pulled my head out of the pool and said,

"Hayden, thank you for telling me you think I'm taking too long to clean out the pool. I'm doing it as fast as I can. You have two choices: to wait patiently or to wait mad. If you want to be mad and scream, you need to be in your room, because it's not appropriate to scream out here."

Back into the pool I went, and as I scrubbed I listened for Hayden's response. Surprisingly, all was quiet so I assumed he had decided to wait patiently. But when I next came up for air, scanned the play area, and didn't see him, I panicked and my eyes immediately came into sharp focus and searched wildly around the yard for him. Only seconds later, I saw that there he was, standing safely and quite still on the front porch at the door, as if waiting to be let in. He had not wandered out of sight. Phew! Crisis averted.

But then it occurred to me: why did he want in on such a warm, beautiful day, especially when I'm getting the pool cleaned enough for a cool, soothing swim, one of his favorite things?

"Do you want the door opened?" I asked.

He clapped, "Yes."

I ran to the porch scratching my head at this seemingly odd behavior. Once I opened the door for him, he walked placidly into the house, then into his room. He moved slowly, though his entire posture signaled deliberation. He was on a mission alright.

Once in his room, Hayden sat on his bed and let out the loudest screams I had ever witnessed him deliver. It was as if

125

a switch had been turned on: he was quiet one moment and the next, the scariest, hairiest monster he could imagine had appeared before him, larger than life and breathing fire, ready to attack!

But I knew better. The only scary, hairy monster in the room was his anger.

"Oh," I said, "You want to be mad. Okay, be mad. It won't get the pool done any faster, but you're welcome to it. Have fun." I shut the door to his room.

"Well, so much for the idea that this autistic kid screams out of control," I concluded. He's in absolute control, even when he rocks violently and screams loud enough to be heard clear up to the perpetually snow-covered, fourteen-thousand-foot peak of Mount Rainier!

* * *

Hayden was five when his dad, Steven, remarried. Steven wondered if I thought Hayden would like to be in his wedding. Well, I didn't think being in a wedding would interest Hayden one iota, but in the interest of his having input into what he did in his own life, having real choices to make, I went ahead and asked Hayden anyway: "Your daddy and Gayla are going to get married. He wants to know if you would like to be in his wedding."

A definite "Yes" was Hayden's response.

This was beyond belief to my astonished mind. Furthermore, upon reading Hayden's subsequent behavior even more carefully, I could tell he didn't just want to be in the wedding, he was excited about it—his heart and soul were already enthusiastically engaged by the very idea of it.

The evening before the wedding came around and the rehearsal was just underway, Hayden walked down the aisle—razor sharp as he heeded his cues—holding his three-year-old sister Chelsea's hand. I sat up front and waited to intercept him as he walked by. Not a hitch in sight, so Hayden beamed like a full moon.

The next day, moments before the ceremony, Hayden and I were in the women's room calmly putting him together. There, now. It's my turn, I thought, after Hayden was done.

While I repaired my lips with a fresh coat of Raspberry Rules, Chelsea decided to practice Hayden by walking him down her own imaginary women's-room aisle all by herself. She was so keyed up that she moved at the speed of a little-kid-at-the-very-beginning-of-an-immeasurably-exciting event, and the dapper, tuxedoed Hayden—who clearly couldn't keep up—went down in the time it takes to spit out a watermelon seed. Then, only seconds later and as if she was topping off our backstage drama with the very bride and groom figures from the wedding cake itself, a woman poked her head in the door and announced, "Children's pictures in five minutes!"

"Great!" I said under my breath, "In five minutes he's supposed to be out there with Chelsea, being cute for pictures. Instead, he's literally screaming mad at her."

Thankfully, I knew just what I needed to do. I asked someone to take Chelsea out of the vicinity immediately. Then I asked someone else to ask the photographer for an extra five minutes. Next, I grabbed Hayden and hurried him into a toilet stall, which afforded a semblance of privacy. I asked him if he was mad at Chelsea.

He clapped a definite "Yes."

His screaming subsided a tad. "Let's be mad at Chelsea then," I said. There was no time to ask if he wanted to work on it. We were working on it! So I sang the 'Mad Song' at Chelsea several times, until he laughed. He laughed!! In fewer than ten minutes after Chelsea had toppled, shocked, frightened, and enraged him, Hayden was all smiles as he posed

127

with her for pictures. All of that animosity for her had vanished into thin air with minimal processing

Hayden did incredibly well with the rest of the wedding. And he thoroughly enjoyed himself, as he strutted among guests at the reception, proud as a peacock in his crisp, minitux. And there was no way he wanted to leave until the party was completely over, which turned out to be almost midnight. We had arrived at 5 pm for pictures! That's right. This severely autistic, auditory-sensitive, five-year-old boy had just spent six-and-a-half hours in an unfamiliar church with a few hundred mostly unfamiliar people, moving at times at the speed of light on high-octane excitement. He sure had proven me wrong! You see, as the special day approached, I had warned his dad by telling him that I would probably have to take Hayden home after the ceremony because he wouldn't want to, maybe wouldn't be able to, stay for the reception." So what did I know, anyway?

This I do know: we all tolerate difficulties, hardships, stressors, inconveniences, and even surprisingly high degrees of pain for something we really want, something that's extremely important to us. Evidently, being part of this wedding was just that important to Hayden, so much so that he worked extra hard at it, did a great job, and the universe awarded him with a fabulous time.

The wedding was part of 'life therapy' for Hayden, as are concerts, games, parks, live plays, and dinners out. Anything Hayden likes and wants to do presents a great opportunity for us to work on how to deal with noise, handle commotion, and practice patience and tolerance (without rocking or squishing). When motivation is high, as it is when we're engaged in Hayden's favorite activities, I capitalize on them as learning experiences.

* * *

Sometimes Hayden's behavior tells me things I would never guess in a million years. For instance, Hayden was thirteen and school was out for the summer. One Thursday I had a haircut appointment to get to. Haircut appointments came under the category of 'boring grandma business' (our description of most of my errands), so I asked Hayden if he wanted me to get a babysitter for him.

"No," he indicated.

"So you want to go with me while I get my hair cut and do some other boring grandma business?"

"No," again.

Puzzled, I asked, "Then you do want me to get a babysitter for you."

"Definitely not!" Hayden took a stand, though it sure beat me what it was about!

"Well," I said, "These are your two choices: stay home with a babysitter, or come with me to my haircut appointment."

"No!" again, this time in absolutely no uncertain terms.

"What on earth does he have in mind?" I tried to think outside the box on this one. I was almost stumped, but then with some quiet reflection, it came to me. "This would be pretty bold for Hayden, but I think he wants to stay home alone by himself."

I had a great deal of trepidation about this, but I also admired Hayden for his desire to be so independent.

"So you want to stay home by yourself while I do my grandma business?" I said.

He did all the things he does when he's in total agreement with me. He was positively gleeful about this inevitable, yet unattainable, desire for the right of passage from childhood to young adulthood. It touched me deeply, this momentous event that arose with no pomp and an impossible circumstance.

I prayed for wisdom, right there on the spot, as I held this baby-man close to me. His pre-speech communication, incongruous in its husky base delivery, expressed a thoroughly appropriate desire to be independent. But the facts—that he was still in pull-ups, made only wordless sounds, and had only a twelve-month-old's motor skills—make it unthinkable.

In my desire to validate exactly what I surmised Hayden was feeling in that moment, I responded,

"You'd like to stay home by yourself and watch movies or play with your toys while I do my boring grandma business, wouldn't you?"

"Yes!" said every part of Hayden, except his most inner voice. Veiled as it was in sadness, it wavered between desperate desire and the sense of this thing's impossibility.

"You are thirteen," I said, "and at thirteen it's appropriate for a kid to stay home and do his own thing while his grandma does her boring grandma business, and I can tell you'd really like to do that."

"Yes," he signed, and determined as he was, the language of his body was growing sadder by the moment.

"I'd like to let you do it, I really would. But there's one big problem we have that most kids and grandmas or moms don't, and that is autism. Because autism gets in the way of your going to the bathroom by yourself, calling 911, and talking out-loud in English if an emergency were to come up, it's just not safe for you to stay home 'by self,' even though you're old enough. No one—no matter how old he or she is—can stay home 'by self' unless he or she can use the bathroom and call 911 in an emergency. So, even though you're thirteen and you're old enough to stay home 'by self' and you want to stay home 'by self,' you'll either need to have a babysitter or come with me while I do my grandma business."

That day, Hayden, defeated only for the moment, or so he hoped, chose to come with me.

"Hah!" I thought to myself, "There's a silver lining here after all!" I knew that such great motivation on Hayden's *part carried on its coattails tremendous leverage with which I could steepen Hayden's learning curve! I was pleased with myself for brainstorming such a win-win solution. But I still had to make the rules crystal clear for Hayden by repeating it.*

"If you want to stay 'by self,' you'll need to know how to go to the bathroom 'by self'—go potty and poo in the toilet, not in your pull-ups. You'll also need to use the phone to call 911 and give your name, address, and phone number out-loud in English, in case there's an emergency

"Most kids who are thirteen do go to the bathroom 'by self' and can use the phone to call 911, so they can stay 'by self' while their grandma or mom does grandma or mom business. When you can do that, then you can stay home 'by self.'"

Hayden remained steadfast in his sense of entitlement about staying home by himself while I did grandma business. But I remained steadfast in my position too, and so, an ongoing disagreement arose between us.

Not long after, I became quite ill. My head and my back ached so, and my temperature shot up precipitously. As I readied myself for a trip to the doctor's—slowly, unsteadily, in near debilitating pain—I asked Hayden if he wanted me to get him a caregiver (I had switched from "babysitter" to "caregiver", hoping to ease the sting), or if he would rather come along with me. He took a stand–he wanted neither!

After I validated his feelings, I restated my position about the staying-home-alone issue. Again, I gave him his options. Grudgingly Hayden chose to stay, so I arranged for Jason from next-door to come over. Jason's mom, who knew Hayden well, would be at home and served as backup. It sounded like a good plan.

When Jason arrived, Hayden became a block of ice: he made me aware of his displeasure about the whole situation by refusing to look at me or acknowledge me in any way.

"I know you're mad about my decision and that's okay," I said. "I know you don't like it and I love you even when you're mad. If you need to be really mad about it—if you need to scream—you may do that in your room with the door shut."

I informed Jason about our rule regarding screaming. And I also let him know that I didn't really expect Hayden to scream. I wanted to cover all the bases before I left for the doctor's, because this was Jason's first time staying with Hayden.

Hours later, just as I arrived home from the doctor's, the phone rang and it was Jason's mom. She had something truly amazing to report: Hayden had called her on the phone!

"What? Am I hearing you correctly?" I asked. "Did you just say Hayden called you on the phone, Heather?"

"That's exactly what he did. Jason told me he held the phone up to his ear to talk!" She sounded just as dumbfounded as I was.

Hayden had, so it seemed, randomly hit redial, and Heather's phone rang because I had called that number earlier to speak to Jason. Though I do think Hayden was in fact attempting to use the phone, it was pure happenstance that he actually reached Jason's mom. But it was a fact, nonetheless, that while I had held the phone up to his ear on several occasions before, I had never actually tried to show him how to use it. In other words, everything about this was a very big step for Hayden. It was huge, even if an element of chance was involved.

I sat beside Hayden, "Heather said you called her on the phone."

His face beamed and he clapped his "Yes."

"Do you maybe want to learn how to use the phone so that way you can stay by yourself while I go off and do boring grandma business?"

"Absolutely!"

"Well, you made a good start by calling Heather. But you also have to be able to call 911 and give them your name, address and phone number out-loud and in English. You have to do potty by yourself in the toilet, too." I could tell how excited he was to work on all of it.

Even by the time he was eighteen, every time I asked Hayden if he wanted a caregiver or if he wanted to go with me on grandma business, he would say "No!" to both. And every time he said "No!" to both, I would not only validate his desire to stay home by himself, but also process the entire rationale for why this wasn't possible yet. And after each and every time we performed this ritual, he never failed to act pleasantly, whether he ended up going with me or staying with a caregiver.

* * *

When I think back to significant times in Hayden's life, I never fail to remember a Christmas when he was only three-and-a-half. Just like every Christmas I can remember from back then, once the season drew near, I dug out my recording of the Messiah *and played it as I did laundry or worked in the kitchen.*

At first I thought it was just a coincidence that soon after the piece started, Hayden would crawl into the dining room, sit on the floor right in front of the speakers, and stare at them, as if he could somehow see the music.

I remember saying to him, "I'm listening to the Messiah. *If you want to listen, okay; if you don't, you can play in your room." But he never budged; he sat and listened to the whole piece.*

As that particular holiday season wore on, I realized that he only came in to listen to the Messiah, *not any other Christmas music. Was he consciously choosing what he wanted to listen to? Could it be?"*

Then one day, when music other than the Messiah was playing, he took his place in front of the speakers. "Well, there goes the notion that he selects the Messiah to listen to," I thought to myself, disappointed, I must admit. I sighed and turned my attention back to folding the laundry.

Shortly thereafter, I heard "eh, eh, eh," Hayden's characteristic something's-amiss signal. I went to see what was up. He was sitting right in front of the speakers, but there didn't seem to be a single thing wrong. But then why did he continue to complain? My answer was imminent.

"Eh, eh, eh," Hayden muttered again—even louder this time, with more edge and frustration.

"Do you want the Messiah?" I asked.

I will never forget how ecstatic I was when his uninhibited claps and laughs answered back. This was the first time ever that he had communicated a preference for one piece of music over another. So I changed the tape to the Messiah recording and he listened intently, right on through to the finale. I recall hoping that his inner glow matched the intensity of my outer one.

A few days later, I looked up from my afternoon chores and Hayden had vanished from sight. He wasn't playing in his bedroom or playroom. I was alarmed because now he could move swiftly on his own. But in the end, I found him sitting quietly in front of the speakers, just staring at them. As I approached him, his expressions of concentration and anticipation transformed gradually into a broad-faced smile. He turned that smile toward me, then to the speakers again and his silent words spoke loudly through his body,

"I want the Messiah," they said.

I put it on and we listened together. And this time we danced joyfully as spirit moved us. I wondered at the time if anyone else in the world had danced to "I Know That My Redeemer Liveth", and the "Hallelujah Chorus"? It almost seemed like sacrilege to me at first, but he knew what I now understand—that all of life is sacred. Dancing through the Messiah *with Hayden was indeed a "holy" experience.*

Recordings of Christmas carols collected dust that holiday season, as the Messiah *held center stage. Nor did the tapes of this great work get put away with the rest of the trappings after the Epiphany. Instead, we marked repeatedly and with great wonder the beginnings of an improbable and long-lasting affair—between a seminal work crafted by a musical prodigy of the 18th century, and an autistic boy of the 20th century. During the subsequent five years, the* Messiah *was a year-round regular in our home. And whenever we set out for long journeys in the car, it was Hayden's traveling music of choice.*

One day during those years, Hayden excitedly brought me the box for the Messiah *tapes. Now that was a first. As a little one back then he would bring me the boxes that held his favorite movies when he had made his choice about what to watch. But the box for the* Messiah *tapes—well, he had never brought that to me before, even though at the time he was well on his way to becoming a* Messiah *expert, having logged hundreds of hours of listening time. No, our communication about the* Messiah *was not centered on the box that held the tapes, as it was for movies and other music; I had just sensed he might want to listen to it and asked him. Usually I was right.*

As I set the tapes up to play, I tried to figure out how Hayden had identified the Messiah *box. It just sat there on the stereo shelf among numerous other empty, semi-discarded cases and boxes for other music and movies he favored. I asked, perplexed this time, if he wanted the* Messiah, *even though I knew I had never identified the box he handed me* as the one the Messiah *came in. Nonetheless, he smiled and clapped, so there was only one thing to do—I set up the first tape, side one, and pushed play.*

"Eh, eh, eh," came from Hayden only moments after the Messiah's opening strains.

"So you don't want that?"

"No," he signaled with a serious look and a sharp shake of his head. Then, of all things, he handed me the Messiah box again!

"Wait," I said, as befuddled as I had ever been. "So then you do want the Messiah?"

He laughed, squealed, and clapped, and this meant one thing only: "Yes!"

"So," I thought, "maybe he has a specific side of a tape in mind. Side three, for instance, began with the "Hallelujah Chorus." I put that on.

But as the chorus' short orchestral introduction began, so did groans of displeasure from Hayden.

"Okay," I puzzled to myself, "so it's not the 'Hallelujah Chorus'." I chose another movement.

"No!" he signaled once more, and he did so over and over until I had exhausted all the possibilities and concluded the impossible—that he wanted the Messiah, but not any of its movements!

By then, we were both beyond frustration. He, because he thought that I couldn't, or didn't want to give him what he wanted, and I, because I had given him what I thought he wanted, but he didn't seem to really want it! We had come to a dead end. I told Hayden that I didn't understand what he wanted and was sorry that I couldn't help him. Then he began to cry. Oh my! How had we come to such cross purposes?

I suggested that Hayden might be mad at me, then asked him if he wanted to work on his madness.

"No!" he motioned. Hayden wanted to stay mad!

"That's a surprise," I thought.

"If you need to be mad," I told Hayden, "you may go to your room and be mad." He walked quietly, somberly, to his room, head and shoulders drooped in dejection, and I said what I always did at this juncture, "Have a great time being mad! I'll check in on you later." But I, too, was deeply saddened. As I closed his door, he began to scream. Over piercing wails that made my heart burn and my chest tighten, I tried in vain to figure out what this was all about.

The same scenario repeated itself seven times over the next few months. Hayden patiently waited while I tried all sides of the Messiah *tapes. I knew it was an exercise in futility, but still, I had no idea what I was doing wrong. What I was certain of was that Hayden would dead-end into a temper tantrum.*

On his seventh attempt, Hayden eagerly handed me the box holding the Messiah *music tapes. Eyes big and bright, mouth sporting an especially handsome smile, he seemed quite determined to get his wish fulfilled. I knew he wanted what he wanted very badly, but I had absolutely no idea what that was.*

I asked for help: "GOD, what am I not getting here? What does he want?"

The answer: "Look at the box he's showing you. He thinks it's a movie box."

The light came on, as it always does when this stubborn grandma finally asks for the help that is always there. "Of course," I thought, "How did I not see that?" The Messiah *audiotapes came in a box the shape of a video box that was just a tiny, almost imperceptible bit larger.*

I took the box in hand, went right to Hayden and asked, "You want the Messiah, *right?"*

"Oh yes!" Smiles and claps ensued.

"But do you want a Messiah movie?" I thought his eyes had shone especially brightly before, but now they lit up like a pair of supernovas as he showed me his full range of affirmative responses: he laughed, rocked, and hugged me mightily because he had finally been heard—because I had finally understood what he wanted!

Still, I didn't have the Messiah *on video. I opened the box and showed him there was no* Messiah *movie inside. But of course he didn't get this. To him, here was a* Messiah *movie box, so there must be a* Messiah *movie in it. Nothing I said to the contrary made any difference to Hayden, and sadly, he ended up in his bedroom screaming again, while I got on the phone and tried frantically to locate a video of the* Messiah *that I could beg, steal, or borrow!*

Six months and many such episodes later, but still unsuccessful in my hunt, I mentioned the Messiah *movie dilemma to my friend, Carol, a piano teacher. She just happened to have a* Messiah *movie and said we could borrow it. I remember how insanely excited Hayden was. He had waited so long! We watched it together, took a break, then went through to the end.*

I held on to Carol's video for nearly a year, and during that period Hayden and I enjoyed watching it repeatedly together. But then I thought it was about time for me to return the video to Carol, because I surmised that Hayden's desire to watch it had been satisfied. Wow, was I wrong!

It wasn't long before, once again, he brought me the audiotape box, and again, I tried to explain there was no Messiah *movie in there. Since I could identify exactly what the problem was—Hayden wanted me to play a* Messiah *movie and I could not—he was ready and willing to work on his madness about the* Messiah *instead of just being mad. So, we sang the 'Mad Song' at me for not playing a* Messiah *movie for him, and there was no screaming because he had been heard.*

Once again, though, I searched for a Messiah *video, eventually ending up with* Young Messiah, *a shortened, modernized version, which he watched in one sitting and then turned off, never to view it again*

Yet another hunt brought me to a Messiah *video in Portland. I ordered it and it arrived just before we left for a vacation.*

"Here is Hayden's own Messiah *movie—to keep!"*

I presented it to him and he was more excited than I had ever seen him. We sat right down and watched the whole performance—plus a special feature, a documentary about Handel's life and his other works. Of course it went on vacation with us, but it definitely had no vacation!

After his initial obsession with the Messiah, *every so often Hayden watched the movie inside and listened to the tape in the car. But I came to see that really, anyone who loves a piece of music that much needs to see it live, in person.*

We had been to a church performance of part of the piece, but when Chelsea called to tell me that the Seattle Symphony would be performing a "Messiah for Children," I decided it was finally time for Hayden to experience live the piece of music he had fallen in love with ten year earlier, when he was just a toddler. Of course, he agreed wholeheartedly. He was then thirteen.

We drove through some of the Northwest's infamous pouring rain to hear the Seattle Symphony's performance. Hayden rocked with great animation beside me in the car; and he squealed in his impossibly high-pitched anticipation. He was happy and turned on, like a radio at top volume. He had nary a care in the world, while I had plenty.

I hated city driving in the first place, always have, and we started to lose time because of the rain. Front-row seats await our arrival, but I began to wonder, "Why was I doing this? What kind of crazy woman takes a severely autistic child to a world-class symphony hall for a performance of the Messiah? *Was I nuts?"*

We arrived late and were seated while the chorus was singing the overture at full tilt. Ah, beautiful Benaroya Hall! Why, it was all "a' wiggle," with restless children so that Hayden's autism-fed rocking was hardly noticed.

But when the overture ended, Hayden immediately knew something was very wrong. I could hear him think: The audience is clapping; there is no clapping after the overture in the Messiah. *Then, a gentleman walked onstage and began to banter with the conductor. I heard Hayden's "eh, eh, eh," and thought, "Oh no!" as I realized I had goofed big-time, and I mean royally! I leaned over immediately and whispered to him, "This is not the* Messiah! *This is not the* Messiah! *You were expecting the* Messiah *and so was I, but this isn't it! I goofed and now I realize this is not the* Messiah. *This is about the* Messiah *and has some songs from the* Messiah, *but this is not the* Messiah."

It was absolutely imperative that I begin exactly where he was and validate him in that place. Mentally, I prepared for the long walk out of the concert hall with this good-sized disgruntled kid in tow. How on earth was I going to explain this to Hayden?

But I continued in the same vein and hoped that I was getting through:

"This is a kid's program about the Messiah. *They're going to do some talking, sing some songs from the* Messiah *and everyone's going to clap after the songs are done. This is about the* Messiah, *but it is not the piece itself. So do you want to stay for this kid's program about the* Messiah *since we're already here?"*

Miraculously, he did. He wanted to stay! I must say, he behaved beautifully and his rocking was simply not a problem, surrounded as he was by a hall full of kids squirming up a storm.

However, I knew that after the ball, I was in for some trouble. Before we were even out of the parking lot, the complaining began. "Eh, eh, eh."

"You're kind of mad at me because I promised you the Messiah *and I didn't give you the* Messiah, *right?"*

"Oh yes," he let me know, "very definitely."

"It feels like I lied to you," I said.

"You bet."

"I made a mistake and I'm sorry. I thought it was going to be the Messiah, *but it was not." All manner of angry sounds emanated from my* Messiah *purist. So we sang a 'Mad Song' at me, until he started laughing. Then we moved on to a 'Disappointed Song':*

You are disappointed.
You are disappointed.
You expected to hear the Messiah,
And it was not the Messiah,
It was a program for kids about the Messiah.
And you are disappointed.

"It is disappointing to expect something you really like and then have it be something different. I was disappointed too. Do you want to be disappointed some more?"

He did, so we sang the 'Disappointed Song' a few more times, and finished with the 'I Love You Song'.

By the time we finished singing, Hayden was perfectly relaxed and relating, but I knew him well enough to know that he was not done. Not yet. What's more, I knew what he wanted, and though I was not certain I could produce it, I couldn't ignore it either.

"You would like me to take you to the real Messiah, *right?"*

He laughed and rocked and squealed and grabbed for me, all in a resounding, "Absolutely!" But I knew that this was the weekend for all the Messiah performances, so I had grave misgivings that everything was already sold out.

"You want me to take you to the real Messiah, but I don't know if I can find one. But I will look. But I can't promise." And suddenly, like the end of a spring shower, it was over. He reached for a music tape to play on the way home. He chose the Messiah. He had been heard and knew I would at least try to give him what he was hoping for.

I had done my homework: this was the weekend for performances of his favorite piece of music, including one by none other than the Seattle Symphony. They had several performances of the real Messiah on their schedule, but tickets were quite expensive and I didn't think Hayden's rocking would be appreciated.

Nevertheless, this was so very important to him. So, a week later, we again headed for Seattle, second verse same as the first. Hayden jubilantly rocked and squealed through the whole trip there.

And once again, I doubted my sanity! However, I also reminded myself that autism should not mean that Hayden be denied access to the music he so dearly loved. Moreover, I also told myself that no one in the audience will have listened to, watched and loved the Messiah more than Hayden.

However, perhaps no one was less welcome to that performance than Hayden, though I'll never know for sure. He rocked throughout the entire piece because he thoroughly enjoyed it and his body was wired. He was not disruptive in a purposeful way. But the fact of the matter was that his presence, when he rocked, was de facto disruptive. That's all there was to it.

I didn't really enjoy that performance, I must admit, because throughout the entire piece, I tried to balance Hayden's need to rock with the needs of the people behind him for him not to rock. At intermission, I asked Hayden if he wanted to go home, but no such luck. He wanted to stay! When it was over, I was wrung out, exhausted through-and-through.

Was it wrong of me to take him, knowing he would need to rock? Perhaps. Would it be wrong of me to deny Hayden access to meaningful experiences because of his autistic behavior? I don't know. I do know that living with and loving Hayden has made a lot of things take on a gray shade, whereas before my whole world had pretty much been black or white. I'm not sorry I took him to this concert, because I promised him I would and because it was very important to him. I do wish I had found a way to apologize and explain to the poor folks behind us...

Not long after this first live Messiah *for Hayden, I received notice of a Mozart program by the Seattle Symphony and Chorale. The Tomatis Auditory Training Program, with which Hayden had logged over 300 hours, features a great deal of Mozart, so Hayden was familiar with a lot of the repertoire. I told him about the performance, and wondered if he might be interested in attending. Perhaps you think I am insane, but I wanted to know how he felt about it.*

Hayden looked at me with a half-smile, which meant he was on the fence about it, didn't really know how to answer.

"You'd like to go to the performance and hear the symphony and chorale do Mozart, but you would not like me to bug you about rocking." I had hit the bulls-eye: he ran the gamut of his usual vocal affirmations—squeals, raucous laughter, claps.

Maybe you wonder why I take Hayden places, why I even consider taking him to the symphony and the theater. And that's a darn good question! I ask myself this very question a lot. I've never been a get-up-and-go-everywhere kind of person myself. Before Hayden, I always figured it would be simpler and cheaper to just stay home.

The answer to this question as to why I take Hayden out and about is not simple, though. It appears to be at least three-fold. First of all, Hayden *does* like to get up and go. Second, I think it's therapeutic for him to be exposed to all kinds of events. And third, I'll be damned if I'm going to let autism control his choices, in particular, eliminate them.

* * *

Kids with autism are frequently thought of as non-communicative and unaware of what's going on around them. Hayden has a diagnosis from the Children's Hospital of Seattle of moderately severe autism. Yet, he understands his emotional environment and a great deal of what is going on and being said around him. The exceptions to this are the concepts of cause-and-effect, logic, sequence, time, and distance. This is true for many kids diagnosed with ASD.

Chapter 7
Traveling Incognito

Once in a while we hear of someone traveling incognito. Why? They don't want to be known for who they are, of course. But why would they not want to be known for who they are? After mulling this over, it seems it must be fear: for a celebrity—fear of invasion of privacy and being disturbed; for a runaway—fear of being located; for a fugitive—fear of being apprehended. My young companion on this journey into autism sometimes disguises himself and pretends he cannot do things that he can, further complicating this already complex journey. I have discovered that perhaps Hayden is in fact hiding from, and in fear of, himself as someone who actually *can*.

Hayden was an infant when I first became aware that he was capable of pretending. He was extremely defensive about his sense of touch—especially in his hands—and simply couldn't tolerate anything coming in contact with his palms. He used his fingers, but never his palms. If something lightly brushed one of them, he instantly pulled away and screamed.

Barb, one of Hayden's early teachers, impressed upon me the absolute necessity of teaching Hayden how to use his hands. How else would he develop any fine motor skills? So, my strategy was to hold the back of his hand in one of mine and tell him I was going to touch his palm. Then I just barely brushed his palm with a finger from my other hand.

145

At first, Hayden's hand jerked away (like mine would if I touched a hot stove burner), and he let out a tremendous wail. I then validated that what I did was scary and felt bad. But I also assured him it was only the two of us so he was safe and all we were doing was getting him used to his own hands. When the fear and crying subsided, we started the whole process again. We repeated this over and over and over, ad infinitum, or so it seemed. This was Hayden's first pre-exercise in fine motor skills, the basis for his learning all others.

Eventually, it became possible for me to tap Hayden's palm lightly—without warning—and get no fearful reaction; his hand and personality remained intact, with no withdrawal of either. But for the longest time, the same sequence occurred: I explained what I was doing, then I held my finger on his palm momentarily, then he reflexively jerked away and cried. Finally, I would soothe him, reassure him, and start all over again.

The trusty kid's song came in handy a lot in those early days: 'Second verse, same as the first; ain't no better, and it ain't no worse!' With Hayden and me, there were third, fourth, fifth, etc., verses. I went ever so gradually from touching his palm with one finger, then two, then three, then four, until I could hold his palm with my entire hand and there was no reaction. Thus, we came to hold hands. We traversed a million miles by only covering a few inches.

When we progressed to putting objects in his hands, however, we landed back at square one. We did get to the point, after much repetition, of my holding a block in his hand for a few minutes. But then we seemed to stall and something strange happened. Hayden seemed to only passively hold the block, depending on me to facilitate the contact between it and me. So I decided to remove myself from the picture to see what would happen.

Good old masking tape to the rescue! I used some to attach a block to his hand, then moved a few steps away. The result: he 'held' a block 'by self. Every day I taped a block, first to one hand, then the other, leaving it a bit longer, but only as long as he could tolerate it. One day, I turned around and saw him with a block in his hand and there was no tape! Excitedly, I acknowledged,

"Look, you're holding a block all by self!" He dropped the block like a hot potato, rolled onto his side, stuck his thumb in his mouth, and refused to respond to my exuberance.

"I did not!" came across loud and clear in Hayden's body language. There was no question that he had suddenly regressed. But why?

Over the course of the next several days, it took much cajoling for him to allow me to tape blocks to his hands again. And it was weeks before he got back to picking one up by himself. His holding the block, and then not holding it—and faking an autistic state—were an introduction to my pint-sized pretender, adding another enigmatic piece to this already perplexing child-puzzle.

When Hayden was about eighteen months old, he plainly said, "Nose." I was so excited that I lavished him with praise. When we went to physical therapy, I told Laurel, "Hayden said 'nose'!" But as it turned out, he wouldn't say it again for years. It was the same with sitting up, getting to his hands and knees, walking by himself, and so on, even though I learned not to make a fuss over his achievements. In all of these cases, he did something new that somehow he couldn't or wouldn't own.

The same thing happened in primary school. One day Debbie sent home a picture Hayden had cut out with very little assistance. She reported, though, that for several days after, he wouldn't touch the scissors.

Hayden still puts on disguises, and he's good, so good that I don't know if he's more disguise than himself sometimes. I'm not even sure if *he* knows. Does he know more than he wants me and others to know he knows? Or does he know more than he thinks he knows? I remember a proverb I learned in elementary school:

He who knows not, and knows not that he knows not, is a fool; shun him.
He who knows not, and knows that he knows not, is a child; teach him.
He who knows, and knows not that he knows, is asleep; awaken him.
He who knows and knows that he knows, is wise; follow him.

Is it my job to teach Hayden or to awaken him? I have always read him pretty well, but on this one, the page is blank. Perhaps it's a combination; or perhaps it's something entirely different:

He who knows, and pretends he doesn't know, is afraid; love him.

* * *

For several years I've been convinced that Hayden can sort. For example, on a number of occasions I've shown him three or four containers with different things in each—a marble, plastic mouse, poker chip, a rubber ball. I've then asked him to add one similar item (from an unsorted pile of items) to each of the containers: "Put the marbles with the marbles, the chips with the chips, etc." Maybe this request felt like an insult to his intelligence, or maybe he could do this but just didn't want to partake in the activity at the moment. Or maybe he really couldn't do it. The one thing I do know is that he would often started sorting correctly, but then put all the rest of the loose items in the same container. On several occasions I heard from his teachers that they didn't think he could sort; other times they said they were convinced he could sort but would not.

There's a word for getting stuck on something and not being able to move on: perseveration; we've mentioned it previously. People on the spectrum often engage in this, as we all know. So for a while I thought Hayden was perseverating. But the little smile that played around the corners of his mouth, and his sly little glances at the correct container, made me wonder...

At one point, I toyed with the notion of offering Hayden Junior Mints as a reward for sorting. If you knew me, you'd know what a cataclysmic, last-ditch idea this was, because I always go for intrinsic rewards and really don't like using food in this way. In fact, Hayden seldom eats candy, but he sure likes his Junior Mints.

During a particularly frustrating attempt to teach Hayden how to sort, he put a number of little green balls in several of the containers I had set out before him, but not in the container already holding the rest of the little green balls! Yet, he most definitely looked at the correct container first and smiled. So I finally decided to try the Junior Mint bribe after all, having purchased a box for just such an extraordinarily challenging contingency. I picked one out of the box showed it to Hayden and said,

"You can have a Junior Mint when you put this little green ball in with the other little green balls."

When Hayden laid eyes on that Junior Mint, he quickly tried to grab it, but I pulled it back and said,

"When you put the little green ball in with the other little green balls."

He looked up at me and laughed, then looked at the container of little green balls, then back at the Junior Mint I was holding, then me, then the balls once again. He held the ball over the container of marbles and laughed, but didn't drop it in. Then he held it over the container of balls, but didn't put it in there either. Then he tried to grab the Junior Mint from my hand again, but I retracted it, and repeated,

"Only when you put this green ball in with the other green balls."

He studied my face intently.

"I've kind of got you in a pickle, haven't I? You want the Junior Mint, but you don't want to put that ball in with the others." I said.

He laughed.

We must have played cat-and-mouse like this for about a quarter of an hour and then suddenly he put the ball in the correct container and grabbed his Junior Mint!

The next time we sat down to do a sorting exercise, we played cat-and-mouse for only about five minutes the first time around, and the next three times he sorted fairly quickly. The last time we did the exercise that day, he held onto his object and looked squarely at me for a few moments, then sorted correctly and received his Junior Mint.

A few days later Hayden sorted correctly each time I asked him to do so, even though he received no Junior Mint for doing so. But after that particular instance, he reintroduced the cat-and-mouse game all over again, so I reintroduced the Junior Mints. This time, he sorted correctly and received his minty rewards. The next time we did the sorting exercise, though, we played cat-and-mouse and continued to do so even after I re-introduced the Junior Mints.

So I'm not sure how to answer my biggest questions about Hayden and sorting, after such a mixed bag of responses. Can he sort? Or not so much? Is he capable of sorting sometimes but not others? Has he somehow learned that he can be in control by *not* sorting? I honestly don't know the answer to this quandary. The important thing to me, however, was and still is to understand what his behavior was telling me so that I can either respond to a need he may be expressing or process the feelings behind it.

As I see it, all behavior is a kind of language to be understood, not a disease to be eradicated. Recently, a speech therapist told me that 93% of all communication is nonverbal. I like to think this means that Hayden, who is nonverbal, gets an A in communication! I may not comprehend his language, but I have no doubt that he communicates.

Think of it this way. If I were to try to do away with some behavior of Hayden's that seemed inappropriate or irritating without understanding what he's attempting to communicate with it, I would essentially be silencing him. I would also, as I see it, have acted in total disregard of his wants, needs and feelings. In addition, it's entirely possible that I'd also be forcing him to shut down or to find other more inappropriate and irritating behaviors to get his point across.

Learning the language of behaviors is not always easy or smooth sailing. Sometimes it's downright frustrating and puzzling. It usually can't be done in a few easy steps, but it can be done. It's a hell of a lot of work, but a heaven's worth of rewards await as your otherwise voiceless children's puzzling, scary, strange behaviors become their "words" to you.

A number of years ago, I was asked to present at an all-day, Saturday workshop on challenging behaviors. I termed my topic 'Behavior as Language.' After brainstorming for just the right thing with which to close my talk—and coming up blank—I just decided to do my own thing, and wrote the following:

Please mom, hear what I'm doing.
See what I'm saying.
The world is a crazy, confusing, scary place for me.
I can't do the things other kids do.
My body doesn't work right.
But inside, I'm just like other kids.
I need to be loved and appreciated.
I need to fit in, to belong.
I need to be useful, to contribute.
I need to be heard and understood.
I want to tell you my needs,
My feeling, my thoughts,
But they get trapped inside me
Because I can't get my mouth to say the words.
So much gets piled up inside me
That sometimes it just blows up everywhere.
And I know you're disappointed in me
And you get angry
And then somehow it's all my fault.
My actions speak so loudly, but
You can't see what I'm saying.
Yet, my actions are my saying.
My body says what my mouth can't.
I act out my feelings,
But often the acting out is such a problem
That my feelings go unnoticed.
But I have no other way to tell you my feelings.
I want to cooperate, to succeed,
To feel good about myself,
But to do that I must be heard.
Please Mom, hear what I'm doing,
See what I'm saying!

    Love,
    Your Child

Chapter 8

The Punisher

One mask Hayden and other children wear is the mask of the *punisher*. Actually, it isn't only kids who wear it: the so-called 'silent treatment' is one with which most of us adults are quite familiar. Our spouse or co-worker might say or do something we don't like and we clam up, walk out of the room, pout, and become completely incommunicado. We do all of this to get across the message, "You hurt me and I want to hurt you back or make you feel guilty," but we make it quite clear that we will not be otherwise communicating about it at the time. This is what I mean by punishing. It's passive aggressiveness at its worst!

Often the behaviors of Hayden, and those of other kids as well, seem to be attempts to punish in this way. Hayden's 'faking' an autistic state around the ability to sort things correctly always seemed to be an attempt to punish me for not picking him up from the cradle even when he didn't or wouldn't reach for me first—this of course goes back to his infancy and early attempts of mine to teach Hayden simple responses.

Hayden was about five when I first came to understand punishment. Walking had finally become functionally possible for him. At about the same time, he also discovered the glorious wonders of the dishwasher. But he also understood that it was well off-limits for him. Though he seldom opened

153

it, every once in a while I found it open and discovered him playing with its contents.

Hayden likes the dishwasher as much as he hates the phone. Rather, I should say, he hates it when I talk on the phone and considers it one of my most annoying habits. Especially irksome to him are my 'serious' calls, when the caller really needs to talk and I really need to concentrate and listen.

One day, as I listened intently to a caller, I also checked up on Hayden; but I didn't find him in his room or playroom. Instead, I found him in the kitchen playing in the dishwasher. I said,

"I'm frustrated that you're playing in the dishwasher, when you know it's off-limits."

He looked at me and smiled.

At that moment, I knew he was playing in the dishwasher expressly because he knew he wasn't allowed to. Why? He continued to look at me with a sly, knowing grin and it came to me. He was punishing me for being on the phone: I did something he didn't like, so in retaliation he did something I didn't like.

I temporarily excused myself from my phone call and asked Hayden,

"Are you trying to punish me for talking on the phone by playing in the dishwasher?"

His laughed and clapped as he validated what I already knew.

"Thank you for telling me you're mad at me for talking on the phone. I don't choose to be punished by your playing in the dishwasher, but thank you for letting me know you'd like to punish me for talking on the phone."

After I finished my phone conversation, we went directly to the talk chair and sang a 'Mad Song' at me for talking on the phone too much. After validating how smart he was for figuring out a way to punish me, I explained to him that punishment has two components—a punisher and a punish-ee. Since I didn't choose to be punished, he could not punish me.

Further, I informed him that even if he played in the dishwasher without my permission, he could not punish me without my permission. I closed the conversation by telling him I loved him even when he was mad at me, but he was still not allowed to play in the dishwasher.

A week or so went by and sure enough, Hayden got into the dishwasher again. But that was the last time he did, though not the last time he tried to punish me, not by a long shot!

During spring break when Hayden was eight, we went over to his dad's apartment complex to swim in the indoor pool there. While Hayden and I stuck our toes in to test the water, a mom and her two boys entered the pool area. One of the boys tried to strike up a conversation with Hayden, who was so absorbed in his own water play that he either didn't hear the other boy, or was ignoring him. The friendly, befuddled boy turned to me and asked what Hayden's age and name were. I answered his questions, but he had one more for me,

"Can he talk?" the boy inquired.

I made a split-second decision to answer simply: "No, he doesn't talk." As soon as the words were out of my mouth, I knew I had goofed big-time!

Several years prior to this poolside incident, I had asked Hayden if he spoke in English in his mind. When he laughed, squealed, hugged me, and clapped with great gusto—and longer than usual—I had my answer. I also sensed that he was pleased and relieved that I finally knew this to be true—it seemed very important for him to have this ability acknowledged. For the most part, then, I'm careful to say that he talks out-loud in "Hayden-ese," but in his mind in English.

When I answered the little nine-year-old at the pool by saying "He doesn't talk," I immediately looked at Hayden to determine if he had heard my response. It appeared not. His activity was seamless, as he continued to float on his back, and blow water out of his mouth while enjoying his cavort in the pool, as usual. "Ah!" I said to myself, "maybe he didn't hear me and I'm off the hook!"

After swimming, we showered, dressed and got in the car. As I backed out of the parking space, Hayden reached over and pinched my neck. I was on the hook, after all!

"Ouch!" I said, "I don't like to be pinched!" Then I paused, changed my tone, and said, "But thank you for letting me know you're mad at me."

How did I know Hayden was mad? Pinching someone is angry behavior, as is hitting, screaming, biting, scratching, kicking, and throwing things. Autistic kids don't do any of these things because they have autism, but because they are angry, frustrated, confused or hurt. Hayden did a lot of pinching when he was younger, but it had been several years since he'd pinched me. So I asked him,

"Are you mad at me because I told the boy in the pool you couldn't speak? I forgot to clarify that you speak English in your mind and sometimes Hayden-ese out-loud."

Angry sounds from Hayden served as confirmation, so I went on to sing the 'Mad Song' at me for telling the little boy Hayden couldn't speak. When Hayden was finished being mad, I apologized and asked if he would forgive me; he did. I promised to work harder in the future to remember to say that he can speak in his mind in English, but that autism gets in the way of his speaking out loud in English. He turned away and looked for the music tape he wanted to hear. This signaled the end of the incident. He was once again at peace.

The pinch from Hayden that day was his way of saying, "I'm mad at you for making me feel bad by telling that boy I'm too stupid to be able to speak, so I'm going to make you feel bad, too." Hayden's feelings justified, to him at least, the *pinch he gave me. I violated him and he violated me—justice done.*

Hayden has a strong sense of justice–the kind that is referred to as primitive retributive justice, Old Testament-style: an eye for an eye, a tooth for a tooth. According to his sense of justice, he had a perfect right to do what he did, so he felt no guilt when he pinched me, even though he knew pinching was not acceptable behavior, just as he knew that saying that he's unable to speak is not acceptable behavior (he obviously considered it a lie).

Perhaps you're thinking about now that Hayden needed to be reprimanded for pinching me, and that all of the above is simply hogwash. You might even believe that children with autism are prone to violence, which in itself is pudding-proof that there's something wrong with my approach here. This is a pivotal point in the discussion of autism.

Hog-washing may not always be nonsensical! If I expect to have a hog in my house, believe you me, I would do some serious, thorough hog-washing before that hog came into MY house!

Since I have a child with severe autism in my house, I do whatever it takes to maintain the serenity of my home. I think you can too. As you begin to look at the world through the eyes of your child, it's really quite simple—though not easy—to understand and utilize that child's point of view to help everyone in the household meet the many challenges of autism.

* * *

Almost every physician who's seen Hayden has asked some version of the question: What about temper tantrums? My answer is and has been always the same: he does not have temper tantrums or behave violently, but he might if I didn't talk to him the way I do." After his appointment with twelve-year-old Hayden, Dr. David Shurtleff of the University of Washington said that he had seen a great number of children with autism over many years of practice, but Hayden's autism was managed far better than any other he had seen. The jungle of autism does have order, predictability, precepts, organization, simplicity, even beauty, after all!

When Hayden pinched me to punish me for what I said to the boy in the pool, in his mind justice had been done; I did something inappropriate, so he did something inappropriate in turn. But it was not really over for him because the wrong done him had not yet been outwardly expressed. It's important to remember that, as has been observed by Deepak Chopra and others, being unable to express what you feel is one of the three greatest physiological stresses for the human organism. (The other two: feeling out of control and like you have no choices.) So even though had Hayden punished me, his body still carried the stress of wrong having been done to him. Needless to say, this transformed him into an outburst-in-the-making. If I were to say to him, "Don't pinch me," I would in effect be saying, "You, don't pinch me," which comes across as a challenge. If he had outloud speech, he might respond, "Well, don't call me stupid!" But he doesn't, so he can't.

From Hayden's perspective, after he pinched me the justice cycle was complete. If in anger I had then challenge him, his sense of justice would have required retaliation, so he would do something to get my goat. If my goat were to kick back—well, so would commence a very un-merry merry-go-round. When would it stop? I'll let you answer that. What I do know is that this negative pattern of reactive, retributive behavior would get rolling if I had scolded Hayden for pinching me.

It's so important to remember that angry behavior occurs because people get angry. There is nothing wrong with being angry; it means, more often than not, that we're not having our way. It is often advised that we may feel angry, but should not act on. Even an important Hebrew scripture admonishes us to "Be angry and sin not." However, there is everything wrong with aggressive behavior we might act out in the moment of feeling anger. Because I advocate 'listening to' a child's behavior, no matter what it is, don't think for a moment I condone or accept inappropriate behavior. I do not.

One of the comments I hear quite frequently about Hayden from professionals and lay people alike, is how well-behaved he is. Because I understand his neurological issues and the extraordinary way his body acts, I am usually able to elicit appropriate, albeit autistic, behavior from Hayden.

For example, upon entering a therapist's office a number of years ago, Hayden immediately put his fingers in his ears. The therapist immediately snapped back at Hayden:

"Get your fingers out of your ears. There's nothing loud happening in here!"

The therapist thought, of course, that he was being disrespectful and perhaps didn't want to hear what she, the authoritative figure in the room, had to say.

But this wasn't at all what was going on. When we entered the office, I noticed the hum of an air-conditioning unit, and so had Hayden. Because I know that his sense of hearing is incredibly acute, I knew he would attempt to muffle the noise by plugging his ears. If he hadn't, his auditory system would have become overwhelmed, causing him to become distracted and irritated. These feelings might well have led him to scream or act out in some other way. The therapist had it all wrong, because she just didn't know Hayden and the very individual way autism manifests itself in him.

159

Aggressive behaviors are inappropriate expressions of anger. In the example of Hayden's pinch after the pool incident, my response to it was forceful but not angry:

"Ouch, I don't like to be pinched (hit, bit, etc.)."

There is no challenge, no punishment in this simple statement. It is just a simple statement of how I felt. I followed it with a pause, a deep breath, a smile, then made eye contact with Hayden and said, warmly,

"But thank you for telling me you're mad at me."

Frequently, when I've worked with other kids who don't usually make eye contact, this is the point at which they will. And that's because they've been heard and their feelings have been affirmed and accepted.

My next step with such children is to ask myself, "Why are they mad?" For a moment, I try to be these children, walk in their shoes, look at what has just happened to them. Often a sentinel event occurs right before inappropriate behavior. When Hayden had waited to express his anger at me for some forty-five minutes after my statement to the boy in the swimming pool, he was accustomed to having his feelings heard and could put off dealing with the incident until after our swim. Most often, though, especially when I first begin to work with a child, the negative behavior will immediately follow the perceived injury.

Next, I propose an explanation for the child-at-hand's inappropriate behavior, then watch for their (behavioral) reaction, which will let me know whether or not I'm correct. When I first applied this strategy to Hayden, he screamed when I acknowledged his anger, but this strong emotional response would abate as soon as I sang a 'Mad Song' a few times. Now, he usually laughs and claps when I hit the nail on the head; if he's really mad he'll make angry noises. If my explanation is off the mark, he will become eerily statue-like still, which I now understand means,

"No, you're wrong; try again. You're getting closer."

When I get it right, he'll let me know. Then I will ask if he wants to be mad at me. If he does, I sing a customized version of the 'Mad Song,' for example,

You are mad at me!
You are mad at me!
I told the boy at swimming you couldn't talk,
But you do talk in English in your mind,
And you felt stupid and put down,
And you are mad at me.

When I got to this point in the pool incident, Hayden laughed and clapped while I sang this three times in succession. Then I asked if he was all done being mad at me. He was not, so I sang it a few more times, and when I asked again if he was all done being mad, and he assented. I apologized for not telling the boy Hayden does talk in his mind; I asked his forgiveness, which he granted; and I promised to work hard at remembering to let people know he talks in his mind, but autism gets in the way of his talking out-loud. I sang, the 'I Love You' song, as I often do at the end of processing an incident. On this particular occasion, Hayden then reached for his tape player, and I knew it was over. Since that incident, there have only been two token gestures towards me that have indicated he was mad at me.

All of us, when we feel put down, unheard, threatened, or hurt, immediately go into fight-or-flight mode. If we feel trapped and cannot 'take flight,' we will fight instead. If we do not have words with which to fight—like toddlers, or kids with autism or other speech-robbing conditions—we resort to whatever kind of aggressive behavior we are capable of.

Every behavior occurs for a reason. Some behaviors are repeated because they were reinforced in the past; however, some may be repeated for a very different reason. When Hayden first opened the dishwasher, it was either purely by accident—the result of exploration—or he was mimicking me. Perhaps the second time he opened it was just for fun, though my responses those first few times must have been emotionally charged enough to give him the awareness that he would 'get my goat' by playing in the dishwasher. By reacting emotionally, the way I did at first, I had, unbeknownst to me, created a means of punishment for him to use against me.

The way not to create an instrument of punishment is to not use an emotionally charged tone of voice in response to inappropriate behavior. Even a small bit of behavior I use to express anger or pleasure about Hayden's doing something may well become a way for him to 'get my goat,' to be in charge, to punish me. If I had chosen to be punished by his getting in the dishwasher, he would have continued to do just that. (This phenomenon is recognized in adult behavior when a relationship between two people develops to the point where Person A 'uses' his/her pathological behavior—often an addiction of some kind, though not always—for the purpose of manipulating or controlling Person B.) There can be no victimizer without a victim; for someone to intimidate, someone must be intimidated; and for someone to punish, someone else must accept being punished.

Emotionally healthy adults can validate themselves, have strong senses of their identity, do not need others to agree with them to feel secure, and are neither a punisher nor a punish-ee. But children and many adults need validation for who they are. They need to be heard, understood, and accepted by significant people in their lives. When they're not validated, they feel unloved and may become angry, and unfortunately, their anger will often find expression in inappropriate behavior.

The appropriate expression of anger seems to involve one's awareness of a feeling as that of anger, and of some sort of expression of that anger (depending on which theory of therapy is followed, for example; in Cognitive Behavioral Therapy, appropriate expression of anger might include the use of 'I-statements' and the technique of meditation to defuse the anger, etc.). Further, the sense that one is loved even while feeling anger seems to help the angered party feel safe and secure while in the initial grip of such a destabilizing emotion. Once anger is appropriately expressed, it often will then dissipate.

When a person inappropriately expresses anger, this expression itself may become a direct form of punishment for others. For example: you hurt me and I want to hurt you back, either physically—by hitting, biting, hair-pulling; or emotionally—by doing things others don't want you to do; or spiritually—by attempting to make others feel guilty.

When children succeed in punishing, that behavior will crop up again every time they don't get what they want. Children with autism have continuous, intense grievances about being in their bodies, as well as limited comprehension and means of expressing these grievances. Is it any wonder their behavior is often inappropriate?

Punishment is often the basis of behavioral problems in children, with or without autism; the answer to dealing with it lies in authentic, detached acceptance and validation of their feelings. This, *not* punishment, breaks the cycle of vengeance.

Thomas Harris' book, *I'm OK, You're OK*,[1] which is based on Eric Burns' theory of transactional analysis (TA), contains some useful concepts for understanding interactions between

---

1. Harris, Thomas A. *I'm Ok, You're Ok: A Practical Guide to Transactional Analysis.*, 1969. Print.

163

individuals. For example, it is posited that the human personality is composed of three aspects: **parent, child and adult**. The parent represents everything we learn externally, such as beliefs, how-tos, facts, and rules. The child is our *feelings* as felt at the approximate level of a three-year-old. The adult is the *choice-maker* who considers both feelings and information in making choices. This particular aspect of the adult is thought to represent the spiritual dimension of people.

In TA, every verbal encounter between people can be seen as an interaction of these three aspects of each person involved. The interesting and helpful concept that concerns us here is that communication flows with the most ease in some very specific ways, allowing someone to influence the response they get by what they say and how they say it.

For example, when I speak to a young child from my parent, I will readily get a response from their child in the form of either rebellion or conformity. If I speak to a young child from my (angry) child, I elicit their (angry) child. If I speak to young children from my adult, I encourage their adult to step forward, when, that is, there is no violence or aggression coming from me, the adult.

Let's look at what happened when Hayden played in the dishwasher. In one of these instances, he did it to get back at me for talking on the phone (Remember, one of his tacit rules is that I am not to talk on the phone!) So initially Hayden's child felt unloved because I had broken one of his rules: if I loved him, I wouldn't break his rules. In order to be more in control of his world, and to punish me, he switched to his parent. In other words, by playing in the dishwasher he assumed the parent role in an attempt to put me in the child role of being bad for talking on the phone. Had I responded in anger, Hayden would have succeeded in getting me into my child mode, in which case he would have been in control. But in my child mode, I would be vulnerable. So I switched to parent and yelled at him in an attempt to punish him. But he did not feel punished. Instead, he felt successful at 'getting my goat' and forcing me into the no-win duality of his parent-child against my parent-child.

Suppose that at this juncture, instead of yelling at Hayden I had tried to reason with him, explain things (a parent-type activity). When seen in TA terms, that would have been like talking to a brick wall, because he was already gone! He had already succeeded at punishing me, and felt insecure about being in charge.

This sort of maneuvering between the different TA aspects of ourselves and others goes on constantly between parents and teachers on the one side, and very young children—as well as those with neurological impairments that affect reasoning—on the other. It also happens with older children, so-called "normal" children of any age, and adults, though it is somewhat counter-balanced by reasoning in the latter.

The most effective way to elicit appropriate behavior from children across the age span and with different degrees and kinds of function, is to lovingly refuse to act punished, to stay in your adult and thereby not let your child get your goat. Once you allow your child to make you angry, they've won: you've relinquished control, and there's a new issue, as far as they're concerned: you've broken their tacit rule, so they feel bad; they break your rule and you feel mad. For them, the situation is over, the cycle complete.

But then, if you yell at them or express displeasure you only break another one of their rules, the one about not yelling at them. So, while the cycle has ended for you, another cycle has begun for your child. And this punisher-punish-ee cycle goes around and around, day-after-day, year-after-year, with the stakes rising higher and higher because your child has cumulative angers, expanded desires, increased size, and greater strength. And lo and behold, autism is blamed for violent children, and:

"Ain't it awful?" We are all *victims* of autism! We try to moderate, pacify, mollify and use restraint to tame the monster, autism!"

You've heard the saying, "Guns don't kill people; people do." In the same vein, "Autism doesn't cause violent behavior. Angry, frustrated people do."

Children with autism do not have to be violent. If I didn't know this to be true, I wouldn't waste my time writing it. One strategy for stopping negative, violent behavior is to refuse to be punished in the TA way. It's simple in many ways, but difficult to carry out, at least at the beginning. As time goes on, however, it can become like second nature. It is, I believe, so much more preferable to living with withdrawal and destructive and violent behaviors.

One day when Hayden was thirteen and we were on summer vacation, I arranged for him to have a caretaker—Marjean—so I could grab some time to write. On the way to Marjean's, Hayden laughed and laughed, and kept it up for at least 15 minutes. This is referred to as "inappropriate laughter." I validated his actions and commented that he was feeling very silly today and the car's a good place to be very silly. After that, I tried to ignore his un-natural sounding laughter. Soon, though, it felt very much like there was something else going on besides a bout of silliness.

As I claimed earlier, behavior is a form of language in that it can tell us what someone without words is thinking and feeling. It seems to me, then, that there is no random behavior. So in this instance of inappropriate laughter, I set out to discover what Hayden's seeming silliness really meant.

First off, I recalled that in the past he had been unresponsive and sullen on the way to Marjean's. This indicated to me that he was mad at me for taking him there. Though he

166

enjoyed playing at Marjean's, he had a tacit rule that I'm not supposed to go places without him. I've pretty much eliminated this problem by asking him if he'd like to play at Marjean's while I do my boring grandma business, so he always says "yes" now. All the same, if I ask him, I have to be prepared to accept a "no."

So on this hot summer day in his thirteenth year, I didn't ask Hayden if he wanted to go to Marjean's because I didn't want to risk a no. But then, what about the laughter? I suspected he was trying to 'get my goat,' push my buttons.

As I continued my analysis of his behavior, I also recalled that in the previous month I had to take him out of a play in which he was performing—the first time in over a dozen live plays in which he participated—for a lot of laughing. So I said to Hayden, on this day I had set aside for myself,

"You've been laughing and laughing a long time, and I'm guessing you want to punish me because you're mad at me."

He looked at me, he smiled and clapped, and the laughing abruptly ended.

"Maybe you're mad at me for taking you to Marjean's while I did some grandma stuff without you, and I didn't even ask you if you wanted to come along with me instead. I just said you had to go to Marjean's."

His clapping verified he was mad at me.

"On this particular occasion, I will not act as if I have been punished by your laughing, but thanks for letting me know you're mad at me because you feel left out, unimportant, and unloved. Would you like to be mad at me?"

He signed his assent, so I sang a 'Mad Song' several times. This didn't quite do it, though—he was not done being mad, so I asked if he was so mad he wanted to punish me and make me feel bad, just like he feels bad. Again, he agreed, so I incorporated that into the next round of the 'Mad Song.'

Usually when Hayden's done being mad, it's over, including the inappropriate laughter. In this very real example, Hayden had somehow learned that adults do not accept continuous laughing; this had probably become one of his many tacit beliefs. Now, he used it as a weapon of punishment. Further, another of his tacit rules seemed to be that adults think nothing is funny. It may be inappropriate to laugh in a particular situation, so adults make an issue of it; so Hayden had learned a compound way to get even.

This type of laughter increased that spring. Reports from school mentioned inappropriate laughing. At a parent-teacher conference, his regular classroom teacher mentioned that one day Hayden just laughed and laughed, and there was nothing funny. I expressed concern that his teaching assistant had not taken him out of the room when he had been disruptive.

Mr. M said, "Oh no, it wasn't disruptive because it was during an activity that included the students moving about the room and talking to one another." He just noted that the laughter continued for no reason.

"For no reason?" I asked myself." Immediately, I knew why Hayden was laughing. I asked Mr. M if students normally moved about in his classroom and he said no. "Do students usually talk during your class?" Again, no.

"So the general rule in your class is students are in their seats and quiet. Is that right?"

"Yes, most often."

Bingo! That's what Hayden found so funny! The rule in Mr. M's class is that students are quiet and in their seats. But on that particular day, for no reason Hayden could see, students were definitely not in their seats and there was a loud din from their lively chatter. Further, Mr. M was not admonishing them for breaking the rules of making noise and being up and about; and it continued like that throughout the entire morning. "Wow—this is great; this is fun; this is hilarious." This was, no doubt, exactly what Hayden was thinking!

Though it made no sense to him, he liked what was happening in Mr. M's class. So from his perspective, laughing at such a situation was totally appropriate. His classmates were breaking the rules and it was okay, so it was fun and funny!

But soon Hayden noticed that the adults got anxious about his laughing and tried to make him stop. Instead of stopping, though, he continued to laugh. That's when he realized he could use this kind of laughter as a weapon of retaliation against adults with whom he was angry.

When Hayden was an infant, he threw himself backwards as an expression of anger and frustration. This was very nerve-wracking for me. It was so sudden and violent an action that I was afraid he would hurt himself. I decided to talk to him about it. I acknowledged that he liked to do this but it was just not safe. From then on when he threw himself backwards I would lay him down on the floor or ground, wherever we were, so he could lie backwards and be safe.

I engaged in this repositioning religiously. I did it wherever we happened to be: in stores, offices, on the ground when we were out-of-doors—anywhere and everywhere he'd try to throw himself backwards. As soon as he began the maneuver, I would immediately and calmly lay him down and step back. Then I would pick him up. If he threw himself back again, I'd calmly lay him down again and say to him that I could tell he wanted to be backwards. He couldn't roll over, sit up, or crawl, so he was stuck there by himself, flat on his back, and didn't like it one bit. It wasn't long before he stopped throwing himself backward.

When Hayden went into long bouts of screaming and I didn't pick him up without him reaching for me first, I came to realize that this screaming was a form of punishment as well. He also went through stages when he hit, pinched, bit, scratched, kicked, pulled my hair, poked my eyes, threw things, withdrew, withheld eye contact, kicked my car, got into things he wasn't supposed to—like the dishwasher—made loud, obnoxious noises, and escaped into a totally non-relating, autistic space.

The good news is that Hayden no longer uses violence of any kind, nor does he use escape into his autistic space or screams, as forms of punishment. Sometimes he gets into the music box on my dresser, I'll give him that. But most often it's sullenness, withdrawal, "eh, eh, eh," sounds, and disruptive mouth play noises that he employs to show his displeasure. When, as above, he discovered the power of inappropriate laughter, he added that to his arsenal for a time, true. All of the above on the list of angry behaviors were simply ways of getting even with adults for breaking his tacit rules.

If you think this is far-fetched and kids with autism are violent for no reason, I invite you to talk to others who have been around Hayden and have seen this all in action, or to follow us around for a few days, or watch me spend a few hours with a young child with autism. I say young here not because my way of working through punishment issues won't work with older children, but because it takes longer with those who have firmly established punishment cycles already in place. The little ones so want to be successful, appreciated, and understood, that they respond quite quickly to having their feelings fully expressed; their tacit rules identified; their punishments refused. And they're hungry to be accepted as children with disabilities, rather than disabled children. In addition, they long for us to simply say exactly what we mean and mean precisely what we say. And of course, they want us to understand their complex neurological issues.

The behavior of children—with or without autism—drastically improves by following my aforementioned guidelines, which are, I'll admit, simple on the face of it, but challenging to enforce at times.

* * *

Several days after the inappropriate laughing incident came to the fore, another example of Hayden's trying to punish me cropped up. One morning, he wouldn't look at me, nor communicate with me in any way. He also made it known that he didn't want to take part in an activity he had previously said he did. These were all indicators that he was mad about something.

I commented that it seemed to me that he might have a problem of some sort.

"Yes!" he said by clapping.

"Do you have a problem with me?" I asked.

More clapping.

"Are you mad at me?" I asked.

More clapping and smiling and I even got a glance, too.

"Thank you for letting me know you're mad at me," I affirmed. "Can you try to use your words ma-ma (meaning, mad at grandma)?"

"Ma-ma," said Hayden.

"Thank you for using your words to tell me you're mad at me! Does it seem to you like I've been a yucky grandma?"

Lots of clapping and laughter. And big smiles!

"It must be pretty awful to feel like you have a yucky grandma."

More clapping and more laughing, as his feelings were validated.

"Let me guess. Are you mad because I talked on the phone too much this morning?" Haden assumed his still-as-a-statue

posture, which I had learned means something akin to 'close but no cigar!'

"Well," I offered, "Maybe you're mad because I took you out of the Music Factory last night before the organ music was done because you wanted to keep laughing. And then I made you sit in the car.

Laughter, clapping.

"Thank you for letting me know you're still mad because I took you out of the organ concert last night. It's time to get ready to go, so we'll get ready, okay? But you can be mad at me in the car if you like." Finally, he began to relate again: he became, once more, compliant, affectionate, and cooperative, as I got him dressed. He even readily went right out to the car and got in.

Once we were on our way, I asked, "Do you still want to be mad at me about last night? He clapped, while I sang a 'Mad Song' at myself several times. But he was still not done being mad, so I sang it some more.

"Does it seem like I'm the yuckiest grandma in the whole world?"

He laughed and clapped.

"It must feel awful to have the yuckiest grandma in the whole world!"

There was more clapping, more laughing.

"Does it seem like I'm a yucky-pucky, icky-picky, stinky-winky no-good grandma?"

The clapping continued.

"Thank you for letting me know. I love you even if you think I'm a yucky grandma. Do you need to be mad at me some more?"

Even more clapping.

"Well, maybe you're so mad at me you'd like to punish me."

Explosive laughter and lots more clapping.

"Maybe you'd like to hit me or kick me?"

Continued laughter and clapping came from Hayden.

Then he finally looked at me directly in the eye, and I ventured an unusual query: "Maybe you'd like to poke my eyes and pull my hair?

He was unequivocally certain that he wanted to do this.

"I see...Well, it's okay to want to, but not okay to do it. Maybe you'd like to pull my hair and bite me and scratch me too?"

He was absolutely sure of this as well.

So I said, "Boy, I can see you're real mad. Maybe you'd like to throw things and kick my car and scream and yell and have a temper tantrum!"

It must have seemed to him I could read his mind, so I continued in the same vein:

"I can see you're very mad at me and you'd like to make me feel bad and unloved like you felt bad and unloved when I made you leave the concert."

Apparently I got that right too.

"Does it seem like a really good grandma who really, really, really loves you would let you laugh as much as you wanted to at the organ concert?"

He assented.

So I acknowledged: "I know. It seems like love should give you whatever you want. But that's not love. Love teaches you what is appropriate, and continual laughing out loud is not appropriate at a concert. If you want to laugh a lot, you may do so, but not at a concert where people are listening to the music. How about being mad at me three more times?"

He agreed, and I sang a 'Mad Song' three more times, then the 'I Love You Song'. Suddenly, it was over completely and totally: no residual feelings to process, no pouting or withdrawal, and no violent behavior.

Some may think I went too far in bringing up Hayden's innermost thoughts and desires to retaliate physically against me. Some may think it awful of me to have exposed such violent, graphic feelings in my grandson.

I maintain that it is precisely when we unmask such otherwise unspeakable feelings and give voice and acceptance to them that we free our children of the masked shadow figure of guilt. Such freedom is absolutely essential for a healthy childhood. In addition, feelings that we acknowledge, express, and accept in love, do not trigger angry behavior. I would much rather openly acknowledge that Hayden wants to hit or kick me or pull my hair because he's mad at me, than let him engage in such actions, which would only reinforce the false notion that kids with autism are by nature violent. Not only is this patently false, but those who believe it take a victim stance in doing so. I refuse to be victimized by autism. And as I have demonstrated over and over again, I need not be. None of us needs to be.

* * *

I readily admit that I can and do control Hayden's behavior with my words, and it's been years since he's exhibited violent or aggressive behavior. Every doctor we've seen for years has asked something about temper tantrums and violent behavior. My answer remains the same,

"No, he does not have temper tantrums, but he could if I didn't talk to him the way I do." And I would further say,

"If I didn't read his behavior as his language and respond in a way he can comprehend, if I didn't validate him as a person, he might rather quickly become aggressive and violent."

When we feel afraid, misunderstood, hurt, or vulnerable, our 'fight or flight' survival instinct is triggered. If we feel trapped, then fight is all we have left. You and I would resort to aggression and violence if we felt as frightened, confused, threatened, trapped, and unheard as our children with autism and other disabilities feel on a day-to-day basis, just being in their bodies. Individuals with autism, solely by virtue of being autistic, are always deeply affected by these three stress factors. And we wonder why they act aggressively? Any time or way we can help them express their feelings, make their worlds predictable, and give them a sense of control in their lives, we can diminish the stress they experience, and thus the need for acting-out. Deepak Chopra's three most stressful things for a human being describe to a tee what life is like for an autistic person.

The 'Mad Song,' for instance, addresses Hayden's inability to express what he feels in many different kinds of situations. My constant explaining—of what may happen, what has happened, why it's happened, what's gone wrong, what's gone right—helps make his world predictable. And, whenever possible, I give Hayden choices about the smallest things to the largest. Giving choices is such a crucial part of caring for and being with a person with autism. Even a small choice is a choice nonetheless. And choices make autistic people feel in control of their lives. Here's an illustration of some of choices Hayden gets to make:

> "Do you want to do physical therapy now and play later, or play now and do therapy later?"
> "Which do you want to do first: cosmic rocker, swing, ball, or spinner (all vestibular activities)?
> "Which chair do you want to sit in?"
> "What book do you want me to read?"
> "Would you like chili or a burger for supper?"

When we're at a park, beach, or swimming pool, I ask, "Are you ready to go home?" long before I plan to leave, just to give him a feeling of having a sense of control in his life by saying, "No."

Obviously, there are many things Hayden doesn't have control over, just as there are many things you and I don't have control over. But when I make a point of giving him control in the many areas where he can have, it is a fairly easy thing for me to do, yet it is extraordinarily important to him. Hayden gives input about where we go for vacation as well as things he does in his day-to-day life. When we decide to take an outing somewhere special for the day, Hayden weighs in on where we go and whether we go by ourselves or take other kids along.

On the other hand, whenever I sense Hayden is frustrated about not having a choice, I verbally acknowledge that it must be frustrating to have something like autism, which sometimes keeps him from choosing what he'd like. In such situations, he never fails to laugh, clap, and hug me to let me know that not only am I right on, but he's glad to be heard. These might seem like little things, but they make a huge difference in how he feels, and therefore, in his behavior.

When he was in school, for instance, Hayden was considered well-behaved by public school personnel, therapists, physicians, friends, family, and people in the community. Marjean, who started looking after Hayden when he was still in preschool and I took advantage of some much-needed respite care, told me once toward the end of her time with Hayden, that she had never, ever witnessed him display violent or aggressive behavior. At one point, I was even told that a school administrator had dubbed Hayden the best behaved kid in the district!

Not long ago, a friend told me she'd been to an early-childhood conference and had attended the sessions on autism. I asked her,

"Did you see any of Hayden in the descriptions of autism?"

She surprised me by saying, "No, his behavior really doesn't fit what they described."

Recently, another friend found herself in conversation about a group of children with disabilities and someone mentioned the challenging behaviors of all children with autism. My friend said,

"Not all kids with autism have behavioral problems; my friend's grandson, Hayden, doesn't." The reply was made,

"Hayden's not autistic; he's not like other autistic kids."

Yet, Hayden is nonverbal, wears pull-ups, cannot dress himself, and was diagnosed quite definitively as severely autistic by a physician from the University of Washington.

Whenever I call the local theater in Yelm to reserve front-row seats for a play, then identify myself as Hayden's grandma, they're glad to accommodate us. Once, even a shoe salesman commented on Hayden's excellent behavior while trying to find a style that fit over his ankle-foot orthotics (also known by the acronym, AFOs). In restaurants, concerts, stores, life in general, people go out of their way to comment on Hayden's behavior.

There is no question that Hayden is autistic: he rocks, chews, perseverates, etc. But, he is not aggressive, violent, destructive or disruptive. The potential is there as it is for all of us, but I use words to keep his stress level down, and thus avoid negative behaviors. I believe this is possible with most children, autistic or not.

Many children with autism are disruptive, destructive, aggressive, and violent, but not just because they have something called autism—I can't say this enough. It's because their bodies are in pain and give them inconsistent, inaccurate, and confused messages; and because they're misunderstood, treated as objects, looked upon as idiots, thought of as weird, disobedient and hopeless; and because they are pitied by many people in their lives. Even though their physical worlds are chaotic, disorganized, inconsistent, threatening, painful and confusing, they can't ask about any of what they experience because autism affects their ability to speak out-loud. Ironically, sadly, it may very well be true that autistic people know at some level just what they want to say.

I can't cure Hayden's autism, although he's come a long way and we're still going for a cure. There are thousands of brilliant and dedicated professionals all around the world advancing their knowledge and theories about how autism is acquired and how it might be cured. Research is also in progress by groups such as CAN (Cure Autism Now) and The Autism Society, as well as physicians, therapists, educators, and family members. All are digging, searching, examining, and exploring in their ongoing quest for causes and cures in everything from genes, casein, gluten, vaccines and heavy metals, to irregularities in skull structure, neurodevelopment, digestion, immunity, and metabolism. Though I certainly stay abreast of their findings, I see that my role, in the meantime, is to utilize as many means as I can to help Hayden's body mature and normalize. I also work very hard at helping him feel good about himself, his abilities and his own world, so that when the magic bullets arrive, he hasn't given up on himself.

* * *

During Hayden's thirteenth year, I arranged for him to play at Pope's Kid's Place—a center for children with disabilities—on Martin Luther King Day. The wonderful thing about Pope's Place is that it's also a respite center, meaning that I could leave him there in good hands and take some time off from being a 24/7 caregiver; that day I decided to use my respite time do some writing at home.

By the time MLK Day came around, Hayden and I had talked about his upcoming date at Pope's Place for weeks on end. So on the morning of the big day, excitement seemed to emanate from every one of his rocks back-and-forth, while the echoes of his ebullient squeals followed him all the way out to the car. I buckled him up and we were on our way. I began singing,

"We're off to Pope's Kids Place" to the tune of his favorite movie, "The Wizard of Oz." This usually triggers even more laughs, squeals, and rocks. But this morning, when I turned around to see why he suddenly became quiet, I witnessed Hayden in stony silence, as if I was not even there, as if nothing had been said, as if **he** was not there.

Many people would say that this was typical A-behavior, and I would agree: A for angry, not for autistic! Still, I was confused at the time. Five minutes ago he had been climbing the walls with excitement; then, suddenly, he had retreated behind a wall. So I asked,

"Do you want to go to PKP?"

"No!" was the surprising response.

"Do you want to stay home?" I asked.

"No!" again.

"You want to go, but you don't want to go?" I asked. "You must be mad about something," I prodded gently. I knew anger was brewing, but I didn't know the why of it yet.

"Are you mad because I'm doing something without you and you feel left out?"

"Nope."

"Have I been mean and grouchy today?"

"Nope." Was his reply.

I reviewed the morning's events several times in my mind's eye, searching for the missing piece, but I came up empty-handed…. No, wait, "I thought, "There was something: ah ha!"

There was a missing piece and I knew this in a way that neither heaven nor hell could shake. This is the bottom line of my work with Hayden and, I believe, the bottom line of all human behavior: behavior is language. Behavior does *not just happen. There are reasons and causes behind all behaviors, reasons such as frustration, fear, insecurity, anger, pain, misunderstanding, sensory overload, rejection. There are certainly reasons for negative behavior. Autism is often associated with negative behaviors because the neurological impairments comprising autism so perfectly set the stage for each of the aforementioned reasons.*

Once we concede that all behavior happens for a reason or a cause, and that autism, in and of itself, does not constitute a cause or reason either, we must conclude that Hayden did not suddenly freeze because of autism. Not at all, though autism may have caused him to perceive something he didn't like, understand or accept. And from what I could tell, in this particular case, Hayden had stopped looking at me, had completely stopped relating to me in every way, because he was mad at me for something I said or did and wanted to punish me for it. Pure and simple, very scientific, all reason, logic, cause-and-effect. I kept sifting through what had happened that morning and the words that had been said, on the lookout for the key to Hayden's precipitous change of mood. Then the veil lifted and I saw the scene and heard the words. As is often the case, everything fit neatly into place: I was the 'cookie thief!'

While I prepared to leave, Hayden was supposed to have eaten his breakfast fruit; but in reality, he had not. Debbie Boone sang "Me and My Blanket"[1] as her daughter, Tessa, adoringly toted her blanket around her world and across our TV screen for at least the 185th time. I had no idea that he was so into the music he was listening to when I mentioned that we really needed to get a move on.

My mind, I believe, was also elsewhere—probably on the fact that this was a respite day, a rare day off for me, a day to

---

1. Boone, Debby. "Me and My Blanket." *Hug-A-Long Songs*, J2 Communications, 1990.

do with as I pleased. But the pears and raisins that still sat in Hayden bowl had not cooperated with me.

I knew there had been ample time to eat, so I said my "one more time" thing, and soon, "one more time" was all done and it was time to go. Before he stood up, Hayden shoved another piece of pear into his mouth. So I said,

"If you want, you can finish your breakfast in the car." Then I proceeded to ready him to leave, amid the happy rocking, squealing, and laughter.

When we have morning appointments, Hayden frequently eats his breakfast fruit in the car. Not only does this save time, but it makes the trip less tedious for him if he has something to eat. As I hurriedly combed his hair on that fateful MLK morning, I asked him if he had finished his breakfast and had received the positive responses of claps and laughter.

"Good! I said, "We're leaving later than I want to and I would just as soon not have a car-breakfast to deal with today."

But when I initially said he could have breakfast in the car, it was settled for Hayden; he would finish breakfast in the car, period. If I hadn't been in such a hurry, I would have been more thorough in asking about breakfast. I'd have asked the same question in another way, at a different time, given full attention to the question, not side-lined it while I was combing his hair.

Hayden does not focus well on questions while something else is going on, and I know that. Yet, my mind was on getting going and not on what Hayden's needs were at the moment. He was mad because I said he could finish breakfast in the car, but I didn't bring it along!

"Are you mad because I said you could finish breakfast in the car and I didn't bring it?" I queried.

Suddenly animated, Hayden looked right at me and made his angry "eh, eh, eh," sounds. So I stated things from his point of view.

"I said you could finish your breakfast in the car, but I didn't bring it. So it seems like I lied to you and you feel confused and hurt and like you can't trust me. So you're mad at me."

Everything about his behavior told me that this was exactly what he was feeling, so I sang a 'Mad Song' at me. I apologized; I mentioned that I did ask if he was all done with breakfast; I sang the 'Mad Song' some more. I said that we could tell Marjean he wanted breakfast. But Hayden was still mad at me, so I sang the 'Mad Song' again and again. This must have been a very serious transgression on my part and in Hayden's view of things, because he steadfastly held on to his anger.

"Maybe you're so mad you'd like to punish me and make me feel bad, just like I made you feel bad," I suggested.

This made him laugh and clap, so I sang the 'Mad Song' some more, but added,

"Are you so mad that you'd like to punish me, maybe poke my eyes and pull my hair? He then made direct eye contact and smiled.

"Maybe you'd like to bite me and pinch me and scratch me?" I added.

Hayden laughed and rocked in enthusiastic agreement.

"Maybe you'd like to scream and have a temper tantrum too?" I suggested, "And throw things and kick my car." Hayden's squeals of affirmation filled the air.

"You'd like to punish me but I don't choose to be punished. It's not okay to hit, kick, bite, pinch, or scratch me, but it's okay to want to. And I love you. Are you done being mad at me?"

He was, so I sang the 'I Love You Song'. Then I asked his forgiveness for not understanding that he wanted the rest of his breakfast in the car, and he readily forgave me. Next I acknowledged my need to be more sensitive to his needs. Then he reached for his tape player, which always indicates that the issue at hand is settled, over.

I'm not sure if Hayden had more breakfast or not that morning, though I told Marjean he might want some more. But my discussion here has not really been about breakfast, *per se*. The real issues on the breakfast table that morning were security, consistency, my trustworthiness and Hayden's 'being heard.' Had I not processed all of this on the way to the park, he might have been withdrawn, belligerent, and non-responsive at Pope's. However, because we had cleared the air in the car on the way there, when I picked him up later in the day, Hayden was happy, relating, and affectionate; everyone said he'd had a good day.

I hope to have imparted some insight with this section into the way Hayden thinks, processes, and responds because I believe many other children with neurological impairments process similarly. Being aware of how they process their world allows us to lower their stress levels and improve their behavior. Moreover, when we unmask the punishers in our kids, we find the scared, hurt, beautiful children who travel through life incognito, and we can free them of their burdens of pretense and self-fear.

Chapter 9

Recall

Every now and then, the news reports a car or even airplane recall, because a specific part on a vehicle has proven unsatisfactory—or even dangerous—and needs to be replaced with a better-functioning, safer one.

Recently, Boeing introduced the world to the *787 Dream Liner*, a graceful, exceptionally efficient airplane. Soon orders from airlines across the globe poured in. Within their first year in the sky, however, a number of *Dream Liners* developed issues with their lithium ion batteries; runway fires actually broke out on several occasions, flights were cancelled on others. Eventually, the entire international fleet was grounded. The FAA essentially recalled every one of the fifty *Dream Liners* that had been operational. No malicious intent was involved, only errors in human accuracy, judgment, and knowledge of the manufacturing process. Adjustments were made to the battery and its casing, and the fleet returned to the skies.

During the past eleven years during which Hayden and I have been on our journey into Autism, I've encountered a number of items that I feel need a national, or better yet, international recall because of the damage they do to children in general and those with disabilities and their families in particular.

The difficulty with a recall of the things I have in mind is that they don't have serial numbers or even brand names. They have no inventory and there are no records of where they come from. They are not objects cast in steel, but ideas formed in the mind. Though they are themselves intangible, the damage they precipitate is very real.

Rules That Need Recall

Our nation has made much progress in social justice and equal rights, yet there still remains much social injustice and inequality within our borders. There is good reason to be concerned about the injustices in Afghanistan; they are atrocious. But it is noteworthy that though our fingers point at Afghanistan, they could just as easily point back at us. I'm not in any way diminishing the situation that existed when we first took up arms in Iraq and Afghanistan. I'm just suggesting that we as a country are not totally innocent.

Psychology tells us that if we want a good look at our own faults, we need only take note of what we condemn, reject, and disdain in others. Perhaps as a nation, it's easier to point a finger elsewhere around the world, than to acknowledge and correct our own social injustices. Some would point with pride to human rights laws that have been passed. I would say that these are just a beginning. Real change only happens when we allow laws of equality, justice and love to be written in our hearts as well as in the books.

We often hear it said that children can be so cruel, usually when a child is ridiculed by his peers. Sadly, this is often the case; bullying has become epidemic in our culture. However, as the well-known prose goes, "children learn what they live." When our children ridicule less fortunate children, we need to look long and hard at ourselves to discover where and when we have fostered this kind of attitude and behavior in our young ones.

"Not I," you may say, "I would never ridicule a disabled person and I get after my kids when they do."

That's great. So you're sure you haven't taught your child to ridicule? Where did they learn it? What do you say when someone cuts you off on the freeway? When someone drives slower than you and you're late? Does your child hear you compliment or ridicule your spouse? What does your child hear about your boss? Your secretary? Your business associates? Your clients? Is that paperboy a stupid %&*#&&! when he misses the porch? Are you always right, blameless, and angry while everyone else is always wrong, a nincompoop, an incompetent? Is your way always the best and any other opinion asinine? Are your politics entirely on target, while those who don't see things your way are idiots? Is the way you dress the right way and somebody else's, dowdy? Or too flashy? At the game, is the ref who calls a close play in favor of the opposing team a blind, incompetent jerk? Are you getting the point?

When a child is in your presence, your words and actions are his teacher. And at a very fundamental level, it seems to me, your examples teach either love or fear. I challenge you to spend a few days consciously noticing your attitudes, words, and actions, then examine them in terms of love and fear. Do you usually think of hate as the opposite of love? In terms of objects, for example, someone might say, "I love pizza but I hate beets." In terms of relationships, however, love and fear are opposites. Behaviors stem from feelings of loved-ness or unloved-ness. And it seems to me that unloved-ness begets more unloved-ness and fear, while loved-ness begets more loved-ness and security.

If your words, actions, and feelings are angry, abusive, violent, critical, demeaning, condemning, condescending, superior, or dogmatic, they may well stem from a deep-seated feeling of unloved-ness that will then go on to teach fear and non-acceptance. This is the basis of all prejudice, whether it has to do with race, religion, appearance, or ability. If your words, actions, and feelings are kind, accepting, understanding, and compassionate, my experience has told me that they spring from an inner-source of loved-ness and will go on to foster love and compassion. Children who grow up in an environment permeated with love, compassion, acceptance, and encouragement will generally be kind to others, including those who have disabilities.

It's a sad commentary on American life that so much of what is considered "comedy" derives its laughs from put-downs. As far as I'm concerned, there is no healthy humor in anyone's being embarrassed, humiliated, isolated, rejected or belittled (think of gentle, though hilarious, humor of Victor Borges as opposed to any of the Late Night Show hosts of the last several decades...).

I would like to issue an immediate world-wide transformative recall: all messages that condemn, condescend, criticize, belittle, bully, or employ sarcasm shall hereby be replaced with kind, loving, compassionate, understanding, authentic, and uplifting ones. The latter cost no more than the former and are also universal in their application; what's more, a positive message causes only positive results and absolutely no negative side-effects.

An edict that absolutely must be expunged from our culture once and for all comes from those who were parents of baby boomers who used the following phrase all too often: 'Children should be seen and not heard.' Only half of this is true: Children should be seen! But they should be heard, too, really seen and really heard! Your child and your neighbor's child may be pint-sized, but they are fully human and deserve the same respectful consideration as gallon-sized adults.

While shopping at a supermarket not long ago, I was privileged to witness a rare and truly beautiful transaction. As a mom pushed a cart, her smiling preschool boy handed her a package of batteries from a promotional display and said,

"Here, mom! Here's some batteries we can get."

I cringed internally, expecting the usual in- validation of an otherwise happy, helpful child. Instead, I was delighted to hear the mom say,

"Thank you for thinking about batteries. We don't need any now, but sometimes we do. We'll put them back."

Together they did just that. I was touched at the loving validation the mom had given her little boy, so when I happened to end up behind them in the checkout line, I mentioned to the mom how moved I was at their little communication. She smiled and knowingly said,

"If I want him to respect me, I have to respect him."

How wise this mother was and what a legacy she had granted her child! She was absolutely, 100% right. The way to get respect from our children is to practice respect for them, and that means to hear them, really hear not only their words, but their actions, their behavior.

We need especially to listen for children's entreaties for validation. Children need their feelings, ideas, opinions, actions, and dreams validated. Often they go un-validated and children are placated instead with expensive materialistic, plastic trinkets of modern society, which, when all is said and done, hold no real value.

As for prejudice, the best way to end it is for all teachers of children–classroom teachers, of course, but also everyone else with whom children come into contact, including parents, aunts, uncles, neighbors, physicians, receptionists, retail clerks, bus drivers, in short, everyone—to acknowledge and respect everyone else, including those from whom we are different. That way, our children will grow up respecting everyone as well, including those from whom they are different. Children's advocate and entertainer, Raffi, expresses this point well in his song, *It Takes a Village to Raise a Child.*[1]

We are, all of us, always teachers of all children. And generally, children learn to be loving, respectful, and happy

---

1. Raffi. "It Takes a Village." *Resisto Dancing – Songs of Compassionate Revolution,* Rounder Records, 1991.

when they experience love, respect, and contentment. The saying, "Your actions speak louder than your words," is especially true when it comes to children. It certainly matters what we say; what also really matters is how we conduct ourselves. Even if we speak the truth, if we live dishonestly, our children will model our dishonesty. If my little child wants me to read a book or play a game when I'm busy or relaxing, and I say, "Not now, I'll do it later," but later never comes, how can I be surprised when, as a teenager, he never seems to get to it when I ask him to clean up his room? Do I then yell at him, punish him, or say, "I can't trust you to do what I say?" Do I shake my head at the younger generation's lack of integrity? Many parents will promise the world to get their children to do something, yet they have no intention of carrying it out and therefore no accountability. These are often the same adults who criticize and condemn the younger generation.

It is incumbent upon us to model, both in word and deed, respect, kindness, consideration, honesty, and integrity, twenty-four hours a day, 365 days of the year, in sickness, difficulty, and play, privately as well as publicly, if we want to see these qualities in our youth.

In the area of medical care, the Terrible Trilogy, which consists of the Physician's Pedestal, the Dire Prognosis and in my case, Autism (it could of course be cancer, brain injury, whatever the diagnosed illness or condition is) deserves to be recalled immediately, in complete totality!

The Physician's Pedestal is available in a variety of styles and sizes, and was first designed, I would surmise, when physicians were educated and the public was not. It is completely outdated but sadly is still in use today in many offices, clinics and hospitals the world over. Though it is invisible to the human eye, it is solid enough to squelch a parent's intuition about their children, and large enough to serve as a roadblock to a patient's chosen path.

Every single Physician's Pedestal, no matter what the size or style, must be recalled immediately! Though I can see an impediment to such a recall—that many doctors and patients alike would find the pedestal comfortable, safe, and convenient, therefore, hard to part with—there's no question that change is in the wind when it comes to this.

How do I know this? Because, largely due to the availability of medical information made available via the internet, more and more people are becoming informed medical consumers and want to participate in choosing the type of medical care, whether conventional or alternative, or a combination thereof, they receive. Likewise, many physicians are broadening their horizons, acknowledging their limitations, and accepting the spiritual component of medicine, which may include personal responsibility, as well as divine intervention, for health and healing.

Physicians did tell me that Hayden's autism was a biochemical brain disorder and there was nothing that could be done; that he wouldn't progress much. Déjà vu. I'd been there before. They were wrong about me and some medical issues I had had earlier in life. They could be wrong about Hayden. So I made a conscious choice to not accept the prognosis of the pediatric experts. Today, at 27, Hayden has many issues, that is true. But it is also true that he went to public school right on through to graduation. He now enjoys dining in restaurants, live concerts, theater, and life in general. I shudder when I realize that if I had believed conventional medical wisdom, it may have been right. That's precisely the way self-fulfilling prophesies work!

Someone once said, "If you think you can, or you think you can't, you're right," which brings me right to the next item that needs to be recalled: The Dire Prognosis. Used in conjunction with the Physician's Pedestal, the Dire Prognosis has caused the death of hope for many people who have autism or who care for someone with autism, or, say, brain injury, cancer, AIDS, you name it. When hope dies, something of the human spirit dies along with it.

It seems to me that at least sometimes, the Dire Prognosis is given by a physician to protect himself from his own limitations. If he doesn't know how to fix it because it cannot be fixed, then he hasn't failed. I believe the solution to every medical problem exists. It may not have been discovered yet, but it exists. And I firmly believe this goes for autism. I will leave no stone unturned, no road untraveled, no possibility unexplored in my search for its cause and cure. When I speak with parents of children with Autism, I hear, more often than not, one or more of the following:

The doctor told me:

- *My child doesn't understand much, so don't use too many words.*
- *There's nothing that can be done about my child's behavior.*
- *My child doesn't know what he's doing is wrong.*
- *Don't bother with a casein-gluten-free diet, because it's very hard to do and it won't help anyway.*

When I hear these assessments, I feel frustrated, angry, and sad. Modern medicine, though truly amazing at diagnosing and treating certain kinds of trauma, musculoskeletal injury, and major infections, appears to me to be in the Dark Ages when it comes to many disorders, like autism, in spite of the progress that has been made when it comes to other disorders and diseases. I'm certainly all for research into the roles possibly played by genetics, vaccines, secretin, diet, the immune and digestive systems, neurodevelopment, heavy metals, candida, and skull structure as possible causes for autism. I have looked into each and every one of these myself. But first and foremost, we all need to recognize that children with autism are more than their bodies. They are human beings with spiritual and emotional needs that are often disregarded. If a child's spirit withers because it is not nourished, what good is a cure for the body?

The Autism (or Cancer, AIDS, etc.) "Sentence" is closely tied to the Dire Prognosis, and it is proclaimed from aloft, atop the Physician's Pedestal. It is, in effect, a living death sentence, unless you've destroyed or returned your own half of the Physician's Pedestal. If it had not been for my journey through my own illness, during which I was tipped off about the Terrible Trilogy, (the Physician's Pedestal, Dire Prognosis, and Autism Sentence), I may well not have had the knowledge, awareness, permission, and power to disarm the Terrible Trilogy and then proceed to set up my own program for Hayden. Once I cast aside the Trilogy, I was able to follow my gut and ferret out the knowledgeable, dedicated, and positive practitioners, regardless of location—they are in practice from Canada to Florida—who make up Hayden's team of healers.

This team consists of practitioners with credentials of all sorts who: grab a notebook and pencil when I say I have some questions; talk to Hayden and listen to me; and say things like, "Let's go for all we can get!" and, "If it's not going to hurt and it might help or give us some useful information, why not do it?" When I heard these two sentences, which pretty much express my approach to Hayden's treatment for autism, spring forth from the mouth of a practitioner, I had a truly earth-stopping moment. I spontaneously ran to him and gave him a great big hug! Hayden's team members are among the many practitioners—their numbers are now growing—who have rejected the Terrible Trilogy and are healers in the truest sense of the word. I am deeply appreciative of them and grateful for them.

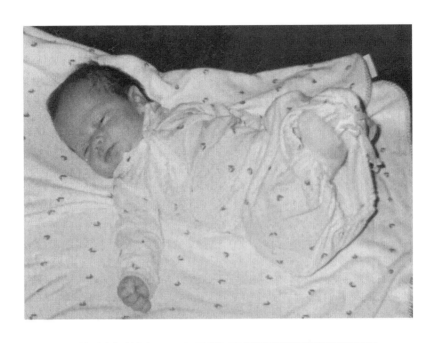

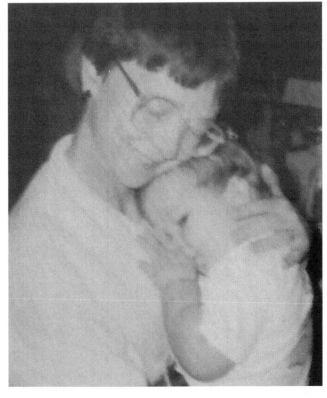

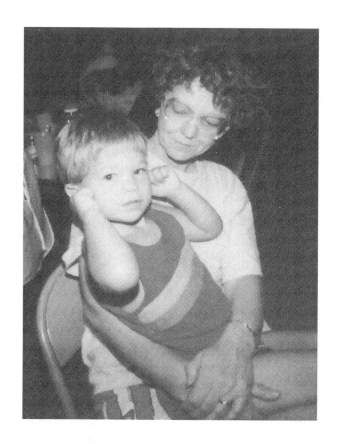

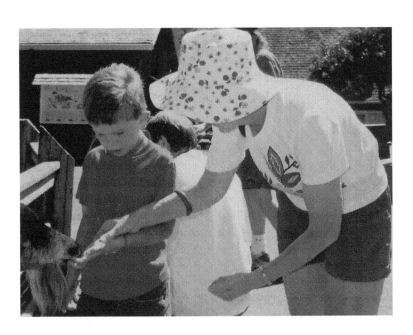

Part IV
Mapping the Journey

Chapter 1

Neurological Aspects of Autism

When you go on a journey, you use maps and travel guides to plan your itinerary. The American explorers Lewis and Clark, however, took to the Northwest 'cold turkey,' gleaning information and experience along the way that provided a basis for the first maps to be drawn up of their route west.

Similarly, soon after my journey into autism with Hayden officially began, we found the existing maps and guides unacceptable, so simply set them aside and created our own. Hayden and I discovered alternate guides, and learned a tremendous amount by trial and error, observation, determination, elbow grease, and prayer; these were the basic research tools that replaced the discarded maps and travel guides.

Up to this point, I've given you a travelogue, an accounting of our meanderings though the milestones of autism. In this chapter, I want to distill out of our journey those concepts that I consider to be fundamental, beneficial, workable concepts about children and autism.

When Hayden was about five, I was asked to do a workshop about autism. I said, "Sure!" It sounded easy. I had been a classroom teacher of biology, and I felt challenged and excited about the prospect of teaching again.

But, as I soon discovered, it wasn't so easy. Autism and biology are different in a key way: there were no texts about autism for me to fall back on, though of course there are in biology.

To deal with this gap, I challenged myself to think like a caregiver and asked, "What do I now know that I wish I had known four years ago when I started caring for a child with autism?" My presentation was based on my answer to this question, and is the foundation of what I impart when I work with parents. It is also the material included in what follows.

We will first look at the neurology of pre-school autism to gain an understanding of the whys of our children's behavior. Along the way, we'll examine feelings, stresses, and behavior as language. We'll also learn more about tacit rules, kids punishing adults, communication, self-esteem, and discipline.

* * *

Sometimes I look at the lonely BA tagging along behind my name and conclude that any attempt on my part to tell you about neurology is surely a case of the blind leading the blind. And you would be absolutely right! I know next to nothing about neurology, let alone the neurology of autism.

If you are keen to learn about jungles, you would undoubtedly check out appropriate books and videos from the library, take classes from botanists, zoologists, geologists and even a *jungle-ologist*, if such an expert exists. Short of traveling to a jungle and learning by immersion, this research strategy would set you well on your way towards picking up a thing or two about jungles.

Suppose, though, that you are able to take that trip to a jungle, but your small plane crash-lands in the middle of it. Wouldn't you be relieved to come upon someone who's lived there for many years? It's in this sense that I feel I can now talk about the neurology of autism. I've learned cold turkey, after landing smack dab in the middle of the autism jungle. And I have survived!

No, really, I have more than survived. Twenty-seven years have elapsed and we—Hayden and I—are thriving, thank you very much. So though I am ignorant of the academics of neurology, I have lived with the neurological disorder called autism for almost three decades. I give you, then, my unique perspective on the pre-school neurology of autism.

Most of us who are members of a family with an autistic child have had no training or experience in neurology in general, or disabilities of any kind. Yet almost overnight many of us are unceremoniously drafted to be an untrained, unlicensed chauffer, therapist, teacher, case-manager, advocate, nurse, dietician, counselor, form-filler-outer and uncertified 24/7 care-provider for a child who has a puzzling and pervasive neurological disorder. Moreover, after a short while, we also function as adept but unpaid researchers, spending hours weekly on the phone, locating providers, talking to insurance carriers, making appointments and accessing services. Autism happens to be my research topic, but it's the same for many other disorders.

When Hayden was diagnosed with autism at eighteen months, the professional advice and instructions I was given by a medical team were quite simple:

- Keep him in the early intervention program.
- Understand that he won't progress much.
- Talk to him only when you are very close to him.
- Don't use many words.
- Get on with your life.

Hayden did remain in early intervention and I have gotten on with my life, though I suspect not in the way these professionals had in mind. The rest of the above? It went right out the window!

I do have some advantages many families do not. I think I have previously mentioned that I was not the chief bread-winner in my family, nor did I have other young children to care for when Hayden came into my life. And I did have the support, both financial and emotional, of my husband, Denny. This is all to say that I didn't have many of the stress-ors that so many caregivers typically deal with. My hat is off to single parents, working parents, and families with other children. I can't even begin to imagine how you do it.

Hayden has significant delays in both gross and fine motor skills. Although he was assessed as a "normal six-month-old boy" at his half-year checkup, the pediatric physical thera-pist, Laurel, assessed him developmentally as a lethargic, listless four-month-old.

Out of necessity, this is when I stepped up and became Laurel's many-hours-a-day physical therapy *assistant*. I took Hayden for PT one hour a week, wherein Laurel demon-strated the exercises Hayden needed to do until the next appointment. For every one hour a week spent with Laurel, I would go on to spend several hours a day working at home with Hayden on the assigned exercises.

Then there was Barb, Hayden's "infant teacher," who came to the house once a week and demonstrated to me the fine motor skills, play and developmental sequences he needed to work on. Again, once Barb left, Hayden and I were look-ing at several hours a day of work before she would return the next week.

In reality, the way our hours of home-PT went was like this: ten minutes on, ten minutes off, every waking hour of every day of the week. Somehow we also navigated a crammed schedule of appointments, meals, naps, bottles, and so on. Obviously, had I been the breadwinner for my household, or had there been other children at home to care for, this grueling schedule would have been impossible. Sometimes it felt that way anyway!

Autism is not considered a disease, but is instead it's considered a disorder. It's not entirely clear in my mind what the difference is, except that most of the abnormal states of the mind are disorders, while those of the body are called diseases. In any case, a diagnosis is made by a medical professional by extracting a very detailed patient history and discerning where this places a child within the main diagnostic tool used for mental illness, the *Diagnostic Manual for Mental Disorders*. Recently a new edition was released, The *DSM-V*[1], and in it, autism is described as a spectrum disorder, meaning there are many degrees of the Autistic Spectrum Disorder, which lie along a continuum of functionality. For the first time, the *DSM-V* places Asperger's on this spectrum as well.

Like the myriad of other disorders in this professional manual, autism requires a qualified professional for diagnosis; school personnel are not so qualified. However, if you as a parent have questions or concerns about your child's behavior or development, however, you have the right to ask questions and expect answers. But the following are not legitimate responses: "Oh, he'll grow out of it, he's just a little slow," or, "You're just a worrying parent." And they are disrespectful to boot; you do not have to accept them.

Rather, you should feel confident and well within your rights to respond to such off-putting responses with the following: "It's nice that you think he'll grow out of it, but I'm concerned, and I want a referral," or, "I may be a worrying parent to you, but I need further information and I would like a referral."

---

1. *Diagnostic and Statistical Manual of Mental Disorders: DSM-5.* 5th ed. Washington, D.C.: American Psychiatric Association, 2013.

The Individual with Disabilities Education Act (IDEA)[1] is a federal program implemented by some school districts to screen or evaluate young children up to three years old. All school districts in the U.S. are mandated to provide autism screening of a child, at the parent's request, for children age three and up. Further, they must provide services to children who fall twenty-five percent below the accepted norm, when this is determined by specific testing.

Parent-to-Parent, a nationwide organization, provides support, services, information, and guidance to families with concerns about their children's development. A less formal website designed to do the same thing is www.firstsigns.org.

As a parent, you know your child better than anyone else. If you have concerns, trust your gut. It knows better than well-meaning family members, friends, or physicians who don't want you to worry. If indeed your child has developmental issues, the sooner they are recognized and addressed, the better it is for both you and your little one. The early years are critical for a child on the autism spectrum; this much we do know about autism.

What causes autism? There's no simple answer to this question. Actually, there doesn't seem to be a single simple answer to anything about autism. Western society is extremely left-hemisphere-oriented, and as such, we've learned to think in terms of concrete cause-and-effect: I push the brake, my car stops. But if my car stops when I don't push the brake, or my car doesn't stop when I do push the brake, I take my car to a mechanic to find out what the problem is—a broken rod or fan belt—whatever it is, we're confident he'll be able to fix it.

Consider this example drawn from a healthcare context: Your child has a high fever, so you bring him or her to the

---

1. *Individuals With Disabilities Education Improvement Act of 2004*, 20 U.S. Code § 1400 (2004).

doctor. The doctor looks for the cause—perhaps an ear infection, sore throat, a suspicious rash. Your expectation is that the doctor will find the cause and then cure it. If something is said to be incurable, there is even an implied sense of control in this label—it somehow fits into the general scheme of things. However, the only truly incurable thing is life. We're all going to die from it.

But autism is a horse of a different color. Actually, it's a beast of many changing colors. For instance, one of the conditions frequently present in kids with autism is heavy metal poisoning; heavy metals are especially toxic to the nervous system. Arsenic, copper, and aluminum were found in highly toxic levels in Hayden's hair at two-and-a-half years of age. How does a child of that age come to have so much arsenic in his system? Do the heavy metals cause autism, or does autism cause heavy metal poisoning by rendering the body incapable of heavy metal elimination? It has been suggested that immature and ineffective digestive and immune systems, frequently found in autistic individuals, lead to heavy metal poisoning because the autistic body is simply unable to rid itself of these materials.

We do know that in some way heavy metal poisoning and immature digestive and immune systems are among the things that plague those with autism. The important question for us becomes: How can we can support the digestive and immune systems and eliminate the heavy metals?

No one in the autism circles I am aware of claims that vaccines cause autism. But trigger it? Yes! It is widely believed that something in an infant's or toddler's physiological makeup reacts to vaccines and triggers metabolic aberrations. These metabolic aberrations in turn result, somewhere down the line, in autistic behaviors. Though poorly developed immune or digestive systems, allergies, candida, and electro-magnetic disturbances do not cause autism, it's been posited that they still seem to play a part—in conjunction with other known and perhaps unknown factors—in triggering a cascading reaction that leads to the disorder.

You may be thinking at this point that a simple, definitive answer to the question, "What causes autism?" does not exist. However, there are many candidates for this distinction: genetics, heavy metal poisoning, vaccines, allergies and sensitivities—particularly to casein (dairy) or gluten (wheat)—but virtually to anything, food, medicine, perfumes, synthetic fabrics, emotional issues, rubella in utero, skull structure, candida, digestive disorders, birth injuries, incomplete or immature nervous system, suppressed immune systems, electro-magnetic disturbances, viruses. The list just seems to go on and on…

In my moment-to-moment, day-by-day interactions with Hayden, though, the 'why' of his autism becomes irrelevant. Somehow, when I can let go of this my load lessens and I become more energetic and focused, more in-the-moment. It is appropriate to do the tests, yes, and to ask the questions, and to find out as much as one can. Thankfully, there is research into all of the things on the list above. But as a caregiver for a child with autism, I have needed to focus on what I can do now so I can enjoy each moment with my grandchild.

Although there are many different disorders and disabilities in the broad autism spectrum, the one common denominator is the range of atypical *behaviors* that most frequently present themselves in those on the spectrum. Although these behaviors may appear bizarre and random, they are anything but that, from the autism side of the fence. This is a very, very important concept to understand. You can't slip in under his skin and feel what it's like in order to confirm this, but acknowledging and accepting it is something you can do. Know that how the autistic child is functioning is not bizarre or random from his side of the fence; to him, *your* behavior appears random and bizarre. Accepting this can help you understand how your autistic child actually feels. Cause-and-effect, logic, numeric sequence–these are Greek to him (unless he's Greek, then they're like Swahili), and much of your behavior makes no sense to him, at best; at its worst, it's terrifying, perhaps even painful.

Fear always raises stress levels. For instance, suppose you pronounce, "We're going to Rome!" a place you frequently visit. But somewhere along the way, you somehow veer off course and end up traveling in the wrong direction. In your continuous world, you are aware that many roads lead to Rome. But in the autistic child's world of separate boxes and discrete, still pictures, there is only one way to Rome and you're not on it! "You said you were going there, but you're not," says the voice of autism. "You lied. What's wrong? Where are we going? Why did you lie?" it exhorts, in confusion and fear.

"Oh, but he doesn't understand words" is something I often hear from parents of autistic kids. When I ask how they know, the answer is, invariably, "The doctor (or John, a friend; or Mary, a family member) told me." Every parent who has said this to me has also said, once I've spent a session or two with their child, "Oh my, they do understand what you say don't they!"

Now, there are children within the autism spectrum who do not hear or process language, just as there are autistic children who are blind or have cerebral palsy. But don't accept this as fact unless and until you know it for sure. Members of Hayden's medical team were certain that he was extremely hearing impaired at eighteen months. They said we would need to be within a few feet of each other in order for him to hear me. This is also what led them to say that I should not use speech as a primary means of communication with him. I absolutely shudder to imagine how much we would have lost had I believed the medical experts instead of my own gut.

As a matter of fact, many children with autism can understand language—especially specific patterns of words—which can help overcome many of the problems that arise due to differences in the way you and your child perceive the world and process language. However, we need to have some understanding, if only rudimentary, of what's behind our children's behaviors and how they process or don't process language in order to be able to take advantage of their specific language abilities.

What follows is a potpourri of information that I've gleaned from books; teachers; therapists; physicians; observations; my own psychotherapist; the late Judy Bluestone; The HANDLE Institute, in Seattle; Dr. Judy Belk, at the Center for Communications and Learning Skills in Lake Oswego, Oregon; one of Hayden's chief practitioners, Pat Omiecinski; Hayden himself; and lots of prayer; all filtered through my experiences and translated into plain English. This is how I understand the neurological aspects of autism: It is the key to understanding the approach I take when working with children on the spectrum.

Autism Spectrum Disorder stems from an immature, irritated, damaged, stressed, and hay-wired nervous system. Keep in mind that the nervous system is our interpretive connection between the outside physical world and us, between different aspects of our body, and how we express things through our body. The nervous system is physical, but bridges to the non-physical world of our emotions and feelings; feelings can be either emotional or sensual, as in from our senses. The emotion of fear, for instance, is usually accompanied by certain sensations (think of the heightened vital signs we experience when we are in fight- or-flight).

The intricate nervous system connects everything in our body to everything else in our body with a network that makes our interstate highway system look like roads in a toddler's sandbox. Our eyes are more versatile than the best of man-made scopes, and the sensitivity of our fingers is nothing short of miraculous. Cranial-sacral osteopathic physician, Dr. Robert Fulford, in his book, *Touch of Life*,[1] claims he can feel a single strand of human hair under eighteen sheets of paper. I tested this myself and found I could feel a single strand under five sheets of paper!

The human nervous system is extremely complex and practically beyond our comprehension. Even more amazing is the fact that this incredible information network is not used to capacity in any of us. An autopsy of Einstein's brain famously revealed he was only using about 10% of his brain. (Where does that leave me?!)

People with autism have glitches in some areas of their intricate, complex brains that sometimes give them extraordinary capabilities. Think of, for example, the mathematical savant illustrated in the film "Rain Man"[2]; Temple Grandin, PhD, who sees detailed, elaborate pictures that she describes in her fascinating book *Thinking in Pictures*;[3] a young man with autism who sees musical notes in color; and Mark Rimland, an accomplished autistic artist. All of these people lie on the spectrum, yet they are able to cross the bridge from the Autism Jungle to the Common Jungle. I suggest that their capabilities are not that unusual, though their

1. Fulford, Robert C. *Dr. Fulford's Touch of Life: The Healing Power of the Natural Life Force*. Gallery Books, 1997.
2. Levinson, Barry, Mark Johnson, Barry Morrow, Ronald Bass, Dustin Hoffman, Tom Cruise, Valeria Golino, and Hans Zimmer. *Rain Man*. Santa Monica, CA: MGM Home Entertainment, 2004.
3. Grandin, Temple. *Thinking in Pictures: My Life with Autism*. Expanded ed., Vintage Books, 2006.

ability to find a way to bridge these two worlds seems nothing less than incredible!

Let's review high-school biology and look briefly at the human nervous system. It consists of the central nervous system, which is broken down into the brain and spinal cord; the peripheral nervous system: twelve pairs of cranial nerves and thirty-one pairs of spinal nerves; and the sensory organs: the skin, nose, tongue, eyes, and ears. The cerebrum, the largest and most familiar part of the brain, controls thought and voluntary muscular movements, and has two hemispheres—right and left—which are connected deep inside the brain by the bridge-like corpus callosum. The right hemisphere develops first and is responsible for subjective thinking, intuition, imagination, musical ability, and visual input. This part of the brain is often highly developed in those with autism, but as a whole, unappreciated and unacknowledged by our highly left-hemisphere-dominant society.

The left hemisphere is where objective and logical thinking, rationality, language, verbalization, writing, following directions, and time management skills are thought to originate. In those with autism, this part of the brain is less developed or develops more slowly than the right hemisphere.

Twelve pairs of cranial nerves leave the brain through openings in the skull, called the foramen, and innervate the nose, eyes, ears, mouth, face, throat, neck, lungs, and digestive system. Thirty-one pairs of spinal nerves innervate the rest of the body.

Autism's effect is global because it cross-wires the interpretive, receptive, and expressive connections between the autistic individual's mind and body. The affect? Terribly garbled messages, mostly. What comes to mind is the switchboard of New York City's telecommunications center being randomly rearranged. The result would no doubt be an endless number of kinds and degrees of mix-ups and general mayhem!

Autistic individuals housed in such terribly hay-wired organisms want and need to be loved and to love, to be accepted and appreciated, to be heard and understood, and to communicate. But the world seems an extremely topsy-turvy place. Some parts of their bodies give them pleasure, while some are terribly clumsy, inconsistent, uncomfortable, irritating, extremely sensitive and even painful. To make matters worse, the rest of the world often exhibits to them bizarre, random, irritating or painful behaviors. This makes life for autistic individuals rife with frustration and fear, which may cause them to act out negatively. It's important to understand that the world is a violent and stressful place for individuals with autism and other disabilities.

You may be wondering how this nursery-level bit of neurology could possibly help you in your day-to-day interactions with your child. All I can say is that it helps me tremendously with Hayden and has done so with other kids I know on the spectrum. Here's how:

- Knowing and accepting that Hayden perceives and processes his world differently means I'm not constantly interpreting his behaviors as disobedient or bizarre. Therefore, I'm not perceiving him as frightening, embarrassing, or threatening. When I see him as just a kid who happens to have autism, instead of a strange, autistic kid, he also sees himself as a kid who happens to have autism.
- Hayden intuitively senses whatever I feel about him and assimilates this into his feelings about himself. In our performance/ appearance/materialism-enslaved culture, kids and adults with physical challenges get a tremendous amount of nonacceptance reflected back to them. I want my interactions with Hayden and other kids to reflect acceptance, love, approval,

and respect. Seeing us as equals, knowing I would act the same if my body were doing what his is, allows me to do that.

- I have come to understand that Hayden's neurological level of organization is roughly equivalent to that of a one-year-old (with regards to motor skills). Because I know this, I don't waste a lot of time, energy, or contemplation about things that require a higher degree of neurological organization. For example, a typical developing child is expected to be in diapers until age three. Hayden's body is not performing at a three-year-old level in speech or motor skills, so I don't expect it to perform at a three-year-old level in the bathroom, either. I offer toileting, and lots of times we catch it, but I tried to never force any expectations on him years ago at school and I asked the same of his teachers, other school staff, and at-home caregivers. It simply makes no sense to pressure myself or Hayden over skills that he is not neurologically or physiologically ready to acquire. There's only so much energy available to each of us every day, and I don't want to waste it. I want to do things to boost Hayden's neurological development, improve his motor skills, help him experience life positively, have fun, and deal with feelings and behavior. When I keep in mind that Hayden's nervous system is immature, I become free of worry about his lack of development of certain skills and behaviors. He used to wet and soil his pants, and still sucks his thumb, drools, spits out hard food, plugs his ears, needs things repeated, wipes his nose all over his face and hands, and goes to sleep anywhere or anytime he's sleepy. He is also challenged in balance, small spaces, and motor planning. I make accommodations in my life for these, but give them no mental energy. What I mean by this is that I accept what is and do not fight it.

I recall one hellish week during Hayden's eleventh year when he wet his bed three times, totally soaking through all the sheets each time. Because of Hayden's auditory sensitivity, I have never used plastic coverings on his mattress (the crinkling of the plastic would drive him crazy), but instead I relied on resistant mattress pads that I discovered were not all that resistant!

Then, I had a stroke of genius. I thought it through in my head: If I expect him to potty at night, why not take him to the bathroom before I go to bed and when I get up at night? This work wonders! In fact, Hayden wet the bed quite infrequently after I adopted this potty schedule, so when he very occasionally did, I would say to myself, "Oh well, I know he wets the bed at night once in a while, so I wash bedding and make the bed." And I give it no energy. It's just what I consider an is-ness of life. The more I accept life as it is and not react because of what it isn't, the less energy I needlessly expend.

These days, I constantly work at being aware of the right- and left-hemisphere differences in styles of thinking. Hayden seems to have little or no left-hemisphere cognition, which makes him a lot like a toddler. Still, sometimes I expect more reasoning from him.

When Hayden was in primary school, I decided to teach him to get his toothbrush and toothpaste out of the drawer by the sink. I began by saying, "This time, you get your toothbrush." At first, he looked at the drawer but made no attempt to open it, so I opened the drawer and showed him the toothbrush, and helped him get at it. Months later, after I patterned each step for Hayden, I could say, "Hayden, get your toothbrush," and he consistently opened the drawer, took out the toothbrush, laid it on the counter, and closed the drawer. After a while, I decided to add put away *to Hayden's repertoire. I said, "Hayden, this time you* put your toothbrush away." *Immediately, he picked up the toothbrush, held it in front of the closed drawer and purposefully dropped the toothbrush—on the floor!*

I scratched my head on this one and silently asked myself, "Why?" I got my answer: No left hemisphere function. Hayden knew where to put it, but he didn't process that he had to open the drawer first. So, I picked up the toothbrush, validated to Hayden that he tried to put it exactly where it belonged, but indicated that, silly me, I had forgotten to tell him to open the drawer first. Before long, he caught on, and solidified the 'put away' routine, too.

I've noticed that when I accept responsibility for mishaps big or small that occur in our journey, in Hayden's eyes, this has the effect of dethroning me. This, in turn, temporarily relieves him of the heavy burden of feeling clumsy and inept. I've also noticed there are two sides to every situation. When I am able to verbally validate Hayden's perspective for him, without denial, guilt, or blame, we each grow both independently and in our relationship with each other. For instance, it was true that I had forgotten to tell him to open the drawer first, even though I am normally extremely clear and give detailed, step-by-step instructions, taking nothing for granted. So this toothbrush issue really came down to an omission on my part.

* * *

Hayden has no comprehension of safety. I believe this is primarily because it involves logical, sequential, cause-and-effect thinking. For instance, he doesn't understand such sentences as: "If I walk in the road I could get hit" or "If I get in a pool it might be deep and I could drown." Hayden very much lives in the moment, in a kind of discreet box or still picture. Though he knows what he wants and needs, these things have no connection to what happens next or what happened in the past. The past, for Hayden, then, is all of those other unrelated boxes or still pictures. I am constantly, vigilantly aware of safety issues for him, but I give them no emotional energy. I just do what I need to automatically now.

Logic, sequence, and cause-and-effect are so intrinsic to our way of thinking that it's hard to perceive how disconcerting it would be not to have them. If I handed you a photograph of someone in India and asked you what happened before this picture and what happened right after, you'd think I was a bit strange to expect you to know. For Hayden, life without logic, sequence, and cause-and-effect reasoning abilities is like a series of these still pictures that have no apparent connection to what happened or will happen or why the still pictures he does have happened the way they did. Yet, everyone else around him seems to have no problem with any of this. There are obviously rules of the game but they are obscure to him; he no doubt feels isolated, confused, insecure, even afraid at times, because he has no idea what's going on around him (We caregivers of individuals on the spectrum will always and forever be indebted to Temple Grandin for showing us how autism presents the world in this way.)

Remember how you felt on September 11, 2001? How uncertain and threatening your world felt? It's kind of like that, but all the time, for autistic kids. Is it any wonder that they shut out the world, insist on consistency in any way they can, or become aggressive? If you and I had bodies that felt, thought, processed and moved like our kids' for just a little while, we'd view our kids with awe and respect for how well they do despite this.

I can help Hayden immensely by verbally filling in for his still-dormant left hemisphere. I talk, talk, talk; explain everything about everything; taking his box or still picture and telling him about its before and after. Every morning I run through what's on the to-do list of the day's activities, so that he'll have some level of preparedness. One day, after Hayden went to school, Chelsea called and I picked her up from school because she was sick and her mom was at work. When Hayden got off the bus and saw her, he turned away from me.

"Are you mad at me because I didn't tell you Chelsea would be here after school, and you're not sure what's going on?" His response was to smile, clap, and make eye contact.

"You're right, I didn't tell you," I said, "because I didn't know. Chelsea was home sick by herself and I went and got her. Thanks for letting me know it's kind of scary not to know what's going on."

Even this little bit of processing cut the tension for Hayden. After all, he likes Chelsea, and although he is sometimes jealous of the attention I give her, he likes it when she comes over. Regardless, he didn't like her surprise appearance, though my explanation was all he needed to feel good about his world again, because I had provided the missing piece of logic, sequence, or cause-effect that made his world more predictable. As a result, his stress level dropped, thereby eliminating the chance of his acting out with negative behaviors.

I can change any situation when I process it as I did above. It's a lot of work to do this all day long, every day. But it's so much less work and so much less stressful than having to deal with tantrums and aggression.

I participate in much of Hayden's education, so it's important for me to understand how learning takes place. There are many modes of learning. Infants begin learning motor skills when innate reflexes are rewarded. For example, a new mom is told to stroke her newborn's cheek, which makes her baby turn toward the stroke, and voila—supper! Soon the little one knows where supper is without the maternal stroke. A month or so later, the baby's head turns automatically as his arms and legs move in a specific way, called tonic neck reflex. This reflexes plays a huge developmental role for new babies: it exercises their bodies, contributes to cross-patterning, and widens their visual scope.

Reflexes jump-start the learning process, after which rep-etition, incentive, imitation, experience, and creativity take over. We have the bizarre notion that schools and teachers are necessary for learning. But they are not! Reflex, repe-tition, imitation, incentive, experience, and creativity are God-given tools for learning. Family members, friends, and instructors who respect and use these tools skillfully, with the child's interests in mind, are effective teachers. Unfortunately, parents, schools, churches, and government agencies are often more interested in their own comfort, agenda, beliefs, and goals than in the development of chil-dren. Nature's learning methods support and encourage individuality and diversity, while society's learning methods foster conformity and compliance to external criteria, which is devastating to all children, especially to those with bodies that are wired neurologically differently from most.

The baby whose cheek was stroked to help find the nipple as a newborn, will reach for the bottle or breast at six months and put it in his own mouth, having learned through reflex, repetition, incentive, and experience how to satisfy that gnawing feeling of hunger. The physical exertion involved in using reflexes repetitively also strengthens the infant's body and expands his visual field. The latter also helps create interest in other things around the baby, and gives incentive to imitate what is perceived.

C.W. Metcalf claims, in *Lighten Up*,[1] that studies show if a baby never sees a smile, he will not learn to smile. Discoveries of "wild" children—those who have grown up in the wild with animals and mimic animal rather than human behavior—remind us how much we learn by imi-tation. Imitation leads to new experiences as the range of

---

1. Metcalf, C. W., and Roma Felible. *Lighten Up: Survival Skills for People Under Pressure*. Basic Books, 1993.

227

things imitated grows. This in turn gives the baby incentive to continue to imitate, especially things that make him feel good. And again, imitation leads to yet more experience. In fact, imitation and the experiential input it gives the young baby continually trigger each other; eventually, this sparks creativity, and the infant's learning explodes, as sight, sound, touch, smell, and taste tantalize and woo them.

Literacy and technological devices are utilized as learning modalities, but often lead to addictive behavior and thereby lose their teaching ability. Learning relies on complex electrical currents that are continually flowing between the brain, nerves, sensory organs, and muscles. When that normal flow is interrupted in any way, a wide variety of aberrant behavioral patterns appear and learning is affected.

Aberrant behavioral patterns have been associated with autism because of its identification as a disorder; they are the basis of diagnosis. But children with autism can learn, though often not in traditional ways. It's important for me to understand as much as I can about the glitches in Hayden's learning profile so that we can maximize on his rather minimalist, though highly individualized, learning style.

Sometimes, kids with autism seem to have no incentive to learn what we want them to learn, so are thought of as dull and disinterested. Though it may sometimes look as simple as this, it rarely is. In order to learn, humans need a sense of safety and stability. But if our attention is always on these two things, we will have no attention left over to give to learning. Imagine, for example, that bright lights flash in your eyes from freight trains rumbling loudly by on both sides of you; or, you sit a few inches from a 30-foot drop; or flying objects buzz around you; or the smell of rotten eggs or an entire spilled bottle of Channel No. 5 permeate the room you occupy; or ants are crawling all over your body. Suppose you experience even one of the above while I attempt to get you to stack blocks, recite the alphabet, learn a poem by heart, or make music. I notice, of course, that you're not even paying attention to me, so couldn't be learning a thing. Would it mean you didn't want to learn these things, or you *couldn't*?

I contend that your desire to learn or not to learn the things I'm trying to teach you never even enters into any of the scenario above, because one hundred percent of your attention is focused on what is happening around you, while what I'm trying to teach you is about as irrelevant and irritating as a pesky fly.

All of these scenarios–trains roaring by, bright lights flashing into your eyes, danger at every turn–are pretty ridiculous, aren't they it? No one would try to teach someone under any one of these conditions. So, we all agree that a pleasant, safe, stable, environment and personal comfort are important prerequisites for optimum learning.

Now suppose your optic nerve relays images of bright lights to your brain when there are none; you hear the sounds of an air conditioner or a fan as loud as a freight train; even though you are sitting squarely in a chair in your room, your sense of balance is so skewed that you feel as precarious as you would standing on the edge of a cliff. And suppose further that you have no sense of where your body ends and the rest of the world begins; your skin feels numb sometimes, hot, itchy, cold as ice, or just plain painful other times; creepy things crawl on it and they give you the creeps, like chalk screeching on a chalkboard. What then? Would you be interested in learning? Would you be cooperative? Would your behavior be normal? Would you be aware of having to go to the bathroom? Or would you be so overloaded that you just shut down? Suppose your life had always been this way? What would you have learned?

What if we call in the experts to figure out why you weren't interested in learning, were uncooperative, wet your pants, and behaved in weird, socially-delayed, spaced-out ways? Suppose the occupational and speech therapists evaluate you; the audiologist assesses you; the neurologist, ophthalmologist, otolaryngologist examine you; the psychologist and sociologist analyze you; the radiologist reads your x-rays; and the educators test you. Yet not one of them sees the "you" behind and beyond their test results.

All other things being equal, you'd be diagnosed with ASD. Then everyone would know why you're not interested in learning, don't cooperate, behave weirdly, are socially delayed, spaced-out, wet your pants. Everyone would focus on your body, which just doesn't work correctly, then would try to control your behavior. But everybody would totally miss you—the intelligent, sensitive person imprisoned in a hay-wired body—who experiences normal emotions and who wants and needs to be validated, loved, accepted, and understood.

The same incentive that encourages the toddler to explore and learn is present and working in the child with autism. But its focus is different. Instead of being focused on learning, it concentrates on self-preservation and security. The more I understand Hayden's world—his fears, joys, and abilities—the better equipped I am to provide incentive for him to *be* in this world and take part in it.

Imitation is another learning mode or tool. The feral behavior of children who grow up with wild animals illustrates how much we learn by imitation. Children dress dolls, drive cars, play house, play school, in a combination of imitative, symbolic, imaginative, and creative play that has as its basis observations of adults doing these things. The absence, or delay of, symbolic or imitative, imaginative play is an important diagnostic criterion associated with autism.

One day when Hayden was in pre-school, one of the activities was simply, "play McDonald's." Johnny, a child who developed in a typical way, held out an empty French fry container and said to Hayden, "Do you want some French fries?" Hayden smiled, reached for the extended French fry container, but there were no French fries. He pushed the container aside and began to look for the promised, but nonexistent, French fries. He became agitated when they did not appear.

I could see where things were headed, so I removed Hayden from that play scenario and explained as best I could that it was only play McDonald's, for which it was not actually necessary to be at McDonald's, so there were no real French fries, just pretend. But this just did not compute in any of Hayden's discreet boxes. In his mind, he'd been 'unfaired-against'—one of our terms for being double-crossed— and the only thing that would resolve the situation was the appearance of the promised French fries.

But I couldn't produce the French fries from thin air! Nor could I explain their absence in terms he could comprehend. So I backed down a level, to his unfaired-against feeling and began to processes why he was mad at Johnny. Was Johnny guilty of anything? Of course not, unless it was of being a typical, imaginative child. Was Hayden guilty of anything? No, except of being a child with autism. On that day, these two little boys were worlds apart, yet sitting in the very same room.

In order to help Hayden survive and participate in this world, I must understand his world and how it looks to him. Then I can use words to build bridges between his world and any other world(s) he wants to explore, or deal with his feelings of frustration when I can't. Hayden's feeling mad at Johnny had nothing to do with Johnny. However, it was extremely important to talk to Hayden about this feeling he had about Johnny.

It is significant to note that in spite of their lack of imitative-imaginative-symbolic play, kids with autism do learn by imitation. Though they do not use it in play, it is an important learning tool. Sign language, for instance, gives voice to some non-verbal kids with autism and clearly imitation is involved in learning sign language. When imitation is used as a learning tool, it's important to remember that incentive is a more basic learning mode than imitation, so activities that feel relevant to a child are more apt to be imitated.

As it turns out, imitation has not been a significant factor in Hayden's learning process. Mimicry seems to be a foreign language to him. At 18, he did very poor facsimiles of *Patty-Cake* and *Itty Bitty Spider*. A great deal of his learning has come from my moving his body—while I explain what we're doing—into a succession of positions he's needed to master in order to be able to sit, crawl, stand, and walk. Hayden took his first steps alone when he was four years old, after which we worked on functional walking: endurance, avoidance of things in his path, managing on slanted walkways or uneven ground, stepping over small objects, and climbing. It took two-and-a-half years of physical assisting paired with verbal cueing of every movement, for Hayden to learn how to climb into the bathtub "by self." But he did it, and were we both so proud!

So Hayden did not walk or climb because he saw people walk and climb and mimicked them. He learned how to walk and climb by learning many seemingly discreet, individual physical movements, then sequences of these movements. And all along the way, he was aided by my words and infamous singing. Without this, he would still be flat on his back, just as he was at eleven months, when he still couldn't roll over or strengthen his body in such a way as to develop that skill.

There are a few physical developmental skills that Hayden has not mastered, that I did not, under the direction of his pediatric physical therapist, Laurel, pattern in. I taught him how to get toys off a shelf by guiding his hands to the toy he was looking at, then helping him pick it up and put it down on the floor. By understanding and using the learning methods that worked for him—patterning, incentive, repetition, and verbal cueing—he has been able to progress far beyond his early doctor's expectations.

Most children transfer learning experiences to new relate areas quite readily. When a toddler has learned to stack blocks, he can stack any blocks. Not so with Hayden. I had to teach him how to stack different kinds of blocks. If I teach concepts A and B, most kids will transfer learning to include everything in between, but Hayden does not. I must teach not only A and B, but also: a-1, a-2, a-3, etc., including all the intervening steps to B.

Hayden is very good at learning each discrete step and retaining those skills. This is why it sometimes *looks* as though he's learned everything from A to B. But upon closer inspection, there are in fact some missing pieces. For example, after Hayden could get in the bathtub and could climb on my bed, I had to pattern in the steps he needed to take in order to get into the car by himself. However, when it was parked on a slant or a couple of inches from the curb, this seemed to present a whole new concept to Hayden, and he was stopped dead in his tracks.

I found this out at Easter Seals Family Camp one year. Everyone was waiting for us at the lodge, and Hayden would not get into the car for the drive down. Because I strongly believe that behavior is a form of language, part of me argued with the obvious reason why he refused to get in the car, the one that most people would posit, which was that he was stubborn and non-compliant.

233

But my inner knowing won. I just knew there had to be a reason why he would not get into the car, so I continued to look for the variable until I found it. As it turned out, the car was parked at an angle, on a slope. When I moved it off the slant onto some level ground, Hayden quickly got in.

For a year or so after he learned how to get into my car he wasn't able to get into any other vehicle; with more patterning and verbal cueing, eventually he could get into other cars as well. But he came with no innate sense of how to or when to generalize. At nineteen, he easily opened car doors and goes in and out of cars by himself, unless the car's parked on a slant or a few inches from the curb: then, as always I guess, he's needed assistance.

No physician, therapist or special education teacher can possibly know the extraordinarily complex and unique learning processes present in their patients or students. As parents or care providers, we know our children best, and are in a position to have figured out which methods of learning are best for them.

Repetition—a basic, innate learning mode for all ages— appears in a mutated form in autism. Even though children on the autism spectrum learn by repetition, just as everyone else does, their unique hay-wiring tends to lead to repetition "quirks" that can abort and limit, or, on the other hand, enhance learning.

For Hayden, the way something is done the first time, or he's successful at doing it, becomes The Rule about the way it's supposed to be done–that's right, a tacit rule. I've mentioned tacit rules before. But there are some specifics that pertain to learning that I have not shared previously.

For one, I need to be diligently alert to exactly what I'm teaching or allowing, so that I do not teach or allow something I will not want to be continued. When Hayden was four or five, he discovered my eyes and touched them with his finger. Because I was pleased with his new awareness of me, and with his desire to know my face, I allowed him to thoroughly explore my eyes with his fingers. Little did I know that in the process, he had formed a concrete rule that he could play with my eyes at any time. Of course we had to work on his coming to understand that it is not okay to so this anytime. It was rather difficult to teach 'no' after inadvertently teaching 'yes.'

My policy of allowing a child to explore something new to get the curiosity out of their system totally backfired with Hayden, because in this eye example I inadvertently set the pattern *into* his system. Now he knows that he's not allowed to poke my eyes, but once in a while, when he's angry with me, he'll reach up and gently touch my eye to remind me he's still ticked off at me for not letting him do that. From Hayden's perspective, he has a perfect right to touch my eyes because he did it *once*.

When he was preschool age, Hayden received a toddler-size accordion as a gift. Totally by accident, he made the instrument produce sound by pushing on the plastic bellows, instead of by pushing the two sides of the bellows together. Now, at 27, this is still the way he plays that little accordion, although I have modeled and patterned the usual way many, many times.

Because I know that the first time Hayden does an activity successfully or I permit him to do an activity, it will become a learned, set pattern, I'm very careful about what I teach him. If I allow him to get away with doing something I don't want him to do, I've effectively taught him that it's okay to do it. I can, with much effort, patience, and repetition, work at it and eliminate the behavior if I need to, but I haven't figured out how to totally erase the rule in his mind that he can do it. Interestingly, this appears to be an aberration of the learning mode of repetition.

Perseveration, or repetitious behavior, seems to also be an aberration of repetition as a learning mode. It's kind of like the stylus on an old phonograph getting stuck and repeating itself...repeating itself...repeating itself. Hayden excels in perseverative play, especially dropping things, all sorts of things, over and over, ad infinitum, it seems. Also, flapping drawer handles, spinning wheels, rocking, repeatedly pushing the same button on a toy and listening to "Hello, Big Bird's Office. Let's play. Choose a game...Hello, Big Bird's Office. Let's play. Choose a game...Hello, Big Bird's Office. Let's play. Choose a game..." or maybe just, "Hel -...Hel -...Hel -...Hel-..." over and over for several minutes. Or maybe it'll be the tinkle of the music box playing, "Mary Had a Little Lamb...Mary Had a Little Lamb...Mary Had a Little Lamb..." *ad infuriatum.* I have not, as yet, found a single educational or social benefit for Hayden's perseveration. No matter how many times he repeats something in perseverative play, he has not improved his skill level—social or otherwise—in any way whatsoever. In fact, if I attempt to join in and socialize, he ignores me, moves away, changes the game, or gets angry. In Barry Kaufman's book *Sonrise,*[1] the boy's parents do perseverative things with him and he accepts it. But Hayden never has. Believe it or not, by total accident, happy accident I might add, I used his aversion to my joining in his perseverative play to eliminate hand-flapping in almost no time, once and for all!

When Hayden was very young we did physical therapy ten minutes on, ten minutes off, right through the day. He always engaged in some kind of perseverative play on his off time. When it was work time, I expected and still expect him to work at the assigned task; but I have always figured his time is his time; if he wants to perseverate, that's his choice.

---

1. Kaufman, Neil Barry. *Son-Rise.* Warner Comm. Co., 1976.

I also discovered, though, that this kind of activity is not as vacuous as I initially thought. Once, years ago, I sat down by myself and perseverated at dropping things, a favorite pastime of Hayden's. I found to my surprise that there was a great deal of sensory stimulation in doing this—tactile, visual, auditory and spatial. There's predictability, thus security, as well. And there's also room for variation. One gets different sounds by dropping the same thing on different objects, at which time one has absolute power and control in that moment. The feeling of being in control is one of the three most important factors in keeping stress levels at a minimum, according to Deepak Chopra. Certainly, this applies as much to autistic children as it applies to kids off the spectrum. I would think that perseverative activity is attractive to Hayden because its predictive nature gives him a feeling of security, and the control that comes from changing things ever so subtly affords him that crucial feeling of control over something in his life.

So, even though I've found no educational or socially redeeming benefit to be had in perseverative play, that doesn't mean there is none, nor am I going to indiscriminately work at eliminating every bit of it. Hayden obviously likes to do it and it seems to calm and center him when he's stressed or in situations that overwhelm his senses. Besides, who can say that perseverative play is less productive than a great deal of what passes as entertainment on TV? Giving Hayden the right to play in ways that he wants to on his time seems to be a kind of corollary to expecting him to do what I, or a teacher or therapist, want him to do during work time.

I need to be clear at this juncture, that though I am quite permissive with Hayden's behavior, there are some absolutes, behaviors I cannot and do not accept. They are: aggression, violence, disruption, and refusal to comply with schedule and routine. But first and foremost, and even prerequisite to the expectation of appropriate behavior from a child, is acceptance, love and honor for a child at the point they are at in their life journey. If the most honest reason I can find to deny Hayden the right to play and relax in the way he wants to is my own fear, prejudice, and embarrassment, then I need to acknowledge that my disability is at least equal to, if not greater than, Hayden's.

* * *

Music, which I consider the language of the brain's right hemisphere and an invaluable communication mode for Hayden, is also useful as a learning tool, just as it is with most preschoolers. It's fun and relaxing and can be used as a vehicle for imparting information, even as a reward.

Though he now uses CD and DVD players, years ago he went through many kiddy tape players, which he uses mostly in the car. He had total charge of holding and controlling them, which was very important to him. He could never manage putting tapes in a player, but he could take them out, choose the ones he wants, stop and start them, and control the volume. Learning how to meet your own recreational needs is an important concept to be learned, even if it's not on school report cards. Frequently I put words about an activity he's learning to a familiar nursery rhyme to give him a point of focus and familiarity, for communication, fun, and to help facilitate the activity.

We do a couple of exercises created by the late Judy Bluestone of the HANDLE (Holistic Approach to Neurodevelopmental Learning Efficiency) Institute in Seattle,[1]

---

1. Simon, Peg. "The Road to HANDLE® Leads to Hope for Children with Neurodevelopmental Needs." Seattles Child, Aug. 2005.

238

called Face Tapping and Skull Tapping, which are still irritating to Hayden, though not the traumatic sensory overload they were years ago. Even so, when we first started very lightly and only did a tiny bit of face tapping, it was neurologically overwhelming for Hayden. So right there on the spot, I composed the following masterpiece to be sung to the tune of "One lit-tle, two lit-tle, three lit-tle In-dians." It goes like this:

Tap-tap-tap-tap, I am tap-ping;
Tap-tap-tap-tap, I am tap-ping;
Tap-tap-tap-tap, I am tap-ping;
Tap-ping on your face.

Okay, so it's no masterpiece! I admit that the music is very common and my rendition surely would have earned an immediate GONG on TV's infamous Gong Show of the 1980s. But let me tell you this: it netted me my own private Nobel Peace Prize for the tranquility it brought to Hayden and the way it facilitated ease in the doing of that activity. Although Hayden truly appreciates Mozart and The Messiah; absolutely adores Raffi and Peter, Paul, and Mary; is fascinated by old-fashioned, hoe-down fiddle music; grooves to the songs of the Cookie Monster, Big Bird, and all the Sesame Street kids; it is the unrecorded, repetitious, raspy renditions of my spur-of-the-moment, decomposed—recomposed nursery rhymes that support his therapy, relieve his tension, help him express his feelings, put an end to his boredom, and facilitate our relationship.

Beginner's math and spelling can be put to nursery rhyme tunes too. I use *The Farmer in the Dell* more frequently than most, but there are hundreds of others. Here are some examples using *The Farmer in the Dell*:

One and one are two;
One and one are two;
Hi ho the derry-oh!
One and one are two.

B-O-X spells box;
B-O-X spells box;
Hi-ho the derry-oh;
B-O-X spells box.

If there aren't enough syllables, just add 'm in. Music is such a versatile, fun tool for teaching. Because I'm aware of Hayden's unique ways of learning, I'm able to make important educational decisions for him. Unfortunately, they're not always in agreement with professionals, school policies, or social norms.

What is the purpose of our sensory organs—our eyes, ears, nose, taste buds, and skin? To see, hear, smell, taste, and feel, of course. But what one general function do all five senses have in common? They give us information about our world. If we couldn't see, hear, taste, smell, or feel anything, how would we know about our surroundings? How would we survive? These five senses seem pretty fundamental, don't they?

But what if these sensory systems consistently gave us unreliable, inconsistent, inaccurate, overwhelming information? How would we feel then? Would the world feel safe? Would we be excited to try new things? Would we be calm, cool and collected, or would we be hyper, hot, and haywired? Has this given you some sense of how disconcerting it would be to live in the shadow of the autism specter?

But this is only half of the sensory picture. There are two sensory systems more fundamental than smell, taste, touch, sight, and sound. Think about the one basic function of these five senses - giving us information about the outside world. What could possibly be more basic than knowing about our own world? How about knowing about our self, our own inner worlds?

Our vestibular and proprioceptive systems develop early and are so basic we aren't even aware of them; for the most part, we take them for granted. Yet, they are fundamental to all of our physical and intellectual endeavors. Our vestibular system allows us to stand upright rather than fall down; to walk a balance beam; to bend over and pick something up without tipping over; to walk without getting dizzy. This is the system that supports vision, hand-eye coordination, and fine motor skills. It is located in the semi-circular canals and otolith organs of the inner ear. If the vestibular system is not providing accurate information about balance, moving may be precarious, or the opposite: a child may need lots of movement just to feel alive.

Movement is fascinating because it's visually satisfying to the vestibular system. Kids with autism frequently have a fascination with spinning, moving objects and activities, as they try to bring balance to their hay-wired vestibular systems. Sometimes, well-meaning but uncomprehending adults do everything possible—scold, bribe, punish, restrain, even medicate—their autistic kids, whose nervous systems are screaming at them to move, climb, rock, twirl, and watch anything that moves as well.

Picture yourself on the beach in sunny California on a typical July afternoon. An eight-foot citizen from the planet Venus–one planet closer to the sun than Earth–has been transported to Earth and has arrived right next to you as you enjoy the relative coolness of your cabana. You notice immediately that he's having a hard time adjusting to the "darkness" of a California afternoon. And he notices you in your shades, in the cool dimness of your cabana and is appalled! He seems to think that you're in great peril and wants to help you, so he snatches your sunglasses from your eyes and effortlessly picks you up and carries you into the bright sunlight. He turns you so that you're facing the sun, and telepathically instructs you to look at the sun and keep your eyes open, because sitting in the dark like that is unhealthy.

Maybe the Venusian tries to bribe you to stay there in the direct sun where, it soon becomes obvious, you are quite uncomfortable. But even his Milky Way and Mars Bar don't tempt you. So he becomes violent and begins to scold you, even slaps you in the face a few times in order to get his way. He feels, you see, that he knows what is best for you and he is only doing this for your own good. But are you going to comply? What will you do if he restrains you in some way so that you can't move, or medicates you to paralyze your eyes?

Of course this scenario is far-fetched. No eight-footer from Venus is going to do this, but five and six-footer 'he's and she's' from right here on planet Earth do comparable things to little earthlings all the time.

That Hayden has vestibular issues means I allow him the freedom to do what he needs to do to comfort himself. At the same time, I use every method available to reduce the imbalances that are stacked against him in the system in which he lives. I am his advocate at school and in the community. I do all I can to educate the public as to the incredible prejudice and burden placed on families and individuals by our culture to be forced into empty social molds that are restrictive, painful, detrimental, embarrassing, and, frankly, unkind and unloving.

The second sensory system that relates us to our own bodies, the proprioceptive system, is responsible for muscle memory. For example, even with our eyes closed, we can write our names legibly. Basically, this system gives us an awareness of our bodies in space. In other words, it gives us a clear sense of where our bodies end and the rest of the world begins.

Proprioceptor organs are located at joints throughout the body. When a child receives information from this system that's inaccurate, he may be clumsy, fall easily, break things, or have difficulty putting his body where he wants it. Simply put, he may just not be able to determine where his body ends and the rest of the world begins.

Aberrations in these two systems, along with the tactile sense, are fundamental aspects of the Autism Spectrum Disorder. They are so intrinsic to those of us who have *normal* neurological function that we can't even begin to conceive of what it would be like if they went askew. While it's possible to imagine being unable to see or hear (we can close our eyes and plug our ears), it's much more difficult to imagine vestibular problems. It's like feeling as though you're falling when all you're doing is walking up a slight incline. Or, it's like wondering if walking through a doorway is safe because you don't know if your body will fit through it. These kinds of issues are daily fare for our autistic kids.

Hayden was three-and-a-half when he started to crawl. He always stopped at the playroom or bedroom door and refused to crawl through. No amount of coaxing could get him to crawl any further. So at one point, I decided to move back a step and I got on my hands and knees over him, as I had done when I taught him to crawl. Interestingly, as soon as I positioned my body over his, he readily crawled through the door, with me over him the whole time. As long as I was over him, he would crawl through any doorway, but otherwise, he would not.

The only thing I could come up with was that somehow doorways frightened him, and my body over him, defining his, made him feel safe. I had not been exposed to the concept of proprioception as yet, but I knew what I was doing was helping Hayden. When I first learned about the proprioceptive system Judy Bluestone workshop, I just sat down and cried, because I finally understood what I instinctively knew. Kids who don't want to go through small spaces, who consistently and repeatedly walk the perimeters of rooms or playgrounds, who are anxious in crowded spaces, or who don't want to move within a group, may be terrified of being hurt by stationary objects or moving people because they don't know where their own bodies end.

I remember Hayden's first day of school at a "regular" kindergarten. Because of his many issues, I stayed the first two weeks to help him settle in and to introduce the teaching assistant to his unique communication methods and bodily reactions. Only after about a half-hour into the morning, I could sense Hayden's discomfort at his table of five other children. I realized he was having a proprioceptive problem: that he was afraid of being bumped into by other children. I explained this to Debbie. As soon as we instituted the change—moved him to another table—he began to relax and become more alert.

Several months later, when the classroom routine, noise level, light, odors, and people were more familiar, Hayden was given the option of sitting at his own table or at a table with other kids, and there were times when he chose to be at a table with other kids. But he always knew, even then, that he was free to move away whenever he needed to. By the end of that first year, he was comfortable sitting at a table with other children, and experienced no trauma doing so. Furthermore, he felt respected for his initial choice of being at his own table long enough to, in his own time, move to the table with the other children.

I've found the following mind game somewhat helpful. Suppose you start to build a new house for yourself, but only as time, energy, and financial resources become available. You might still be working on the foundation six months after you start.

Next, suppose that a contractor comes along and asks you how long you've been working on the foundation.

"Six months," you say.

"Incredible," he exclaims. "At six months the foundation should be done, the sub floor should be down, and the walls should be going up! Stop what you're doing and put up those walls! After all, it's six months since you started!"

Of course a contractor wouldn't say such an utterly ridiculous thing. No one, in fact, would advocate putting up walls until the foundation and sub-floor are laid. They must be finished first, regardless of how long it takes. This is just plain common sense.

When it comes to building a house, society is very much in agreement with common sense. However, when it comes to bringing up children, our culture throws common sense out the window. "How old is he? Six months? Oh, at six months he should be able to . . ." or, "She's six? Well, at six she should be able to ..." or, "He's in the third grade? Well, he should be doing..." All of these responses display total ignorance of the fact that the vestibular and proprioceptive systems are the foundation for all physical and mental learning, and may not develop according to what we consider a universal chronological time table.

If you don't have a solid sense of safety in, and awareness of, your own body, how in the world can you learn about the world? Yet, children who have very immature and therefore weak proprioceptive and vestibular systems are often expected to learn as other children do. But they cannot. Consequently, they are often labelled as retarded, lazy, and even rebellious.

On the other hand, children who are seeing- or hearing-impaired are provided adaptive learning materials to maximize their learning potential. No one expects a child with severely impaired vision or hearing to learn to read in the same way as other children; nor are such children labeled retarded or lazy because they cannot learn in the usual ways. Yet, many intelligent, interested, industrious kids are ignored, scolded, ridiculed, failed, isolated, restrained, punished, medicated, all to compensate for society's lack of awareness and knowledge of their unseen, yet pervasive, biological and neurological proprioceptive and vestibular deficits.

There is a growing awareness of these needs of such kids, and sensory integration therapy is now gaining more recognition at such neurodevelopmental programs at HANDLE and the (these are the ones in my neck of the woods). These programs evaluate clients through observation, and develop unique home programs designed specifically for each client's needs, taking into account their unique proprioceptive and vestibular issues. In addition to these individually designed programs, general activities to be engaged in at home or school, are suggested to help soothe and strengthen your child's irritated sensory nervous system.

Hayden was three when he was evaluated by Judy Bluestone. She went on to found and direct the HANDLE Institute in Seattle after she made a series of home visits to treat Hayden; he also went to the Institute for treatment. The vestibular activities she recommended for him have proven over and over again to be exactly what is needed to bring him down from overload, which used to manifest in the following ways: violent rocking; jutting of his lower jaw; loud, eerie, wordless vocalizations; copious saliva production; increased auditory and tactile sensitivity; and a definite *not-being-there-ness*. This would frequently escalate into the inconsolable screaming for which kids with autism are famous—or infamous.

However, by doing the exercises daily, I was able to gradually decrease, and just about eliminate, the intense episodes of overload that were as ordinary in our house as a load of laundry.

When Hayden was thirteen, we went to a family Christmas get-together at my niece's. We don't normally do large family gatherings, but this one was fairly close to home. After we were there for several hours, Hayden began to rock violently. I also noticed his jaw begin to jut out. And soon he started to squeal at a piercingly high pitch and decibel level. As soon as we got in the car and headed for home, however, he calmed right down.

The only case of full-blown overload that's taken place in recent years occurred at a local movie theater when The Grinch, who stole Christmas from the kids of Who-ville, managed, at the same time, to steal sensory equilibrium from Hayden! He screamed at the top of his lungs. As soon as we were out of the theater, the screaming stopped, and he calmed down.

Not only has working the exercises daily decreased the number of overload incidents Hayden suffers by strengthening the vestibular system, but the same exercises are capable of aborting cases of overload in progress. Engaging in them at the right time can eliminate the screaming stage altogether and move Hayden from violent, loud, spaced-out overload to his totally calm and relational self in just a few moments.

When Hayden was eleven, we traveled to Coquitlan, Canada for twenty days of hyperbaric treatment. The schedule he was put on consisted of two such treatments daily, which made for a very full day. In the waiting room one day, about half-way through the twenty days of treatment, and about fifteen minutes before we were to enter the chamber for the second, afternoon session, Hayden began showing signs of overload: pronounced rocking, jaw-jutting, high-pitched squealing and a lack of presence. He had been doing so well with the treatments, far better than the staff expected. Had I taken him into the chamber already in a state of overload, however, I would have been not merely courting disaster, but proposing to it!

There was no time to go anywhere, and no place to go if there had been time. So I did what I needed to do. I tuned out the crowd milling around the waiting room, sat down with Hayden on the floor, and did Judy Bluestone's side-to-side rock with Hayden. In less than three minutes, he was completely calm. A few people wanted to know what I had done and if it would work with their kids, because it was so dramatically effective. I explained that it was a vestibular activity I had learned from HANDLE, and some children would respond to it, though others might need a different movement to calm their own, very unique vestibular system.

These are the specific vestibular activities I have used to calm Hayden's hyperactivity and overload: side-to-side rock, roll-backs (also from Judy), somersaults (backwards and forwards), and spinning. When Hayden was a little guy and we took excursions to the zoo and to parks and beaches, he frequently exhibited signs of stress and overload early in the outing. I would take him aside, put one hand on his chest and the other on his back and flip him over my hand backwards three times. The result was what I came to denote, "re-March-able" - he'd go into it like a lion and come out like a lamb! We were always able to continue our outing without another trace of tension, hyperactivity, or screams.

When Hayden entered pre-school at three-and-a- half, so did I. At the time, he was non-verbal, not yet walking, had extreme auditory sensitivity, was somewhat light sensitive, reacted defensively with his hands to uncomfortable tactile situations, was super-sensitive over most of his body, had unreliable vision, and had pronounced vestibular and proprioceptive issues. All of this combined to make new people, places and things terrifying and painful. And it frequently send him swiftly into overload.

Also, by this time, Hayden and I had been to hell and back together. We'd been through evenings on end of night terrors huddled together in the rocking chair; hours of his screaming, my praying; day after day of physical therapy; his frequent physical attacks of me—hitting, biting, pinching, scratching, kicking, hair pulling. At that time, I was still ignorant of his auditory, light, tactile, vestibular and proprioceptive sensitivities; I was totally unprepared for understanding what was involved with caring for a child with his issues; the social climate at the time was characterized by a total lack of knowledge, compassion, and wisdom about him and his care, and about my needs as his full-time care-giver. Yet somehow, we emerged from those first two hellish years. I walked upright, and he crawled. Yet the two of us came through it all side-by-side and victorious!

Hayden surpassed all expectations in the progress he made. It was slow, to be sure, but he was getting there. He was happy, affectionate, interested, and well-behaved. And he was cute as a button! I had not succumbed to burnout as predicted, although I had burned the candle at both ends and in the middle sometimes. GOD was and still is, my abiding source of wisdom and serenity.

In our first years together, Hayden and I had forged a bond of love, trust, understanding, communication, and mutual respect—each of us both teacher and pupil for the other. Because I knew Hayden's aggressive behaviors were his way of expressing anger, frustration, confusion, and strong feelings, I always asked myself "Why?" when he felt angry, frustrated, confused, or unloved and exhibited aggressive behavior. I became quite perceptive about determining the causes for his behaviors. When I coupled this with singing a custom-designed 'Mad Song,' Hayden's aggressive behaviors were reduced to infrequent token gestures towards me, from a few times a year to perhaps a bit more frequently as he entered his teens.

As a whole, our days were full but they went smoothly. Most of his screaming, physical aggression towards me, confusion, and fear, were miles behind us in most ways, though of course in some, just a few steps away. I constantly assessed the environment vis a vis sounds, lights, commotion, temperature, and space. And it became second nature to do the same with Hayden' bodily states. I was at all times aware of whether he was hungry, thirsty, tired, bored, sleepy, overloaded, or suffering from some tactile issue. I learned to identify, without consciously knowing how, the slightest turn toward potential overload, consequently, I would frequently abort it before it even began. Because I spent more than two years learning the language of his behavior; establishing a consistency of expectations; using words to give him security; expressing feelings for him; adeptly reading his body's warnings of impending over-stimulation, I grew really expert at knowing how fast and how far he could go in a few minutes and how long it took to bring him back. Given all of this, can you even begin to imagine taking him to preschool and leaving him there with people he didn't know and who knew nothing about him and all of his 'stuff?'

I certainly couldn't. It was school policy that parents not stay in preschool; however, it was my policy not to leave him anywhere I was not comfortable leaving him, and I was not comfortable leaving him at preschool. I would rather have kept him home or taken him to a private preschool where I could have stayed. I located several private schools that would allow my full participation, but the public school decided to let me stay on a trial basis after all, so I agreed to work with the teacher and staff members to assimilate Hayden into the class and phase me out.

It was a difficult, rocky year, but we worked together to make Hayden feel safe, heard, understood, and accepted. I would say we used this time to smooth out all the rough spots and pave the way for an overall positive experience in school that continued on to his last day as a student.

By Hayden's second year of preschool (with the same room, same teachers, same teacher's aides, and some of the same therapists), all of us—including Hayden –were ready for him to be there without me. The first day I took him and left . . . to my car with a book to read. It was forty minutes home and forty minutes back, and school only lasted for two-and-a-half hours, so I didn't go home during class all year. But I did leave the school grounds after the first few weeks. So Hayden did exceedingly well. His teachers knew and understood him, which made all the difference in the world.

The other thing that made the year go so well was my knowledge of Hayden's vestibular and proprioceptive issues. Hayden would not have been able to cope at all with the stresses of preschool without the calming, centering, neurologically stabilizing effect of his *vestibular stuff,* as we called it then and still call it.

My first goal for Hayden in preschool was for him to be in the classroom, not in overload. When I sensed he was moving towards overload, I would hold him and speak to him calmly and soothingly. If that didn't do the trick, I led him in vestibular activities. For instance, if necessary, I took him out of the room, we talked and then performed some vestibular exercises; almost always, this would calm him right down.

However, one day, a few weeks into preschool, Hayden began screaming, his face took on that spaced-out look, and he just couldn't calm down, no matter what I did with him. The only option was to take him out of class and home. When his teacher called me that evening, she said she hoped I wouldn't give up on preschool. I chuckled and told her not to worry, that I didn't give up on things, and that we would be back when I felt he was ready, on my terms.

A week or so later we went back, but with some changes. The most significant one was that Hayden attended school fewer days of the week. During our timeout from preschool, I worked with him on the things I learned were the most problematic for him. When we went back, there were still times we had to leave the room, most often because of excessive noise. But as far as being at school, he never again reached the point of such dramatic overload that he simply was not there and just sat and screamed.

How can you tell if your child has vestibular issues? He will tell you loud and clear, even if he is non-verbal. The body never lies. In the same way that you immediately and unconsciously squint in bright light in an attempt to normalize your visual system, your child's body will do its level best to normalize its vestibular system when it goes out of sync.

Kids with vestibular problems may seek out intense movement. Or avoid it. They may be fascinated by moving, spinning objects, or with the feeling of rocking their own bodies. Hand-flapping, leaning on things, and slumping are also popular among autistic kids. They may prefer sitting on the floor rather than in a chair. And they often have trouble with eye coordination. Many autistic kids also feel insecure on slopes, stairs, or uneven surfaces; some may always feel unsteady on their feet. Frequently, autistic people have difficulty with speech, language, and hearing. Keep in mind, the vestibular system is foundational. If it's askew, all other sensory systems are likewise weakened.

The semicircular canals and otolith organs in the inner ear are all part of the vestibular system; and, they are stimulated by many different kinds of movement—rocking backwards, spinning in both directions, log rolling, rocking sideways, jumping, bouncing, swinging (especially sideways and kitty-corner), somersaulting (backward and forward), dancing, teeter-tottering, sliding, flipping over (small child). This is why kids love to be, for instance, tossed onto the bed and going on carnival rides.

When it comes to muscles, building occurs by pushing them slightly beyond their comfort level. Not so with the nervous system. With activities involving the nervous system, they must be terminated at the very first sign of discomfort, dizziness, or neurological disorganization.

If a child loves to do somersaults, for instance, the child may want to do many, but they may not necessarily have a calming influence. If one somersault makes your child dizzy, it's likely this is a movement he needs, but only once a day. In fact, in such a case as this, doing multiples might actually end up being counter-productive.

With Hayden, movement on a daily basis in various directions, to stimulate all three semicircular canals and otolith organs, produced visible calmness. When he was about five, once a month I'd have a weekend of respite care. Because he loved the music at church so much, I would pick him up on Sunday morning before church. After a few months, several observant people at the service could accurately identify his respite weekends by his increased hyperactivity, which was the result of not having done vestibular exercise on Saturday or Sunday.

I use vestibular activities in two ways: first, as daily activities to meet Hayden's specific vestibular needs. When used this way, they generally reduce stress and overload and enhance the system. Secondly, I use them as a side-effects-free calming regime for hyperactivity, stress, and overload. There is no one-size-fits-all program, though, that works for all kids, because each child's body is unique and has unique vestibular needs based on their particular vestibular wiring. By carefully experimenting with one type of movement at a time and observing its effects, it's possible to come to a set of activities that reduce hyperactivity. When Hayden started preschool we did vestibular activities at home on a daily basis. I also taught his teacher and aides how to do these same activities with him in order to calm him down, if need be, and abort overload.

When doing vestibular activities, there are a few important things to keep in mind. First and foremost, respect your child's body and don't go beyond its comfort level. One swing sideways at comfort level is more productive than five or ten swings sideways at discomfort level. It might be difficult to imagine how a slight movement could be dizzying or neurologically disorganizing because it is totally outside our experience. However, just because we can't imagine a situation, doesn't mean it can't occur. When I use to do Hayden's vestibular exercises with him every day, I regarded this as an inexpensive, non-technical, interactive, mostly fun, at-home way I could have a positive impact on his comfort level and behavior, and thereby on his other activities at home and school, as well as in the community. It's also a great way to avoid using medications to treat these issues!

The other sensory system that tells us about ourselves but is weak in individuals with autism, is the proprioceptive system. Proprioceptive receptors are located in muscles, tendons, joints, and the inner ear. A child who has proprioceptive issues may be: clumsy; prone to falling and other kinds of accidents; uncomfortable in small areas and in crowds of people; all over the bed and even on the floor when asleep; especially fond of intense hugs and rubbing against people; afraid of small spaces; prone to obsessively walking the perimeter of a room or yard; a wanderer in an effort to find where they end. Joint compression, blankets, beanbags, weighted vests and cuffs may help such kids "find" their bodies. Also doing things with eyes closed forces a child to find his body without visual input. Playing games with fingers or nose; putting on hats, gloves, boots; listening to songs that use finger play–these are all fun ways for children to learn how to locate, feel, and identify parts of their bodies.

Hayden wore a Support Pressure Input Orthosis (SPIO)—a custom-made Lycra body suit—for a number of years to help with his proprioceptive issues. Individuals with weak proprioceptive systems expend a lot of energy trying to locate their body and protect it. But how can you protect something you can't even find? When Hayden was in kindergarten, his classmates would all move into circle-time after attendance was taken. Although Hayden did not want to do circle-time with all the other children as they moved about, he was happy to find a place in the circle once everyone else had settled down in theirs. He was not anti-social or non-compliant. All that movement was scary because he felt he could get hurt. He waited quietly in his chair until there was no more moving around, then he felt safe and happy about joining the other children. If a child's major concerns are to stay upright and not get bumped, he will have little time or energy for making friends, vigilantly checking the boundaries of his body, and learning academics.

The sense of touch develops very early on, along with the proprioceptive and vestibular systems. These sensory systems support, and are supported by, each other, and form a working foundation for learning that takes as its model a symbiotic relationship not unlike that between the fingers, thumb, and palm. I have found it helpful to draw the following analogy to help myself and others understand how these three systems work together. Think of the thumb as representing the vestibular system, governing movement and stability; the fingers represent the tactile system, sensitive to texture, temperature, pressure, and pain; the palm represents the proprioceptive system, establishing location and coordinating tactile and vestibular senses. Together they form a functional unit that supports and enhances learning in all other areas.

Autism Spectrum Disorder is characterized by weakness, immaturity, or aberrations in at least these three sensory systems, thereby affecting learning in many areas. It is not a matter of intelligence or ability, but of body mechanics. For example, aberrations in the tactile system result in a wide variety of atypical sensory perceptions, ranging from numbness to extreme sensitivity to touch, pressure, and textures. They are also responsible for unusual interpretations of painful stimuli, temperature, hunger and thirst, all present in unpredictable, inconsistent, pattern-less patterns, adding their unwelcome contribution to the frustrating, confusing, heartbreaking, enigmatic behaviors that characterize our kids, challenge us, and chafe many uninformed observers.

There is a Navajo proverb: "Never criticize a man until you have walked a mile in his moccasins." Those of us who have walked many miles in the ASD tennis shoes have felt the sting of criticism, ostracism, and superiority from im-perfect strangers in stores, restaurants, and other public places; from health professionals; even from friends and family members who think they have all the answers. To these people, I would like to say: If you do have the answer - if you have walked in my tennis and learned something useful, please teach me. But please don't criticize me. I'm doing the best I can. If you haven't walked in my tennis and you don't understand, have the grace to acknowledge to yourself that you don't understand, so you won't need to criticize me and my child. Then you'll be free to love me and support me. Because you know what? I need your support. I really do. The tears streamed down my face as I wrote this because it reminded me how very true it is…

On one level, we get used to being the sideshow—to the stares, the pointing and whispering, the disapproving looks, the silent withdrawal, the spoken and unspoken comments. We've come to terms with the fact that we have a very cast-conscious, yet officially casteless, society, and anyone who doesn't fall in the middle of the infamously curvaceous Ms. Bell is a social outcast. We know that kids who poke fun at kids who are different have learned this intolerance from adults around them whose own insecurity and poor self-esteem compel them to be critical and judgmental of those who are different from them. Being a recovering critic and judge, I have walked many miles in those spiked heels, and feel experienced enough to comment. Yet, when we stay open and vulnerable, it hurts like hell to be shut out from love, acceptance, and companionship, to be essentially alone, isolated.

Regardless of how it hurts, however, we have no choice but to feel the pain and go on, because we know that pain is minimal compared to the pain our children suffer. They are the essence of vulnerability, because they feel all. But they don't have the logic or experience to understand that the criticism, condemnation, isolation, and humiliation directed their way has nothing to do with them. Unfortunately, our ASD children cannot see that they only serve as mirrors for others and their own unacknowledged pain, vulnerability, weakness, fear of not being good enough, incompetence, and isolation.

Young children are open and have a healthy curiosity about new and different things, so of course they're going to point and stare. That's okay. Unless you have lived, worked, or visited in the shadow of the autism specter, Hayden's behavior will seem markedly different from that other young men. When walking, for example, his hands are up, his head tilted; his gait is awkward, likely at a snail's pace or lumbering straight ahead like a bull-dozer; he squishes loudly and drools prolifically at times; he makes many non-speech-like sounds; he uses toys uniquely, for example, he flips pages of a book like he's shuffling a deck of cards; he may appear to ignore the whole world, by sitting down on the floor in the middle of a hallway, room, sidewalk, drive-way—anywhere—and begin to rock violently; he sometimes engages in hysterical laughter or claps loudly; if tired, he will lie down just about anywhere; he may totally ignore some-one who is talking directly to him, yet reach out to touch people anywhere, especially their hair, whiskers, eyebrows, face, and eyes; he balks at stairs, curbs, hills, uneven surfaces and narrow or crowded passageways, indiscriminately grabs anything close by (including people, again, anywhere) for support. Hopefully, I'm close enough so it's me he grabs. I offer my hand, which he takes in a vice grip that sometimes hurts, as I slowly walk and talk him over, up, down, around or through an offending obstacle.

Hayden is taller than I am. I know we're an odd couple and it must look strange when I pull out a long cover-up and a big unbreakable bowl to feed this young man, or wipe his nose, unzip his coat, or go with him into a stall in the wom-en's restroom. Kids from two to ninety-two are going to look. But curiosity is not in and of itself evil; when I see kids watch-ing him, their faces full of puzzlement, and the situation lends itself to conversation, I catch their eyes, smile, look toward Hayden, and say,

"Maybe you've never seen anyone with autism before?"

They frequently respond with, "Why does he do that?" referring to the rocking, squishing, or strange sounds.

I'm careful to smile and make eye contact with any accom-panying adults, so they're okay with the child's questions, then answer,

"He's rocking and making noises because he's very excited. When he's excited, his autism makes his body need to rock, kind of like you need to scratch when it itches. He does that with his mouth because his mouth itches inside, and he's trying to scratch it."

Usually, when I say this about the itching in his mouth, Hayden will clap loudly. Then I add,

"He's just a kid like you who happens to have autism." Frequently that's all that needs to be said. They've had their questions answered openly and acceptingly, and they're able to move on.

Sometimes kids will ask more questions, however, such as,

"How did he get it?" "Does it hurt?" "Can he talk?" With Hayden listening and clapping his agreement, I respond,

"Hayden's had autism since he was a baby. A lot of sounds hurt his ears. He talks in his mind in English. He says everything he wants to say in his mind. His autism gets in the way when he tries to talk out loud, and it comes out in "Hayden-ese."

I welcome questions, and answer them as simply and honestly as I can. Often, an accompanying adult will say,

"Thank you. I didn't know what to tell him."

I don't mind people looking and staring. My hope is that they will do so with understanding, compassion, support and love, rather than with condemnation, prejudice, pity, criticism, and superiority.

`You may be wondering where this previous little conversation came from. Me, too! Since it wasn't in my plans, it didn't come from my head; it must have come from my heart! But why? It seems to have come out of the blue, in the middle of my discussion about our sensory systems, as part of the neurology of autism. The aberrations that trigger the very behaviors that are not understood or accepted by our society, occur in the nervous system. I keep feeling this doesn't belong here; but it does. What doesn't belong is prejudice in a free, democratic society. Let us recall our country's Declaration of Independence:

"We hold these truths to be self-evident, that all men are created equal, that they are endowed by their Creator with certain unalienable Rights; that among these are Life, Liberty and the pursuit of Happiness."

Our society has come a long way from established slavery: child labor; restricted voting; limited education; discrimination based on race, color, gender, ethnic background; witch burning' insane asylums, and dehumanizing institutions for retarded people. But prejudice still exists in un-American American hearts the world over for people with many disabilities.

I want to acknowledge and express my appreciation to the chorus of kind, loving, accepting, helpful people, from friends to family members to professionals to strangers, store clerks, kids and everyone else who does accept Hayden and his stuff with love, compassion, and acceptance. I am grateful for family members where we're welcome with all of our paraphernalia and special accommodations; physicians who talk to Hayden and listen to me; friends who call and ask, "Would Hayden like to go on a boat ride?" or "How are you doing?", strangers in doctor's waiting rooms who *chit* with Hayden, even when he doesn't *chat* back; store clerks who respond to his obvious excitement about a toddler toy or book with "Looks like you're going to have fun with this at home!"; kids who include him and talk to him, but are nonplussed by his seeming disinterest or unawareness of them; many smiling, friendly people in all kinds of public places who are accepting, kind and understanding. You gladden my heart, lighten my load, put a smile on my face, and remind me that not only is social change possible, it is happening; that prejudice can be eliminated.

Before I got on my soapbox and exposed my heart, we were looking at sensory distortions caused by tactile system aberrations occurring in ASD. Some kids have an aversion to touch because it's actually painful. This makes them: dislike clothes, certain fabrics, tags in clothes, waist bands, hats, mittens, glasses, or shoes, and being touched. The anticipated pain of being touched would explain why often these kids avoid or withdraw from being hugged, held, holding hands. They may also dislike sitting still, because their bottom or legs itch or hurt. In addition, they are also prone to rub off kisses; not want to get their hands dirty; hate face, hand, or hair washing; avoid using their hands, except for fingertips; become aggressive when touched; touch others too hard, just like a person who's hard-of-hearing might speak too loudly; want hard bear hugs, rub very hard on people or things; engage in excessive mouth play; hold a pencil incorrectly, if at all; reject certain textures of food, or certain silverware or dishes.

When I began offering Hayden liquid in a glass or cup, for instance, he would drink only out of my glass and not his. I thought he just wanted what I had, and I was partially correct. He wanted my drinking vessel, which was made out if glass, not his plastic kiddy cup. I prefer drinking out of glass so I always have glass. When I poured him a glass made of glass, he readily drank from it. He also accepts hard, glass-like plastic. When he was young, I didn't use paper cups for him, as he had no concept of a soft grip (which is actually a proprioceptive issue); but now I can. Interestingly, a change in utensils might make a meal go more smoothly.

I must stress that these issues do not begin as power struggles or acts of noncompliance, but rather, as neurological irritations; negative behavior may become a part of such scenarios if the situation is treated improperly.

The feel of some textures and pressures may be grating, irritating, and neurologically disorganizing, much the same way as chalk screeching on a chalkboard is grating and irritating to many people. Some kinds of steel wool give me the heebie-jeebies to hold, and I have no diagnosis of neurological disorder.

There are three broad categories of tactile issues in ASD: (1) over-sensitivity to touch; (2) under-sensitivity to touch; and (3) inability to distinguish kinds of touch. Sad to say, it's not at all unusual for autistic people to have these sensitivity issues *inconsistently*. This of course makes things another whole level of difficult for their care givers. Thomas McKean, who wrote about his own autism in *Soon Will Come the Light*,[1] says that sometimes the keys of his computer keyboard feel like ordinary computer keyboard keys, but sometimes they feel as hot as fire. Because something feels one way this hour or day doesn't mean it will feel that way in a few hours, or tomorrow or next week. How disconcerting and frightening that makes the world for the person with these sensitivities!

One part of a child's body may be over-sensitive, while another area is under-sensitive. Hayden's hands are supersensitive, so that holding onto things is a challenge for him. Yet, his way of snuggling is to rub his head and arms against my head and shoulders with such tremendous force that I sometimes have to stop it because it's painful for me.

When Hayden was an infant, he preferred to be naked as much as possible, and was always more relaxed with no clothes on. When I worked with him, I kept the room extra warm and dressed him in only over-sized cotton training pants, so I would be protected and he would be comfortable.

1. McKean, Thomas A. *Soon Will Come the Light: a View from inside the Autism Puzzle*. 2nd ed., Future Horizons, 1994.

When he was a toddler, Hayden's chest was so ticklish that just buttoning up his bib overalls would render him totally limp and reduce him to a small 'Hayden-ball.' But on the other hand, he just couldn't tolerate any tightness whatsoever around his waist.

At eighteen, Hayden tolerated regular jeans, but often wanted tags removed from his shirts, needed his socks to be turned inside out, and disliked hats and mittens. He doesn't like writing or art because of the discomfort it causes him to hold a pencil or crayon. But, he's come a long way from the days when he screamed in pain if anything touched his palms, that's certainly true. But, tactility is still an issue for him.

What can you do if your child has tactile issues? Understand and accept it, even though you can't really understand because it's so far from your realm of experience. Again, neurodevelopment programs, such as sensory integration therapy and developmental preschools may provide some help. Go very slowly, introduce touch and textures a tiny bit at a time and speak calmly and reassuringly.

Earlier, I described the method I used to help Hayden's extreme tactile defensiveness. When he got a bit older, I brought out a dozen mixing bowls, each one filled with a different textured item. One was filled with rice, for example. There were also bowls of pinto beans, elbow macaroni, marshmallows, pennies that had been through the dishwasher, marbles (he wouldn't put anything in his mouth), water, poker chips, sand, birdseed, feathers, and cotton balls. If you decide to try this, just remember to go very slowly, gently, and reassuringly. Don't force anything, but at the same time, be encouraging. I thought I had pretty well represented all textures, but I inadvertently left out gooey, sticky stuff. I only realized my omission when Hayden adamantly refused to feel the gooey insides of his Halloween pumpkin. So we went back to the bowls, some of which were then filled with

Play Dough, some manufactured goo's, shaving cream, water and flour, and pudding.

If your child is comfortable, you can rub, massage, or tap on their body using your hand, a ball, a soft brush, a washcloth, or fabrics of different textures. Do not use a brush on the face, neck, chest, or stomach, because these areas feel especially vulnerable to these kids.

Some kids like battery-powered vibrating toys, massagers, and toys like the Bumble Ball. Don't forget teethers, which provide oral stimulation. Hayden wore a nubby, figure-eight teether around his neck on a shoestring for many years. We referred to it as his "lip stick."

The tactile, proprioceptive, and vestibular systems integrate first, that is, very early on in a child's neurodevelopment, and are basic to gross and fine motor skills, eye movement, hand-eye coordination, academic skills, and self-image; they are always involved in some way in ASD. The remaining four senses - sight, hearing, taste, and smell - may also have exhibit distortions early on.

The auditory sense is super-sensitive in about seventy percent of people with autism. Sounds that the rest of us would consider ordinary can be extremely painful, neurologically disorganizing, extremely loud, distorted, even muffled to people with ASD. Such a person's auditory system may be so hypersensitive that even noises made by internal bodily function—which most of us cannot even detect—such as blood rushing through arteries, or peristalsis, for example, may become irritating. Sometimes, certain sound frequencies are painful regardless of volume. Sounds most people don't notice or hear at all may be painful or neurologically disorganizing to someone who is autistic.

During Hayden's first year of preschool, Denny put studs on my car for the upcoming winter, since I had to drive over an hour a day on the rough and at times slick roads of a *military reservation to take Hayden to school. It took me a few days to ascertain why Hayden, suddenly, for no appar-*ent *reason, would not take his fingers out of his ears on that ride to and from school. I finally figured out that the culprit was the noise from the studded tires, of which I was totally unaware, but which drove poor Hayden a little crazy. That winter he never did take his fingers out of his ears on the way to or from school!*

When sounds hurt your ears, the world is not safe; you never know when or where you will be assailed or what the assailant may be. Unusual and unpredictable sounds are, without question, the worst. As with other sensory systems, auditory aberrations in ASD kids may not be consistent from hour to hour or from day to day. As a baby, Hayden's ears were extraordinarily sensitive. If I cleared my throat or coughed in a room where he was asleep, he would wake up screaming with ear pain. You can just imagine how difficult it was to go anywhere because of the possibility of exposing Hayden to this acute pain. In fact, it was pretty much par for the course to have to remove Hayden from his preschool class screaming as many as two or three times in a two-and-a-half-hour class. The reason: ear pain.

In December of that first pre-school year, I contacted Dr. Judy Belk, then director of the Center for Communications and Learning Skills in Lake Oswego, Oregon, near Portland, because I heard she did auditory training. After Christmas, Denny, Hayden and I went to Dr. Judy's for an evaluation. Judy does both BCG and the Tomatis auditory programs, and felt he might benefit from either. We chose the Tomatis program and Judy said we could begin in early January with two hours of listening a day for fifteen days. Hayden would have to wear larger earphones for this work.

My sister Gerre lived in Portland, so I knew we'd have a familiar place to stay. But I was quite concerned about the

265

earphones and how they were going to work for him given his tactile sensitivities. He couldn't even tolerate a soft cap on his head—off it went! How would he tolerate those huge earphones? I sensed we might have to work up to this—and I was right—and I was glad we would not begin the heart of the program immediately.

I started to plan my strategy and told Judy I needed six weeks to get Hayden used to the earphones. First I got some Walkman headphones and cut off the cord. I sat Hayden down and told him we were going to learn how to wear earphones so we could maybe make his ears not hurt so much. I put the Walkman headphones on; he pulled them off. I put them back on; he pulled them back off. I put them on; he pulled them off. This was Phase I: On - off, on - off, and so on. We started out maybe half a dozen times, several times a day, for the first week. I made a game out of it. I talked about how yucky they felt but how safe they were. On - off, on - off, on - off. I was building familiarity and predictability, and also giving Hayden some control over the headphones.

Phase II began when I told Hayden we were changing the rules; now I would hold his hands for a second and he'd wear the headphones. When that was no longer traumatic, I held his hands for a few seconds, gradually increasing the time to ten minutes and phasing out my holding his hands.

In Phase III, we used a second Walkman headphone set and I began to play his favorite tapes over the headphone until he would contentedly listen to music on Walkman headphones for fifteen minutes.

Phase IV began exactly like Phase I, except Hayden was using the large headphones instead of the smaller ones. Phase V was a duplicate of Phase II, again, using large rather than small headphones. Phase VI, which we implemented at the beginning of the last of our six weeks, consisted of Hayden wearing large headphones and listening to music for thirty minutes several times a day. After all of this, Hayden was as prepared as he could be. But I was not prepared for how difficult this therapy would be.

There was a huge difference for Hayden between listening to familiar music at home in non-distracting surroundings for thirty minutes, and enduring four thirty-minute sessions of unfamiliar music in distracting surroundings. Especially challenging was that the low tones were progressively filtered out, leaving really only scratchy, screechy sounds coming out of those huge headphones.

Not surprisingly, Hayden frequently pulled his earphones off, stiffened his body, and screamed. I kept putting those earphones back on Hayden and spoke softly and gently to him for hours on end. Frankly, this wore us both out, kept Judy hopping, and relegated us to the back room with the door shut, while the other kids did their listening up front.

This process was such an incredible struggle, with those earphones coming off and on so much, and Hayden screaming so loudly and often, that I wondered if the program would be of any benefit. But Judy didn't feel as negative about it as I did. The thirty hours of listening required by the program felt like a hundred and thirty and challenged my patience, endurance, and resourcefulness.

However, in spite of struggles and inconsistent listening, the Tomatis program dramatically decreased Hayden's auditory sensitivity. Whereas I had been taking Hayden out of his preschool classroom two to three times a day because of his searing screaming, at the end of this training I only had to take him out of the class one time for the rest of the school year. In retrospect, this was an amazing outcome, and well worth the struggle.

By age eighteen, Hayden had been through eight and a half thirty-hour rounds of Tomatis and one ten-hour round of BCG, but he still had some residual auditory sensitivity. Actually,

267

he had quite a bit of it left. But overall, what remained was so much less than it had been that it seemed minimal. Also, and this is key, Hayden learned to modulate the remaining sounds around him by putting his fingers in his ears. This has enabled him to tolerate a lot of loud and irritating sounds. Consequently, it has also had the effect of enlarging his world. For instance, some things that Hayden really enjoys— attending concerts, fairs, plays, improvisational theater, and athletic events—involve a lot of noise. But the auditory training has diminished that so much that the residual is controllable by Hayden, which puts these activities back on the calendar for him.

As with other sensory systems and ASD folks, the only auditory system consistency is that it is inconsistent! Sounds that are tolerable today may be intolerable tomorrow or in a few hours, but may be fine again the next day. The air conditioner or furnace at home may go unnoticed, while the air conditioner in the bank elicits cringing or disruptive behavior and screaming. Someone yelling at home may precipitate aggression from the same child who chooses to go to basketball games where he knows everybody's going to be yelling. Hayden may flap drawer handles or repeatedly activate an electronic toy, but then might plug his ears and retreat when someone else does the very same things. A child may ignore some loud sounds, yet grow exceedingly agitated over sounds you would consider insignificant. Your child may catch a whispered conversation across the room or even in the next room, and yet when you're standing right beside him and talking to him, may totally ignore you as if he were deaf, making it appear as if there's nothing wrong with his ears and he's just being non-compliant. Oh, if only it was just that simple!

For those of us with fully integrated sensory systems, life is kind of like a basketball game: there's only one ball in play at any given time, and only one basket to get it into–your basket. Almost all effort by you and your teammates goes into putting that one ball in that one basket.

For those with ASD, it's more like a game of pool: there are many balls, several different baskets, and the path of any given ball that's struck influences the way all of the other balls go. The latter is how it is with sound, which is to say that the way Hayden perceives sound is not a straight shot. It depends on: the nature of the sound itself; how tired, hot, hungry, thirsty, bored he is; how bright the lights are; how new the present environment is; how his vestibular and proprioceptive systems are functioning at the moment; what emotions are triggered by the sound; what tacit rules he has about that sound, or any sound at that point in time; and how expected or unexpected the sound is.

Sometimes I feel as though I've become pretty skilled at predicting when Hayden will have a negative reaction to a sound, when I work hard at taking all the things above into consideration. But it's such a complex thing that it seems there's always some other factor I have neglected to consider that throws things off. But on I must go, so I then add that to my list of predictors and hope for a better result the next time.

Hayden can tolerate much more sound when he's controlling or expecting it than when he's not, just as I can force myself to sit calmly while a technician takes blood from my arm, but would jump and holler and who knows what else, should that same technician sneak up on me in the mall and jab a needle in my arm while I'm window shopping!

Stress is cumulative for us all. If I'm tired, hurt, or scared, for example, I will respond differently to difficult life situations than when I am rested, comfortable, and calm. The same goes for Hayden. It's just that because of his neurological issues there are a whole host of unexpected things that stress him, things that I don't readily see and that he can't tell me.

The world sounds totally different when you're hearing it from the autism side of the fence. Have you noticed how terribly loud it sounds when you drive over railroad tracks, even slowly? Or hit the turtle bumps on the side of the road? How your child cries in pain every time you run your car over these bumps? How they plunge their fingers deep into their ears when they see a railroad crossing sign? How they even become very loud to you? How loud the dishes and silverware rattling at a restaurant sound once you attend to them? The world is a very noisy place. We humans have acknowledged many ways by which we've polluted our planet's air and water, but have only given lip service to noise pollution. There is no question that this kind of pollution poses a real challenge to those on the spectrum.

How can you help your extremely auditory sensitive child? Understand and accept that his ear pain is real, frightening, neurologically disorganizing, unpredictable, and perhaps intense. Honor your child's pain by validating all of this. Keep in mind that by honoring your child's pain does not mean feeling sorry for him; this would be pity, which we have already discovered is tantamount to demeaning, victimizing, and down-putting. Honoring your child's pain does entail empathy, however. It's all about feeling their pain with them, and being compassionate. This empowers your child and creates a bond between you.

The Condescendingly Approach says: "Poor thing, isn't it awful that your ears hurt." If you feel sorry for him, he will learn from you to feel sorry for himself, and that is self-pity. It is isolating, victimizing, perpetuating, depressing, and immobilizing.

However, the Matter-of-Fact Approach states: "A plate fell and broke. It was awfully noisy for you and made your ears hurt. I think that's it for plates breaking now—it won't happen again anytime soon. I'm sorry your ears hurt. I don't like my ears to hurt, either. I can't make your ears stop hurting, but I'm here with you and I love you." If you respect your child and his feelings, he will learn from you to respect himself and his own feelings too. This self-respect is a form self-worth; it accepts, affirms, and empowers.

We continually teach our children attitudes and perceptions about themselves, as surely and effortlessly as we do language. You cannot speak English and tell your baby to speak Spanish instead of English; so you cannot pity your child because of his disability and at the same time expect him to develop a positive sense of self-esteem, self-worth.

The first way to help your child with auditory sensitivity is to matter-of-factly acknowledge and accept its validity. Respect your child's right to cover his ears in self-protection. You and I might think that goes without saying, but I'm stating it very clearly here because I've been living with the autism specter long enough to have been told numerous times that Hayden needs to keep his fingers out of his ears. That's right! I've actually seen professionals remove his fingers from his ears for him, then tell him it's not noisy. This has of course prompted me to consult with supervisors and discontinue specific therapy.

When Hayden was young, there were places I chose not to take him because of the noise level. When we go to some local places, my husband and I take two vehicles, so I can take Hayden home immediately if he needs to leave. That way, Denny has a choice to stay or go. Sometimes I plan ahead and find a place for Hayden and me to go for a breather.

Sometimes, even practices can be changed. Hayden's school teacher changed the daily welcoming song for each child from ". . . stand up and we'll clap for you" to "...stand up and we'll wave to you." At a family reunion when Hayden was three-and-a-half, family members agreed to wave their hands in the air instead of clap during their gatherings.

Earplugs, which are helpful for some kids, worked for Hayden only when he was doing therapeutic horseback riding, because the helmet strap secured the knit hat which prevented his pulling out the ear plugs. In addition, his side-walker, Terry—a tall, gentle man who wore a cowboy hat and whom Hayden adored, was the one who put on his helmet, his knit cap, and the earplugs.

Through the years, I've also laid down some "quiet rules" for home and in my car. Only quiet voices are permitted in my car; no noisy toys, paper or plastic sacks are allowed. Hayden's room is available for other kids to play in if the door is open, but when he goes inside and shuts his door, this means he wants space and quiet. If Hayden watches a movie in the playroom/vestibular room, no games or vestibular activities are allowed in that room while he is watching.

At first, I said kids could play quietly in the playroom, but I soon recanted this rule when it became obvious that Hayden's definition of playing quietly and other kids' definitions were not always compatible. The same is true with playing in our swimming pools. Each summer I have two pools so that Hayden can play fish in one—stay in as long as he wants to, since there are so many activities he cannot do. Meantime, there's another pool for kids who want to swim. Hayden really loves water: to watch it, feel it, but especially, to be in it. Washington State's cool summers and Hayden's less active play initially entailed carrying enough buckets of hot water from the kitchen to the pool to heat it up. As you might expect, this just became too much for me. But the handy local hardware store manager, to whom I explained my predicament, recommended I purchase an inexpensive little gadget that allowed me to attach my hose to my kitchen sink. Voila! Bathtub-warm water instantly filled the pool.

There are auditory sensitivity programs available to do at home, and others that need to be done with a therapist at a center. Hayden has done both. The Tomatis program proved to be world-enlarging for Hayden by dramatically decreasing his auditory sensitivity.

Everywhere we go, I name and explain sounds to Hayden, including how loud they are to me, acknowledging they could be very loud to him as well. New, loud, and unexpected sounds tend to frighten him, so reassuring him that it's a safe sound and that I'm not afraid of it are important, along with giving Hayden some idea of their likely endurance and intensity. If we walk into a quiet room and he puts his fingers in his ears, I listen for traffic sounds from outside. Our house is a bit off the road, so we don't get much noise from traffic, air conditioner or heater fans or any other normal noises. I might say, "I hear an air conditioner fan. It isn't loud to me, but it might be to you. It is a very safe noise; the air conditioner keeps it cool in here. It won't get any louder; if it gets cool enough it will go off. If it goes off for a while, it might come back on." With that information in hand, Hayden can assess the situation; in his late teens, for instance, he frequently felt safe enough to take his fingers out of his ears. If a place becomes loud and Hayden covers his ears, I offer him the option to go home, take a break, or stay. Sometimes just knowing he's in charge of staying or going helps him feel okay about staying.

Several years ago I took Hayden to his first Heart Sparkle Play-Back Theater workshop, dinner, and performance. Because it was a new place and a whole new kind of situation for him, his fingers immediately went into his ears. And they stayed right there, because in addition to the newness of the whole experience, a tremendous amount of ambient noise accompanied this performance: loud talking, clapping, laughing, and people moving about constantly. When everyone stood up, he refused, and instead slouched down in his chair, drew up his legs, and put his fingers in his ears. At the time I thought, "This isn't going to work for him!" and expected to take him home.

When I crouched in that position, as I often did during my early years of bouts of depression, I said with my body, "I don't want to be here." At the time, I assumed his body was saying this now too. But I also have a very important rule for myself: **Make no assumptions based on what you think he wants. Always ask him.** So, I leaned in close and said, "I can tell it's loud for you. Do you want to go home now?" Still slouched in his chair, fingers in his ears, feet drawn up, he shook his head—no. I was so startled with the dissonance between his body language and his assent, I just had to ask again: "Do you want to stay?" With his fingers still deep in his ears, he moved one pinkie up and down, which affirmed that he still wanted to stay.

Nevertheless, he looked so forlorn I almost wanted to just take him away. But I had to stand down and recognize my smother love *desire to parent him, which in this case seemed to emanate from me not him. I also needed to remind myself that he has the right to choose for himself. Once I got all of this straight in my mind, I could see that I was being a real* butt-in-ski.

For the first hour or so, Hayden stayed in his huddle, fingers in his ears, as I participated in the activities. But when Rich started playing music, the butterfly Hayden emerged from his invisible cocoon of fear, and with his fingers still in ears, he went to investigate the music. The two and one-half-hour workshop was followed by set-up time for the pot-luck supper, the supper itself, then the performance. After the workshop I again offered Hayden the option to go home or stay for supper. We stayed. A little before the performance at seven, I once more gave him the option to head home or stay. Again, he chose to stay.

At the conclusion of the performance, Debe, the leader of the troupe, asked if we would come back next month. I told her I just didn't know if Hayden would want to because it was a pretty loud evening. Except for eating and playing a few instruments, his fingers had been in his ears most of the evening. I appreciated her offer to have everyone do palm rubbing instead of clapping, and said I would check with Hayden: "Next month there will be another Heart Sparkle Workshop. Do you think you might want to come?" Absolutely! I didn't mention the palm rubbing. In spite of the obvious intenseness of the evening, he was, and still is, excited about Heart Sparkle; we've gone back several times and he gets very excited when I mention Heart Sparkle. He never turns down an opportunity to be at one of their performances. These occasions push him way beyond his comfort zone—I know it, he knows it— because he wants to be involved, become part of things. When we partake in these acting improvisation events we at least bruise one of autism's ugly heads, and strengthen Hayden's connection to the world. What could be better?

If you were to spend any time around Hayden and me, you might hear me tell Hayden I don't think his ears hurt, and you might then think I'm disregarding my own teaching. First off, I'd be tickled pink if you were so aware and observant! And secondly, I would agree with you! The first time I did this, Hayden was about eight. He had his fingers in his ears, although we were home and there were no unusual noises. But was he ever mad. Because I know how readily emotions translate into bodily sensations and bodily sensations into emotions, I ventured to say, very matter-of-factly,

"Hayden, I don't think your ears hurt; I think you're mad. Are you mad about something?"

Angry sounds were his response.

"Then let's get your fingers out of your ears and be mad."

While Hayden took his fingers out of his ears, I did a mental review of what had happened leading right up to his fingers going into his ears. I looked specifically at what I had done and tried to identify any alleged transgressions on my part. This was the very first time I realized that putting his fingers in his ears could be a signal from Hayden that he was mad.

Many years earlier, I had an experience that gave me insight into Hayden's 'fingers in ears' meaning "I'm mad" for him. About a year after pretty much conquering my emotional illness, I was writing—perhaps what is referred to as "journaling"—about my cold-bloodedness. In those years I was always cold, and I hated it! I literally slept under ten blankets, the bottom one in the pile an electric blanket turned all the way up on high, summer and winter, while Denny slept with a sheet and maybe one blanket. I had a house coat - and I don't mean one of those frumpy mixes between a real dress and a nightgown—but a lined, outdoor jacket that I always wore in the house.

A few years earlier, while visiting Disneyland with my daughter and son-in-law, I was a real whiny, party-pooping, wet blanket because I was so cold. I could even be miserably cold on a beautifully mild, spring evening in California, so cold that I wasn't able to enjoy anything, and always wanted to be inside.

That night, while I wrote sitting in my comfortably overheated room, in my very own house, I explored, via journaling, the issue of my coldness and why I was always so cold when others were comfortable or hot. What I discovered was something really terrifying about always being cold - it totally dominated me and morphed me from human to beast. In my mind I saw a ball, a huge ball. As I watched it, it became two colors; then each color sent projections into the other. I continued to watched, fascinated, as the two colors pulled away from each other and then suddenly, became two different-colored balls. As soon as I asked, "What does this mean?" I had this awareness: the original ball represented coldness; the separate colors represented the emotional coldness of feeling rejected and the physical sensation of coldness.

It then occurred to me that I had melded these two feelings into one. When I was very young I had transposed the coldness of feeling rejected into the feeling of physical coldness, because physical coldness was less threatening. This meant, then, that when I felt rejected I felt physically cold, but also that when I felt physically cold, I also felt rejected. I had made emotional coldness and physical coldness into one entity, resulting in my panicky behavior, when cold, of feeling rejected.

Looking at the two separate balls, I realized that I had, unconsciously of course, made cold a monster. It was at this point of inner revelation that I was able to separate the two kinds of coldness and demystify both. Neither could control me any longer. I can—and do—accept myself now, so someone else's rejection or perceived rejection of me does not need to be devastating. This was a huge piece of self-awareness to uncover. I became very peaceful when I came upon this understanding of myself, and I fell to sleep mid-sentence.

When I awoke, I was surprised and very pleased to find that the pile of blankets I always did my writing under was on the floor, and the heater had been turned way down. And I wasn't cold! I still prefer to be warm, but being cold is no longer traumatic.

So this all went through my mind when I thought about Hayden's ear pain. It occurred to me that when his ears hurt, he was angry, just as I had felt rejected when I was cold. Anger and ear pain became melded for him, so much so that when he felt angry he perceived that his ears hurt, which meant that they did. For a few months I really focused on trying to differentiate between madness and ear pain in Hayden, so often that I frequently asked Hayden, "Are you mad, or do your ears hurt?" Consequently, he came to know the difference. Regardless, sometimes now when Hayden puts his fingers in his ears it's still an indication of his feeling truly mad and not in pain.

At twenty-seven there are yet more things Hayden might be saying by putting his fingers in his ears. It can still mean something's too loud. Or it can mean that he's in a new setting and afraid something will be too loud, as in: "I remember this place being loud before; I remember a place something like this that was loud; I don't want to hear what you're saying so I'm shutting you out or me in; I'm mad."

If putting his fingers in his ears is related to loudness, it does not necessarily mean Hayden wants to leave where he is, however. He may well want to stay there, but protect himself by doing manually what our ears do automatically for us—adjust the decibel level of sounds around him. When I see his fingers in his ears, I try to assess what's going on. I'm pretty adept at reading him and the surroundings, but I try to follow my own rule and not make determinations about the nature of his feeling, needs, or wants without checking with him first.

* * *

I've written pretty extensively here about the sensory systems of vestibulation, proprioception, tactility, and audition for two reasons: these are Hayden's most affected systems, ones he deals with on a daily basis, therefore I deal with all the time as well. And secondly, it is important to note that they are typically problematic with many ASD people.

Vision, as it turns out, is also frequently an ASD issue, either in the form of extreme light sensitivity, multiplicity of vision, poor eye movements, dominant peripheral vision, depth perception, or exceptional acuity. Visual aberrations can be as overpowering for some kids as audition was for Hayden in the beginning. He was mildly light sensitive when quite young, but I'm not aware of its being a problem today.

Both Dr. Nancy Torgerson, developmental optometrist with special training in autism, and Judy Bluestone from the HANDLE Institute, evaluated Hayden as seeing at least double, possibly fragmented, with poor eye coordination. Both thought there might be some pathology because he watched movies with his head cocked in a peculiar way. Dr. Torgerson thought perhaps he blocked out one eye to avoid seeing double. Also, at the time, Hayden seldom made direct eye contact and seemed to use predominantly peripheral vision.

As it turns out, Hayden does have some astigmatism and near-sightedness, but has always been resistant to wearing glasses; and I will not force him to do this. Good vision needs a firm foundation of tactility, proprioception, and vestibulation, all of which are immature in him. For whatever reason, Hayden says loudly and clearly, with the language of behavior, that glasses are just not comfortable for him. I defer to the wisdom of his body. How can I possibly know more than he does about what he can handle?

You may say, "But he needs to see clearly;" and I would say, "Yes, he does." However, comfort and safety are more basic than sight; he needs to be comfortable and feel safe more than he needs to see clearly. At this point, he can focus on one image at a time, he does use central vision, and he has fair to good eye contact. For Hayden, vision most likely does not give a consistent, accurate view of the physical world, but he does enjoy looking at books and pictures of people he knows, and he likes to sight-see and watch movies as well.

Kids who like to be under tables, wear billed caps, and are often found in dark corners are unconsciously trying tell us something–that they're over-sensitive to light. On the other hand, kids who stare at lights and seek out bright lights in general are under-sensitive to light. Florescent lights are neurologically disorganizing, so often contribute to inappropriate behavior in our ASD kids when we take them shopping at mega-food stores. That is definitely something to keep in mind.

Irlen Syndrome, a condition caused by the brain's sensitivity to full-spectrum light, causes varied vision difficulties. If light is painful, the world is not going to be a friendly, safe place for a child, particularly when denied the right to protect their eyes with blankets, hats, tables, or by seeking out darkened corners. If a child doesn't feel safe, all their energy will be directed towards safety issues, and academics and socialization become of secondary importance; not because they can't or don't want to socialize, but because their primary need is to feel secure.

The senses of taste, olfaction, and smell can also be affected in ASD. The main problems that come up regarding taste are aversions to certain tastes, and it's opposite, insensitivity to certain tastes. If a child has gustatory issues coupled with oral tactile sensitivity, which also may create aversions to food with particular textures, it's easy to see how he might be labeled an extremely finicky eater. Hayden, for example, doesn't like hard textures like little bits of rice or un-ground meat. But overall, he eats well and heartily when familiar things appear on his plate!

It is well known that olfaction is a dominating sense. It's also true, though not as well known, that its objects are processed more directly in the brain than any other sense. What this means practically is that if olfaction is over-stimulated in an ASD child, this can land him in a state of extreme neurological disorganization, wherein he may be unable to attend to other sensory input. All the while, you and I may be totally unaware of the offending scent. Kids who constantly smell everything around them and ignore you and what you and the world say, may be sort of *locked into* olfaction, it is that powerful a sense. Just be aware that because you may not smell something, that doesn't mean your ASD child doesn't. Make sure to acknowledge what your child smells, even if you don't smell anything.

Before I wrap up this section on neurology, there's one more thing I'd like to mention. Parents have frequently said to me,

"My child does fine at school, but when he comes home, he falls apart."

Or,

"When we go out, my child does well, but when we get home his behavior goes to pot."

Before you conclude that your child's misbehaving because he has autism, consider this: in a marathon race, some racers cross the finish line and collapse. Does anyone say:

"Well, you just ran twenty-six miles, so why are you falling down now? Just to get attention? Why don't you just walk to your car?"

Of course not! We understand that these runners have just completed a grueling race that pushed them beyond their physical limits, and that by sheer force of will, they accessed enough adrenaline to just make it over the finish line. If the finish line had been ten yards closer or farther away, very likely they'd have made it across that line too, and then collapsed. We understand the strength of will power when it comes to a marathon, and celebrate as heroes those who go beyond normal endurance and cross the finish line.

I suggest that there are many unsung heroes who push themselves beyond endurance, not for a marathon, but simply for a day at school or an afternoon at a family outing. These are the kids I've been writing about, those who live in the shadow of the autism spectrum, kids who every-day face demands, as much stress, and a comparable degree of exhaustion as a marathoner. Like the long-distance runner, they hang in there, supported by guts, determination, desire, will power, and adrenaline—for *their* many finish lines!

These kids won't collapse physically because their battle is not physical, it is neurological. They will collapse neurologically, however, which may well appear as falling apart or behavior gone to pot. And most of the time, there are no cheers for their tremendous effort, just jeers for their horrendous crash. While there is never an excuse for negative behavior in our kids, there may very well be good reasons for it. And when we examine those reasons, it is not to excuse the behavior, but to understand the contributing factors behind it so solutions can be explored.

With Hayden, I must say, the above scenario doesn't often arise anymore. When he was still in school, he came home, I welcomed him, then I asked him about his day; we then headed straight for the bathroom. After toileting, his time was free, which meant he could do whatever he chose to do, within accepted parameters, of course. I learned when he was in preschool that he needed down time when he got home, the same as he needed down time when he did his PT as a baby.

Keep this in mind as well: kids like to be acknowledged and appreciated for their hard work, and enjoy validation for a great day at school. For example, I used to say to Hayden,

"You must be pooped out and need some time 'by self'," which would help him feel understood and respected.

It's been a long trip through the autism jungle to reach the point when I can look at things from the perspective I have shared with you here. I hope this has been enlightening. I have mapped the neurological material first, because it's the basic terrain we're all dealing with and it affects every interaction we have with our kids. This last chapter specifically dealt with understanding the physical aspects of autism and their fall-out.

The next eight chapters are not autism-specific, however. Rather, they look at parenting as a whole from the perspective of allowing, accepting, honoring, and validating feelings in such a way that the language of negative behaviors becomes as uncommon in daily use as, say, Latin.

The method of parenting that is described in the next several chapters is based directly on my own experience of therapy, which allowed me to move from fear, self-hate, perfectionism, insomnia, nightmares, denial of feelings, rigidity, judgmental-ism, critical-ness, superiority, and prejudice to a point when I could join the human race and experience the "Kingdom of GOD" within. This way of being has developed in me during the time Hayden has been in my care. And I must add that during this time, Hayden has been both my student and my teacher.

Chapter 2

Feelings

There is a massive—though seemingly invisible—series of brick walls that often prevent parents from understanding their children's behavior. Even though they seem totally impossible to dig under, climb over, or blast through, there is a simple key that unlocks all the doors and allows easy passage through all the walls.

First of all, these walls are not really invisible. It's just that as a culture we've been taught not to see them because they're too threatening, the idea of them too unthinkable. One of those brick walls is a child's feeling of un-loved-ness. Right about now, I would guess you've probably decided this doesn't apply to you and your child. But humor me and please continue to read because, for example, it applies to Hayden and me daily, often several times a day. Recognition of a child's feeling of un-loved-ness is the key to understanding these seemingly invisible brick walls, and awareness allows us to turn the key.

To say that Hayden feels unloved at times doesn't mean I don't love him or that he doesn't generally feel safe and secure in my love. Nor is it to say I act as if I don't love him, am unkind or inappropriate with him. The feeling of un-loved-ness belongs to Hayden, and it stems from an erroneous belief of his that:

285

"Love should give me everything I want, when I want it, and only what I want." This is often the underlying factor in fear, anger and negative behaviors, as well as illness.

Spiritually it is true that we have everything we need and that we are loved unconditionally. Young children know this intuitively. However, when a two-year-old transmutes this spiritual principle into its physical counterpart and comes up with:

"If I want it, it's mine and if you love me you'll give it to me," it's akin to bringing me a mud pie and telling me it's supper!

It is perfectly normal, natural and healthy for a two-year-old to make mud pies and pass them off as all kinds of delicacies, and for us to be appreciative and pretend to eat them. It would not be appropriate for us, however, to treat a mud pie as a reality and actually try to eat it. Nor would it be appropriate for me to scold the child for lying, and tell them "It's not pie, it's mud."

In the realm of the physical, we accept the childishness of children and their world of pretend, and often play grownup with them. But in the context of feelings, unfortunately, this is not so. We get scared because we assign adult realities to children's perceptions. Thus, a child's "I hate you, Mommy" elicits parental feelings of inadequacy and fear, which morph into anger and get expressed as reprimands.

But in reality, the child's statement has no connection to hatred. It simply means: "You don't do what I want you to do (or let me do what I want to do) and I feel bad, so I will punish you and make you feel bad."

On a deeper and unacknowledged level, we think our kids mean: "I feel unloved and scared because you don't meet my criteria for love, so it feels like you don't love me."

If we dare go even deeper, it seems to mean: "I want you to love me," and then, at its most basic level, we seem to come to the realization that "I hate you, Mommy," is just a silent scream of, "Mommy, please love me."

When an adult responds in hurt, horror, or anger to, "I hate you, Mommy," or "I'm mad at you, Daddy," the child's 'I-am-not-loved feeling' intensifies and he wants to not love back. But he's scared of not being loved or cared for, so becomes divided. Either he acts out in anger at mommy, or buries his anger, along with his unacknowledged and fear-induced love, which has just been created. But this fear-induced love is not really love and does not feel like love. What's more, it creates even more fear.

In love, there is no place for fear. I do not need my child to love me to make me feel good. So, when my child says that he doesn't love me, I am neither shocked, nor hurt, nor angry. I understand he feels unloved when I don't do what he wants me to do. Since I know that, I'm not surprised. I can respond to him from the Adult Position—one of power, love, and strength—with:

"Oh, you're mad at me. Maybe you hate me. Thank you for sharing your feelings with me. I love you. I guess it seems to you like I'm very mean to you when I don't let you do what you want. Would you like to be mad at me?"

Since Hayden is non-verbal, I sing the 'Mad Song,' while, for a verbal child, I'd let them say what they feel in an 'I-message,' though I would challenge a 'you message.' When I use an 'I-message,' I tell others about me and me alone—who I am and what I feel. An 'I- message' always begins with 'I.' Examples are: "I am angry," "I am sad," "I hate you." A 'you-message' is one in which I tell you who, what, how *you* are. Examples are: "You are lazy," "You are stupid," "You are a brat." In an 'I-message,' I accept ownership and responsibility for who I am. Any feeling is acceptable; it is appropriate to share feelings in an intimate, loving relationship and be heard and accepted.

So, a child (everyone, of course) has the right to express exactly how he feels and who he is. But he does not have the right to tell me who I am. If my child says, "You are a mean old witch,"

I would validate him by saying, "It seems to you I'm acting like a mean old witch." This validates his feeling, but it does not entail I agree with what he says, that I agree with him. I would further say:

"Thank you for letting me know you think I'm a mean old witch. You do not have the right to tell me who I am, only who you are, and you've said you think I'm a mean old witch. It must feel pretty bad to think your mom (teacher, aunt, grandmother) acts like a mean old witch. But I'm not a witch; I'm just me. Would you like to tell me why you think I'm like a mean old witch?"

The purpose of my child calling me a witch is to sidestep the issue, whatever is getting to them, to 'get my goat,' to be in control. I cannot overstate how critical it is to listen at this point, really listen, with their ears, from their shoes and orthotics, their wheelchair, their side of the fence, and accept that their feelings about it are valid for them.

And, as it turns out, this is the perfect place to start. Once I do this, I can take them where they need to go. I just might find out in the process that I'm not nearly as innocent as I'd like to believe. If I have been in error, acted rashly, been inconsiderate, etc., I need to acknowledge this and apologize.

Children seldom receive apologies from adults or acknowledgement from them that they are wrong. As a culture, we have some deep-seated concepts and attitudes about children that are as antiquated and inappropriate as a seven-year-old working on an assembly line. As I see it, they stem from our general lack of respect for children as full human beings. "Children should be seen and not heard" or "Don't interrupt when an adult is talking" are phrases that express exactly this.

Just as a child does not have the right to define me, I do not have the right to define a child. "You are a brat" is never appropriate, true, kind, helpful or loving. Never. If define that child in this way, I thereby expect him to act as a brat. But this sets up a self-fulfilling prophecy. No child's essence is to be a brat. Although my child may at times—even often—act like a brat, it is not his true nature. I do my child, society and myself a great injustice when I pin the stereo-type brat on him, and thereby program him to continue to act bratty. It is, however, appropriate to acknowledge—without condemnation, anger, or judgment—but with a simple, declarative statement of fact, that his behavior is bratty when in fact it is.

On a few occasions, I received messages from school that Hayden had misbehaved. On these rare occasions, when he returned home from school, I sat him down and matter-of-factly said,

"Your teacher told me you've been acting like a brat in music class. Is this true?"

If so, he laughs and claps, knowing and agreeing that he has misbehaved (perhaps you remember the story awhile back about Hayden having issues in music class.)

"There must be some kind of a problem for you to act like a brat, because you are a fine boy," I added on this particular occasion. Hayden clapped and laughed in agreement.

"Acting like a brat in school is not appropriate, but thank you for letting me know you have a problem," was my response.

With this interaction, Hayden and I moved from the effect, which was his inappropriate behavior, to the cause, which was his feeling of being unloved, hurt, rejected, inse-cure, or afraid. When I deal with the cause, as I did in this example, and settle on what that is, the bratty behavior falls away.

There's a universe of difference between saying "You've acted like a brat," and, "You are a brat." It may seem like a minor distinction, and that I'm nit-picking, but it really isn't and I'm not. For example, one month, a number of years ago, our home was visited by the hated head lice, and believe me, I was, out of necessity, obnoxiously nit-picky! I had to get each and every one of them.

I like to draw an analogy between those lice and the all too prevalent, name-calling you-messages, which are insidious, and far more damaging than head lice because they infest not a head of hair but the very psyche of a child, where they latch on and multiply, just like lice do. "You brat," "You lazy bum," "You sure are stupid," "You're such a bad boy," "You never do anything right," "You're a real slob," "You always spill your milk." These are all insidious you-messages and their use as a way to deal with a child's problems is simply never affective, appropriate, healthy or loving.

I must say that validation is one of the most powerful concepts I use with Hayden and other children with whom I work. Validation is the non-judgmental recognition, acknowledgement, and acceptance of feelings, ideas, and non-aggressive behaviors. Validation serves as a mirror for children to see themselves and how they experience the world. A simple example in which we intuitively validate Toddler Jeremy, is as follows: Jeremy points to a dog and says, "Dog," and we respond, "Yes, that's a dog."

We invalidate Jeremy when he points to a cat and says, "Dog," and we say, "No, that's not a dog, it's a cat." It is true that a dog is not a cat. And we want Jeremy to learn the difference. We can validate, instead of invalidate, him in the process, though, if we recognize, acknowledge and accept that to him it looks like a dog.

Actually, Jeremy was quite observant and intelligent when he called that cat a dog. He had a new experience, of a cat, and categorized it in the same way as he did a past experience, of a dog. The two species do in fact have many similarities, which made him draw his conclusion that the cat is a dog.

Jeremy was correct on many levels. Scientifically, in fact, the two species are related. They're in the same order: carnivore. Since they belong to different species, however, it's easy to ignore what was right about what Jeremy said and focus on what was wrong about it. But this, then, invalidates his reasoning.

If Jeremy feels invalidated, he may also feel confused. Or he may feel certain he is right, and say "Dog," again. The adults may all laugh, while Jeremy feels confused, made fun of, inadequate. Sadly, with his creativity dampened, his faith in himself would be undermined in this scenario.

Studies have shown that whereas most Western children score high in creativity at a young age, by the time they enter school, most score low. Their ideas, perceptions, and observations have been invalidated so often that their creativity is squelched and they can no longer access it.

So the question remains,

"How can we teach Jeremy that a cat is not a dog without invalidating him?"

It takes a different approach, but it's really very simple. We start with Jeremy, who points to a cat and says, "Dog," then bring ourselves to his level and thereby make us psychological equals. I look at the cat and say the following:

"Hey, you're right! It sure does look like a dog. It's furry, it has four legs and a tail, just like a dog, and it walks like a dog. But, even though it looks like a dog and walks like a dog, it's not a dog. It's a cat! They're different but they sure do look a lot alike. Dogs say, "Woof," and cats say, "Meow.""

291

Jeremy's reasoning powers have been affirmed, his perceptions have been acknowledged, and this makes him feel confident about himself. He's been validated and has learned a new concept, "Cat." Validation is important for every child, and adults need it too. But for a toddler and a child with neurological impairments, it is absolutely critical because their world feels so chaotic. Such kids have so many limitations and failures that they need to have their as many of their ideas, observations and abilities validated as possible.

As I have pointed out previously, Hayden has auditory sensitivity. Several times when we've walked into a room where there's a furnace or air conditioner running, Hayden has put his fingers in his ears, and before long, a perhaps well-meaning adult has said to him, "It's not noisy in here." Without any awareness, this adult totally invalidated Hayden, whose response was to keep his fingers in his ears, but to also become confused, because he experiences the motors running in these appliances as quite loud. The likelihood of any true connection between Hayden and this adult is now minimal, because Hayden would always feel that he couldn't trust this adult.

Until Hayden entered my life, I had never heard of auditory sensitivity, and was unaware of how painful and neurologically disorganized ordinary sounds can be to someone with hypersensitivity. Back then, I could easily have been the adult who said, "Why does he have his fingers in his ears? It's not noisy in here!"

While most people are unaware of auditory sensitivity, and this is the vantage point from which they see Hayden with his fingers in his ears, I know Hayden's dis-advantage point. He thinks, "Something is noisy, and I don't know what it is. Maybe it will get louder and I'm afraid it will hurt my ears."

Knowing what I do now, I would say to him, "I hear a furnace fan. It isn't loud to me, but it might be for you. It's helping to keep the room warm and I don't think it will get any louder. If it gets warm enough, in fact, it will go off. It's very safe." Hayden would then, most likely, take his fingers out of his ears, because he'd been validated and had his concerns addressed.

When Hayden was younger and his auditory sensitivity was even more acute, he frequently kept his fingers in his ears for hours at a time when we were away from home. We attended our first live play, Fiddler on the Roof, at Yelm's Drew Harvey Theater, when Hayden was about eight. He sat entranced, but with his fingers in his ears.

A concerned woman who sat next to me suggested that I take him home since it appeared his ears hurt. So I asked Hayden,

"Do you want to go home?"

With his fingers still in his ears, he shook his head,

"No."

So, with the intention to validate him, I responded,

"It's very loud, but you like the play and you want to stay. Is that right?" His smile grew wide and his eyes said,

"Yes!"

As a matter of fact, Hayden had solved his own problem. By putting his fingers in his ears, he dampened the sound for himself. I wondered if his arms would become weary, but if they did, he never let on. When intermission came, I again offered him the choice to go home. It was 10 o'clock, he'd had a full day at school, and he'd been holding his fingers in his ears for over two hours. But he definitely did not want to go home. So, we stayed for the rest of the play, and his fingers were still in his ears when the curtain came down!

The first few times we went to The Enchanted Village, an amusement park near Federal Way, Washington, Hayden spent the entire day, both in and out of his stroller, with his fingers in his ears. Again, kind strangers suggested I take him home because his ears must hurt. But again, he didn't want to go home!

The first time I took him there, I wasn't sure he'd want to stay there at all, in truth. We arrived soon after the park opened at 11 am, and thereby missed the bigger crowds. I had made arrangements at the gate for a refund if Hayden didn't want to stay once he got inside and found out how noisy it was. But again, he wanted to stay! I figured if we could stay just a couple of hours, we would bruise one of autism's ugly heads, but we flat out gave several of them severe concussions! We left at 8 p.m., to Hayden's consternation, because the park was about to close! Most of the day he had his fingers in his ears.

It's easy to read behavior incorrectly. Fingers in ears may signify pain, but it may also mean, "It's pretty loud here, but it's interesting and I want to stay so I'm going to protect myself." It may also mean, in Hayden's case, any of the following: that he hears an unidentifiable noise that he believes could get louder; that he's afraid of a particular noise he hears; that he has a memory of a noise in a similar situation; that he doesn't want to hear what's being said; or that he's mad.

The world, from a child's point of view, may be surprisingly different from ours. When we look at behavior as a kind of language, we must check to make sure the behavior is indeed saying what we interpret it to say, so that we validate the child's feelings and not our own. When we read behavior as language, we often guess, based on our own feelings, wants and needs, at what our child is saying. That's great! It's all we can do, since we're not mind-readers. So we think such things as: "What would I mean if I were to do that?" Then it's necessary to check with our child to see if what's done is in fact what they mean by their behavior.

With Hayden, I eventually began to understand how he thought and processed his world. At some point, after years of experience, I just knew, so that now, I'm fairly adept with Hayden and am usually correct in how I read his behavior. Still, I always check, because I'm sometimes wrong; more important, he needs to know he is validated and honored.

Feelings are neither good nor bad, they just are. It is true that some *feel* good and some *feel* bad, but feelings themselves are just feelings. They're a lot like the weather—they come and go—unless we deny and disown them: then they come and grow, and eventually they blow! Frustrated, hurt, confused, angry feelings, when they are unexpressed, unacknowledged, and unaccepted, are often the basis of negative behaviors (pain, metabolic imbalances, allergies, and sensory overloads sometimes precipitate negative behaviors and these physical issues need to be addressed.)

The way to eliminate feeling-based behaviors is to catch the signals early and put the feelings into words. It is just as helpful for our children to be able to "talk out" a problem they're having as it is for you and me. Our kids may not have out-loud words, but they certainly do have powerful feelings.

Soon after I began my journey into autism with Hayden, I read books claiming that children with autism have no feelings and don't care what people think. I haven't heard anything as asinine as this in my entire life. People with autism have been invalidated, unheard, misunderstood, coerced and dehumanized to such a great extent, that, like individuals in abusive domestic situations, even like prisoners of war, they often shut down all feelings entirely, only to live continuously in 'fight or flight' mode. Since they might have an internal environment (neurologically, for instance) as abusive as their external environment, they cannot 'take flight' physically or psychologically, so are often in 'fight,' seeming not to care, when in reality they care very, very deeply.

Everyone has feelings, wants, and needs, when it comes down to being accepted. Most people with autism are very sensitive individuals; some shut down emotionally, while others act out aggressively because their feelings are not acknowledged or accepted, their bodies are driving them bananas, they can't express themselves, and the world is an abusive, chaotic, overwhelming place to be in. Only recently has an understanding of the neurological distortions present in autism been advanced enough to clarify that they may well be the true causes of some of the bizarre and violent behaviors traditionally thought to be unexplainable, integral parts of autism.

Approval or praise is often used instead of validation and although very important in building self-esteem, it does not build self-worth. Validation is the entrée, praise is the seasoning; validation is the cake, praise is the icing. When Barb, Hayden's infant teacher from the Olympia School District, first introduced me to the importance of validation over praise in response to positive behavior, I was quite resistant. Hayden, a year old with the motor skills of a four-month-old, wasn't successful at much of anything and I certainly believed he needed praise—and lots of it.

Barb, on the other hand, said it would be better for me to state what he did, rather than to praise him. Still, I wanted (needed) to praise him. When he put the blocks in the container, I said, "Good boy, Hayden," whereas Barb thought I should say, "You put the blocks in the box." When she suggested that if I absolutely needed to praise him, I should say, "Good job," instead of "Good boy," I felt she didn't understand. But in the end, I finally saw that it was I who didn't understand.

Barb's thinking was that "Good boy" is a judgment statement and opens the door for his also being a bad boy. Young children intuitively feel good about themselves, until they learn to feel otherwise from adults, situations, life itself as it unfolds with all of its challenges. All children—all people— are good because they and are not good because they do a task correctly, efficiently, or as directed.

What Hayden needs, then, is validation of himself, to have himself reflected back to him, without judgment, so that he can know himself in relationship to his world. With much internal resistance and many external botched attempts, I finally retrained myself to use "Good job!" instead of, "Good boy!" so thoroughly that now I cringe whenever I hear someone say to a child, "Good boy!" for an activity done well.

I began to use "Good job," even though Barb added a description of the action, such as "You put the blocks in the box." But something about it still bugged me. It was too ordinary. I still needed to praise. Yet, as I watched Barb and Hayden, it intrigued me. Barb's comment was not invasive, while somehow the praising part of mine was. I gradually came to understand why I somehow needed to praise Hayden, and it was all about me, of course, not him or what he needed. Perhaps some of my own childhood feelings of guilt, worthlessness and want of praise had colored my perceptions. I was simply projecting what I had needed as a child onto Hayden.

What I now understand is that Barb was engaged in the play therapy equivalent of active listening and reframing, excellent tools of good communication and psychotherapy. When I listen actively, I do not comment or give my input, but instead encourage the other person to freely express himself. As an active listener, I focus my eyes on the speaker, and allow eye contact if they desire it. I smile, am alert, nod my head, and use phrases like: "I see," "Oh," "Uh-huh," "Do you want to tell me more?" In reframing, I reword what I hear and offer it back. For example, "Is this what you're saying?", "Let me see if I understand you correctly." This allows the other person to see himself clearly, without judgment or intrusion, and thus gain a new way to understand himself. As a graduate student in psychology and counseling, I was trained to perform these very skills. While Barb demonstrated the use of these techniques on Hayden, I demonstrated how to be the "butt-in-ski-opinion-giver." Thank you, Barb. Hayden and I are deeply indebted to you!

It may seem like a minor thing, but a child's feelings of self-worth are a major thing. When a child ties his shoes for the first time, for example, it is appropriate to acknowledge that. My original inclination was to say, "Good boy, Johnnie, you tied your shoes." But suppose that the next time he tries to tie his shoes he's in a hurry or tired and he can't tie them. Will I then say, "Bad boy, Johnnie, you didn't tie your shoes?" Of course not!

Johnnie's not bad for not completing the task of tying his shoes. Nor is he good for tying them. Johnnie has intrinsic value because he exists. The jobs of tying shoes, getting straight A's, shooting the game-winning basket, are activities done well, just as not tying shoes, making C's, and missing the potential game-winning basket, are activities not done as well. Yet, ultimately, they have no relevance to the value of a child. Our children need to know, really know, that. When we praise the task ("Good job!") and not the child ("Good boy!") we help them differentiate between their intrinsic value as a human being, and the extrinsic values of doing things well. Praise is for the special stuff. Validation, is for the minute-by-minute stuff.

Praise is a value judgment by me that my child has done well on my terms; it is external from them; it is dependent on an outside source. Validation, on the other hand, is a non-judgmental acknowledgement and acceptance of my child, of what they're feeling, doing, who they are and how they see his world. It is internal, in that it is on their terms. I don't have to agree with or understand something to validate it. I simply acknowledge, without judgment, what he's feeling or what activity he's engaged in.

It's my goal to continuously validate Hayden's feelings with such language as: "You're feeling sad," "You're mad at me," "You'd rather play than eat supper now," "It seems to you think I'm being mean." In addition, there are the everyday activities I would acknowledge for a toddler, such as, "You're putting your pants on," "You're playing with toys," "You're listening to music." If their behavior is inappropriate, I validate the feeling I believe is behind it, but remind them the behavior is inappropriate. For instance, if we're in a doctor's waiting room and Hayden wants to sit on the floor and rock, I'll say to him,

"Thank you for telling me you want to sit on the floor and rock. But we are in a waiting room and there is no room to sit on the floor here and rock. So even though you want to, you may not."

Aggressive and violent behaviors are never validated, however, although I will validate the feelings behind them after dealing with them. It may seem strange or inappropriate to validate feelings that are not in touch with reality, such as, "It seems like I'm mean because I won't let you play out in the rain." But it's just this kind of case that is of crucial importance. Hayden, like many other kids living in the shadow of the autism specter or with other neurological issues, along with toddlers, have very immature logic-sequence, cause-and-effect reasoning. On top of that, they have intense feelings, so sometimes there's nothing to balance out the feelings. Considered the universally known **Toddler's Creed**, which I read about years ago and rephrase as follows:

If it's mine, it's mine.
If I want it, it's mine.
If I had it, it's mine.
If I see it, it's mine.
If I can get it, it's mine,
If I want it, and you love me, you'll give it to me.

By the time a child is three or so, if development is "typical," both physically and psychologically, the child has learned that not everything belongs to him just because he wants it. His left hemispheric functions of logic, reasoning, and cause-and-effect are in a developmental phase. If development is not typical, the child is apt to get stuck in "Whatever I want is mine, and you'll let me have it if you love me" mode, and no amount of reason, logic, explanation, cajoling, begging, scolding or threatening is going to change that.

Of course, bribes, physical force and physical punishment might change the behavior momentarily, but the anger will remain, poised to pop up at a later time. Kids are often labeled stubborn, belligerent, noncompliant, disobedient, uncooperative, then aggressive and violent, over what often seems to adults to be foolish or insignificant issues. But the feeling of un-loved-ness is always significant.

Suppose your two-month-old baby is just feet away on the floor on a blanket as you make your way through a mountain of laundry. And further, you discover you're out of laundry soap and have to make a quick trip to the store for more. You pick up the baby, carry him to the car, put him in his car seat, and run your errand, right? Why should you have to go pick him up and carry him? Why not just have him come to you? It would be faster.

However, you could call, reason, explain, cajole, beg, threaten and punish, but to no avail. The baby will not come to you. Would you then call him stubborn, belligerent, disobedient and noncompliant? Of course not! The baby cannot walk to you, so you must go to where the baby is and pick him up. Then you can take him anywhere you want to go.

Let's change things up just a little. Suppose the child on the floor is Hayden, he's about six years old, and he's been diagnosed by a University of Washington physician as being autistic to a moderately severe degree. Now suppose, on a typical school-day morning Hayden is glued to a screen as he watches a movie. From across the room I say,

"Hayden, come get ready for school."

But he doesn't move. I could reason and explain that the school bus is coming soon. He would likely just tune me out. I could yell, but he'd just plug his ears. I could go take his hand and try to pull him. He might come, but he might also refuse to get up, scream, or become aggressive. Is he stubborn, uncooperative, noncompliant, belligerent and disobedient?

My answer would be, no more so than the baby. Yes, Hayden can move his body, but not his feeling. Hayden is stuck in his feeling–the desire to watch the movie. And feelings are primary. So I can go to his feeling and guide him from there to where he needs to go.

Let's start again and show how, step-by-step, this would be attempted. Let's say Hayden is on the floor in the middle of watching a movie. In a few minutes he needs to be ready for school, so I say, "Hayden, you may watch your movie one more time, then it's time to get ready for school." Now, suppose he doesn't budge. Then, from across the room I say,

"Hayden, one more time is all done. It's time to get ready for school."

Usually, he comes the first time I call him, but let's suppose he doesn't this time. I respond to his behavior as if it were a language. Since he hasn't come, obviously he does not want to get ready for school now, but wants instead to continue to watch his movie. His behavior has *told* me that. So I validate this with the following:

"Thank you for telling me you don't want to get ready for school now. You want to watch your movie. Even though you want to watch your movie, it's time to get ready for school, even if you don't want to."

Usually, Hayden comes immediately. Why? I've gone to where he is emotionally: he *wants*, more than anything, to watch his movie. Knowing this, I can take him where he needs to go, that is, to get ready for school, even if he doesn't want to.

But, what if he still doesn't come? This is not the place to get into punishing behavior (we discuss this later), but let me say at this point in the discussion if I were to yell, become irritated with him, or in any way move out of my neutral position, I would set the stage for an attempt by him to punish me. This is because from his position, he's innocent. Remember he has a whole list of toddler's axioms, and is likely acting according to the following one at this stage of the game:

"If I want it, it's mine, and if you love me you'll give to me, and you're guilty for trying to take it away from me."

What exactly is his behavior saying? He really wants to watch his movie, his movie is very interesting, fun, or exciting, even though I'm positive it's the million and third time he's seen it; I'm being a pain and why can't we just get ready after my movie?

Remember, temporal sequence, thus deadlines, were not clear concepts for Hayden at six. Very slowly through the years, he has developed an inkling of these things, though it is very difficult to say how he understands time now. However, regardless of how it appears from our side of the fence, Hayden, in the school morning scenario we have described, is not non-compliant, uncooperative, rebellious, or disobedient. He simply has no comprehension. Hayden at six had no more capability to understand the concept of time than the two-month-old on the blanket has the ability to walk across the room. Because I understand and accept this part of Hayden's disability, I use verbal cues to compensate. If he is still not coming when I call him to get ready for school, I'd walk over to him and say,

"Boy, I can tell you really, really want to watch your movie now, and it seems to you like we could just wait until your movie's done and then get ready, and maybe you're kind of mad at me for interrupting your movie. Even though you really, really want to watch your movie, and it seems like we could just wait, and even if I seems like I'm being mean to you for making you get ready now, it's still time to get ready for school."

Now, if Hayden didn't begin to come immediately, after this mouthful of validation, I would calmly stop the movie. There have only been a few times I've turned off a movie when Hayden needed to be doing something else. And after my turning the movie off, he's always come, with no problem (I'm not at all suggesting that the first time you work with this, you'll only have to ask a few times, particularly with an older child. I am saying, however, that with patience, persistence, and practice, it is possible).

What if Hayden still didn't respond, even after I turn the movie off? What would this mean? Remember, behavior is a form of language. So the question we ask is, "What is he saying with this behavior?" Perhaps he does not want to go to school because there's been a problem there. That's a totally different issue; I usually know if there's been a problem at school, but sometimes I don't.

I'm reminded, in particular, of one morning years ago. After I gave Hayden a one-more-time-warning, I said it was time to get ready for school and saw him start to get up. So I busied myself, and listened for the sound of the bell in the bathroom (I had rigged a bell up in the bathroom for Hayden to use in case he needed help). But the bell never rang, so I went to the bathroom, and there was no Hayden either. Where was he? Not by the TV...

In a bit of a panic, I hurriedly looked all over the house, and found him on my bed, which was very atypical for Hayden. Such unusual behavior would mean Hayden was having a very intense feeling that he needs to express.

Unfortunately, I wasn't "listening" at that moment because I had another agenda—to get him ready for school. So I said, "What are you doing on my bed when it's time to get ready for school? Come on, now, let's get to the bathroom."

Hayden obediently followed me into the bathroom and pottied, but when I started to wash his face, he covered it with his hands. Again, this was totally unprecedented behavior. But again, I still did not listen, but instead said,

"Hey what are you doing? I've got to wash your face."

His hands remained on his face, covering it from all to see.

"Hayden, what are you doing? It's time to get ready for the bus. I can't wash your face with your hands there."

Finally, I put a pause on my previous agenda and asked myself the correct series of questions: What does this behavior say? Why did he get on my bed? Why did he cover his face? Do these behaviors say he doesn't want to go to school? Then I was ready to ask Hayden the appropriate questions out loud:

"Are you telling me you don't want to get ready for school?"

His hands came off his face as smiles snuck out around his eyes and lips. Then he hugged and kissed me. I had no idea what was going on, other than he didn't want to get ready for school, which I had erroneously translated into he didn't want to go to school."

It bears repeating that this was very unusual behavior for Hayden, because he normally wanted to go to school, at least after his movie was done. So I asked,

"Did you have a problem at school yesterday?"

"Most definitely!" his behavior told me.

But this puzzled me, because I usually heard about problems at school as soon as he got off the bus and burst in through the front door, and he most definitely didn't go to the Talk Chair after school yesterday. But I realized, nonetheless, that we needed to talk, because he had surely indicated that there was a problem.

As Hayden headed towards the Talk Chair, I called the bus barn to say he wouldn't be riding the bus that day. Then I sat down beside him on the Talk Chair and by way of validating him said,

"You had a problem at school yesterday and you don't want to go to school today." He didn't respond yes or no, so I tried again:

"You do want to go to school today." Again, neither yes nor no.

So I was confused, of course, and decided to go back to what I did know,

"You had a problem at school yesterday."

That got a definite "Yes!"

So I continued, "Was it a problem with a teacher?"

His frozen pose said "No."

Then I asked, "Then it was with a kid?"

He remained in that eerie frozen state, which, nonetheless, told me it wasn't a kid issue. So I tried a restatement:

"You had a problem at school yesterday, but it was not with a teacher and it was not with a kid. It was something else."

Hayden became very animated, which was tantamount to an affirmation.

So I asked myself, "What? If he had a problem at school and it's not a teacher and not a kid, what could it have been?"

And then the answer became obvious. It must have had something to do with the bus. Hayden dearly loved his bus, and had ever since I added a one-way bus ride to his school schedule in second grade. He just adored it, and soon thereafter began to ride the bus twice a day. Our only bus problems had been with his loud, excited squeals, but he'd pretty much learned that squeals—even happy, excited squeals—are not appropriate on the bus. But here we were with a bus problem. Hmmm...

I rephrased, once again, to make sure I was on the right track:

"You had a problem on the bus yesterday."

"Absolutely!" his behavior told me. I followed with,

"You want to go to school but you don't want to ride the bus." Hayden was in full agreement as he rocked, laughed and squealed, which told me that I had finally gotten it right. He wanted to go to school but he didn't want to ride the bus.

But then, something else came into focus as I shed the light brightly back onto what had happened yesterday regarding the bus. Yesterday when Hayden got off the bus, Lisa, his bus driver, said that Johnny had screamed the whole time on the bus and she knew it bothered Hayden because he'd had his fingers in his ears and was hunched over the whole time. When we entered the house together yesterday I had said to him,

"Lisa said Johnny screamed the whole time on the bus and made your ears hurt. Is that right?"

"Yes!" his behavior had told me.

And so I had said, "I'm sorry Johnny screamed and made your ears hurt. Do you want to talk about it?"

He had indicated that he didn't want to talk about it. He had already been validated by Lisa and Donna, the bus monitor, as well as me, so it should have been over. In this kind of scenario he normally would have just moved on after the validations. But I realized that today, the day after the bus incident, there was still some residual anxiety for Hayden. He didn't want to get on the bus because he was worried that his ears might hurt.

So I drove Hayden into school and promised him I'd pick him up after school, because he had indicated he wanted this. In the meantime, I went to the bus barn to chat with Lisa. I explained to her that I would drive Hayden to and from school as long as he needed. Then I asked about Johnny's usual bus behavior. As it turned out, he was always quiet in the morning and frequently somewhat noisy in the afternoon, but never like the previous day.

When I picked Hayden up after school that day, I told him I had talked to Lisa and that she had said that Johnny was not usually loud in the mornings. Nonetheless, I promised to take him to school and pick him up as long as he needed, but that he could also choose to ride the bus whenever he wanted. The next day, Friday, he chose to ride the bus to school but have me pick him up at the end of the day. When I arrived at school to bring him home the following school day, Monday, I kept my word and our agreement but he turned away from me; which "told" me that he wanted to ride the bus.

Lisa and Donna got together and brainstormed and purchased some toys to occupy Johnny on the bus ride home, and there were no major problems from that time on during Hayden's school-bus days. Truth be told, Johnny continued to be occasionally somewhat noisy. But because Hayden has *been heard and validated, and promised he didn't have to ride the bus, that he had a choice about that, this became a part of his life over which he had gained some freedom.*

Had I forced Hayden to get ready for the bus, or reprimanded him for covering his face that day, I'm quite certain he'd have had a bad time of it, perhaps would have been withdrawn and sullen, belligerent and aggressive, or would have alternated between the two, which would have given those around him some challenging times, indeed. Instead, I actively listened to him, heard him, and helped him feel safe and protected. In the end, I gave him the power to choose, and in so doing, he was able to handle a challenging situation and grow from it.

Now, suppose Hayden had not gotten in the car with me to go to school that day? I would have continued, calmly, to validate him, keeping in mind that: he *didn't* want to get ready for school, he *did* want to watch his movie; he *did* think I was bugging him: after all, why couldn't we just wait until his movie was over to get ready for school?

When I state calmly and plainly what I think a problem might be, Hayden's behavior lets me know when I hit the mark. Once I know what the problem is, I can process it, as I did above. The validation of feelings is one important, inexpensive way to decrease stress, thus improve behavior. It may be awkward in the beginning, but it's not difficult. However, it does take a willingness to look at things in a very different way.

How can you begin to validate feelings if it's a totally new concept and your own feelings were never validated? Well, it's kind of like learning a new language. Decide you want to learn, and practice. Then practice some more, and so on. Below are the steps I use.

How to Validate Feelings

- Accept that all feelings are okay—valid and real.
- Assume that angry behavior means "I am angry." (Hitting, biting, scratching, etc., are angry behaviors. If a child engages in them, but then says, "I am not angry," my response is, "Hitting is angry behavior.")
- Put yourself in your children's tennis and see the world from their vantage (or dis-advantaged) point.
- Strive to remain detached, neutral.
- Ask yourself how you might feel in the situation at hand.
- Ask your child if he is feeling that way.
- Acknowledge then validate his feelings.
- Let your child express, as much and however he can, his feelings to you. Then, if you're just not getting it, express for your child the feelings you have.
- Bring closure to feelings by asking your child if he is all done. If he isn't, suggest he finish up.
- Express love for your child: let him know that you love him however he feels, whether he is angry or not.
- Thank your child for sharing his feelings.
- Let go. And let GOD.

Chapter 3

Behavior is Language

If we actively reduce stress in our children's lives, we promote more positive behavior on their part. As I mentioned earlier, endocrinologist (among other things) Deepak Chopra has pinpointed three factors that lead to the most physiological stress:

1. The inability to express what one feels.
2. The feeling of being out of control of one's life.
3. The feeling of the unpredictability of one's life. Children with neurological issues and very young children are often stressed in all of these areas, but we can—with awareness, effort and patience—reduce these stressors.

Feelings, all feelings, as they come upon us then dissipate, are natural, healthy responses to life, especially when expressed and acknowledged. As such, they are like the steam from an open boiling pot. But when feelings build up in us, as if in a pressure-cooker, when they go unexpressed therefore unacknowledged, they become capable of producing a lot of stress and, subsequently, potentially negative behaviors. When we speak openly and frankly with our children about their feelings–with appropriate detachment–and help them express them if they cannot, negative behaviors will disappear. the 'Mad Song' is my template for expressing any feelings whatsoever for Hayden.

311

But the 'Mad Song' is in no way set in stone. Whatever gets your child's feelings out into the open, expressed and totally accepted—that is all that is needed. It's important to note that when you accept your child's feeling, this does not necessarily mean you must think it's reality-based or that it is appropriate for your child to act on it. It simply means you understand that at this moment that's what your child is feeling and you accept their feeling as valid.

When Hayden is mad at me—and he frequently is, often several times a day—it means I'm not doing what he wants me to do. But it is not my responsibility to make him happy, though it is my responsibility to meet his needs. Much of the time, I know I'm not going to do what he wants me to. But acknowledging what he wants and that he wants it is therapeutic for him. When we validate and express feelings for children their stress is physiologically reduced, which means that reactive, angry behaviors are minimized too.

As a culture we have been programmed to minimize, deny, and ridicule feelings. Consequently, we often feel uncomfortable when we attempt to accept a child's anger. It may be difficult to identify with how they feel and awkward to try to express it verbally. To do this in our culture is to execute a paradigm shift, and that is never easy. New things are usually awkward and cumbersome when we first try them, but become easier with practice. After doing just this for decades, it's become second nature for me, though I sometimes feel like a broken record that's stuck on "You are mad at me!"

So what exactly do I do at such times? VALIDATE! I validate myself all the time to dispel my own feelings of frustration. Sometimes, I grow weary of being mad at myself for Hayden, and I'd like to yell at him and tell him to hush up and leave me alone. Next I might smile and say to myself:

"You're darn right. Right now I may be sick and tired of dealing with autism, and I don't want to express feelings for him, I want to express feelings for me. I'm mad! Mad at Hayden! Mad at autism! Mad at the world! I'm just so tired of always being the bad guy! I'm really sick and tired of the jungle of autism!" But then, at some point, GOD always pipes up and says,

"Boy, you sure are mad; and I love you. You don't have to sing the 'Mad Song' ever again. In fact, you can ignore Hayden if you like. But know that you'll have to live with the consequences..." Naturally, that's always the clincher. Regardless of how I feel or what I'd like to do, I must ask myself which consequences I can live with. As I write, the fact is that tears run down my cheeks. I don't know what this means, I just know this: a few decades after I officially entered the Autism Jungle—during which I read extensively about the ASD, talked with many professionals and parents about it, studied many approaches to dealing with autistic behavior, and worked with the behavior of a number of children diagnosed with autism—at which time I discovered that the only consequence I'm willing to accept is the one I consistently get from the 'Mad Song.' Autism is not easy to deal with. But it's far easier to deal with expressed feelings than with aggressive, destructive behaviors.

We all want to feel we have some control over our lives. That's what freedom's all about: making choices for ourselves. Children in general, and children with disabilities even more so, have little control over their lives. While there are many areas in which they may not have control, there are also many situations that can afford them small choices. They don't have to be major decisions. Little choices go a long way for little people. Many seemingly insignificant and disparate choices can have the cumulative effect of making a child feel valued, capable, and in control of life: what to wear; where to sit; what book to read, toy to play with, movie to watch; when to do something. Anything. Granting children choices is a way of restoring their sense of power and control over their lives.

Sometimes I ask Hayden about whether or not he wants to do something I plan to do, even when I know full well he'll want to do it. For example, he is our household's official Spaghetti Kid. The amount of spaghetti he can devour is truly amazing. So, any time I plan to fix spaghetti for supper, I'll ask, "Hayden, would you like me to make spaghetti for supper?" "Of course!" is his immutable response. He would probably like me to make it every day, but I don't ask every day. And since he's non-verbal, he as yet doesn't have a way to ask me to make it every day. But on this day, he had a choice, or so it seemed to him that he did.

If I ask Hayden, "Do you want me to watch a movie with you, read to you, push you on the swing, play a game with you?" he has some control in his life. Any time, any way I can give him choices, I help him feel more in control of his life and I reduce his stress level, therefore his negative behaviors. If you have predictability in your life, you have the third of the three most important factors of a stress-free life.

I've spoken previously about the fact that most adults have a basic level predictability in their lives just by virtue of understanding the relationship between cause and effect as it manifests in the physical world. We will begin to help our children feel more secure when we understand that the logical thinking we can engage in, and the consistency of the physical world we observe—which are what give us predictability in our lives—are absent or diminished for them. We can compensate for these deficits by building our children a predictable world with words, by explaining what's going on, where, when, why, by whom, and for what.

Numerous times parents have said to me of their ASD children, "He (or she) doesn't understand language so don't use too many words." When I ask how they know this, what I invariably find is that this well-meaning, highly-educated person has simply made a huge assumption that is simply not true. How do I know this? From experience, lots of it. Without fail, after a mom who has asked me to work with her and her ASD child watches me interact with her child for a few sessions, she will say something like, "Wow! I think he understands you!"

Now, I don't deny that some ASD children are completely deaf, are hard of hearing, have garbled hearing, or are unable to process heard language in some other way. But I don't believe this is the norm. Whatever the percentages may be, don't take someone else's word for it. You are the expert on your child.

For example, Hayden's hospital team assured me that he was quite hard of hearing and suggested I not use language as a primary means of communication with him. As it turned out, they were just plain mistaken. Hayden hears, processes, and understands language extremely well, and I use quite sophisticated vocabulary to explain things to him, as I do with other kids. Children are fluent in body language and tone of voice too, so much so that at times they "hear" a lot we'd just as soon they didn't! I'd rather assume children do understand language and talk, talk, talk to them—only to discover down the line I'm wrong—than to assume they do not comprehend language, never talk to them, and later find out that they do comprehend.

My response to queries about Hayden and temper tantrums, violence, and aggression is always the same: he does not have temper tantrums now, though he did when he was much younger, but he hasn't had one in a very long time. He is not aggressive or violent, but he might be if I didn't talk to him the way I do. Until Hayden was twenty-one, every morning as I dressed him I went through something very like the following delivered verbally:

"Today is Friday, November 10, 2006. Yesterday was Thursday, November 9; today is Friday, November 10; tomorrow will be Saturday, November 11. Yesterday, on Thursday, you went to school and in the evening we went to Chelsea's choir concert. Today, on Friday, you will go to school. Tomorrow is Saturday and you don't go to school. I need to do some Grandma business tomorrow. The month is November. November is month number 11; last month was October. Halloween is in October. November is month number 11. Veteran's Day and Thanksgiving are in November. My birthday is in November. December is after November. Christmas is in December. Poppa's birthday is in December. The year is 2006. Last year was 2005, this year is 2006; next year will be 2007. It will start after Christmas... The season is autumn; sometimes we call this season fall. Last season was summer; this season is autumn; next season will be the season of winter."

Sometimes I would go into more detail about a season, or name all the days of the week, or go through all the months and all the seasons, or talk about the last ten years. Sometimes I would talk about numbers, that there are seven days in a week, four-and-a-half weeks in a month, twenty-eight to thirty-one days in a month, and so on. I simply went on and on—like a broken record— until he was fully dressed. This would, of course, be redundant and terribly boring for you and me. But for Hayden, it was reassuringly predictable, both in its content and that I said it every single day.

Do ASD children engage in repetitive behaviors? Do they like things done exactly the same way every time? What about toddler toys: does your ASD kid constantly push buttons that make things spin, sing, swing, say, sound, stop, start, spin, sing, swing, say, sound, stop, start, spin, sing, swing, sound, stop, star, and so on, *ad go-nuts-um*! What about that movie that gets played over and over until you think you'll lose your mind? How many books do you know by heart from reading them over and over and over again? What do you suppose your child is trying to say to you with these repetitive behaviors? I believe it is this or something very much like it: "I need something to be consistent, be the same, so I can feel secure!" As a corollary, I also help Hayden feel more secure by telling him when something's going to be different and if it's *safe* from his perspective, because the unknown holds a huge element of uneasiness for him.

Hayden has always loved movement. During the fall of his eighteen-month birthday, Denny hung a baby swing inside the house after the typically soggy Pacific Northwest weather had literally dampened swinging as an outdoor activity. The inside swing was an instantaneous hit with Hayden. Unfortunately, there was a down side for all of us to the swing, which, however, I was able to transform into a tremendous learning experience for Hayden. As you might have already guessed, no matter how long I pushed Hayden in the swing, he'd scream when I stopped. So I realized that I needed to look for the meaning behind this screaming.

It occurred to me that, for example, if I were to sit down to read from my favorite book of the moment and someone came along and grabbed it out of my hands, I would be pretty miffed! This helped me see that my abrupt end to Hayden's swinging sessions must feel the same to him; and screaming was his only way to express this when he was young.

So, I began to tell Hayden, "I'll push you one more time and then we'll be done swinging" to soften the blow. At first, when I gave him the one-more-time- warnings, he would still cry when we stopped swinging, regardless. Then I noticed that when I only said, "I'll push you one more time" he also began screaming, without even hearing the "we'll be done swinging" part. The takeaway for me: he was none too happy about this one-more-time thing, not at all! So, I said the following as a step toward addressing his displeased behavior at a deeper level:

"Thank you for telling me you don't want to stop after one more time. Even if you don't want to stop after one more time, we're going to. You can choose to swing this last time with a mad feeling and some screams, or you can have fun on your last swing for now."

Once Hayden realized that experientially "one more time" could not be erased, altered, or bargained away by screaming, nor would I be punished by such behavior, he finally accepted that "one more time" literally meant one more time.

The one-more-time mantra was then easily transferable to other situations. For example, when Hayden was in his teens, giving him one-more-time warnings before transitions made them happen without resistance and in a timely manner. If he hesitated at all, I would say, "Thank you for letting me know you don't want to, but even if you don't want to, it's time." When I employed this formula, he readily left an activity, even when he didn't want to.

Of course, when Hayden was two, five, or even seven, I could pick him up and take him wherever I needed to go and therefore *de facto* end whatever activity he was engaged in, if it ever came to that in, say, an emergency. I figured, however, that if my greater physical size and strength were my only methods of control, Hayden would eventually outgrow these and then where would I be?

If, on the other hand, I taught him to respect and respond to words when he was two, four, or even seven, when he reached his pre-teens he would be well versed in his appropriate response to words. There was no question, I thought, that words could be an asset for Hayden and help give predictability when the physical world did not. Yet words could also be another source of confusion and stress in a crazy, mixed-up, physical world that makes no sense.

* * *

For years, Hayden was very dependent on me. But because I gave him a baseline of consistency and predictability as early on as possible in his life, he's been able to move out into the world without me because he knows that he has consistency to come home to. Though Hayden is now twenty-seven I am still careful about where he goes, who he's with, and what his environment is like. And I always, always want to stretch him though never do I want to break him. To these ends, my words must be as clear as possible. When they're not, I still need to be accountable.

Recently, I gave Hayden the choice of doing physical therapy now or something else now and physical therapy later. No surprise: he chose to watch a movie now, then do physical therapy later. I said, "You may watch one movie," I said, "then we'll turn it off." While Hayden watched his movie, my sister Donna dropped in and we got lost in a sisterly gab. When Hayden then came to me after his movie was done, I told him that even though I had said we'd do physical therapy after the movie, I would talk to Donna a little bit more and he could pick out another movie to watch. I explained the change of plans to Hayden several times, then off he went, happily, or so I thought, to the second show of his double feature.

When Donna left and I finally got back to Hayden, he wouldn't even look at me, wouldn't acknowledge me in any way whatsoever. He was steaming mad at me, no two ways about it, but not because his therapy had gone undone. He was angry because I didn't keep my word and that made him feel uneasy and insecure.

Because I understand the way Hayden perceives the world and processes information, I can handle it when he's frustrated with me. In this particular instance, I easily processed his anger at me with a 'Mad Song.' Without this, however, he might have remained withdrawn or become uncooperative, even aggressive.

I must be as consistent as possible with my words in order to provide Hayden with the predictability he needs. This is why I felt it was imperative for me, if you remember the incident recalled earlier, to take him to a "real" performance of the *Messiah* a number of Christmases ago—I had promised it. There was just no way he could comprehend the monumental mix-up about the programming— why, that is, he had ended up at a performance for *kids* and *about* the *Messiah*, rather than what he expected. Had I not been able to arrange for him to see a real *Messiah* performance shortly thereafter, I would have accepted his anger at me, because to him, it would have seemed that I had lied or not kept my promise. I would have apologized for not taking him to the *Messiah* when I said I would, and then I would have asked for his forgiveness. Asking his forgiveness is a part of what I must do when things go awry like this, even when I'm not really responsible. It does not mean I am guilty of violating the Law of Love. It means I understand that in Hayden's eyes, I am guilty of breaking a promise to him and of thus violating his trust. Such a scenario would cause a rift in our relationship that I would then need to mend. I can accept responsibility for a difficulty such as this without feeling guilt or blame.

The second way I need to be consistent and predictable for Hayden is to be centered in my 'I am.' By this I mean I must accept ownership of my feelings and not let them control me or Hayden control them. Nor can I blame Hayden for my feelings—when I am mad, happy, sad, or when I have any other feeling. Whatever the feeling is, I am having that feeling. Consequently, I am 100% responsible for it, 100% of the time. No exceptions. No excuses. None. I don't care what Hayden or anyone else does or says, or how much of a pain Hayden is in the moment. If I'm mad and I respond in anger, I take full responsibility for how I feel and how I react.

For example, if Hayden gets into the dishwasher, a big no-no in our house, and I say "Hayden, you make me so mad," this would parse as follows: "Hayden, your behavior is not pleasing to me; I'm responding in an angry way in order to coerce you into doing what I want. That is, my anger is meant to intimidate you or make you feel guilty."

This is what I believe is the underlying meaning of "You make me mad." And in reality, this is not a helpful thing to say. It's a dishonest, blaming, ineffective, guilt-producing, relationship-destroying, victimizing thing to say that would generally elicit a Hurt-Child or Angry-Child response (*a lá* our transactional codes of earlier).

The reason I say this is a dishonest statement is that our feelings come from within ourselves, not from someone else. It's blaming because it's a 'you statement' not an 'I statement.' It's ineffective because it takes the focus off the behavior in question (Hayden getting into the dishwasher) and lays it onto the perpetrator's feelings of defensiveness, anger, guilt, and worthlessness. It's guilt-producing because the inference is, "You are bad for making me feel mad." It's relationship-destroying because no relationship flourishes on blame, guilt and dishonesty. And it is victimizing because if I give someone power over me (e.g., to make me feel mad, as in this particular example), I become their victim. This last makes it akin to a Child- stance because it is said with a great deal of feeling.

During WWII, POWs taken by the Nazi's were often given shovels with which to dig their own graves. If you say to someone, "You make me mad!" this is sort of like digging a relationship grave. It also hands that other person—on a silver platter—a weapon of punishment to use against you.

Being centered in my 'I am' not only entails that I accept ownership of my own feelings, but it also involves being able to feel anger without behaving angrily. What does that look like? Something like this: In a firm but calm voice, I would say to Hayden, "Hayden, I get frustrated when you get into the dishwasher because the dishwasher is not for play and you know that." I would then pause, smile and go on, "But thank you for telling me you're mad at me." Why have I added the "mad at me" piece? If I tell Hayden I'm irritated about something he's done, chances are he's doing it because he knows it's unacceptable and he could just as well have chosen not to do it. But if he's chosen to do it, that means he's using it to get even with me about something.

Note, the second time Hayden misbehaves my response will be different from the first time he does that thing. If, say, he breaks my favorite serving bowl, I would likely feel pretty ticked off and might scold him. And I might also feel quite justified in doing so. I might even go so far as to express the desire to punish him, to make him feel bad just as he's made me feel bad by breaking my bowl. But surely we see that this is easily characterized as a Child retaliating against another Child (TA-wise), which is pretty much the same as a school-yard fight. How so?

Autistic children are like minor leaguers playing on a major-league team. From their eighteen-month-old or two-year-old, or even five-year-old perspective, nearly everyone else on the team is bigger, smarter, more experienced, more powerful, and more competent than they are. Try as they might, their bodies say "No!" to many things they want to do and many exciting places they want to go. What's more, their minds say "No!" to words they want to say. Meantime, it seems to them that the big, powerful major leaguers run around and say, "No!" to almost everything else, and can get into anything they want to: they can go anywhere they want, do anything they want, have anything they want.

Further, ASD children's major-league counterparts never get their noses wiped, their diapers changed, their faces washed, or have to take naps or go to bed at all if they don't want to. And they miraculously make food and drink appear and disappear. Somehow, they make that big box come alive with people and animals and cars that do all sorts of exciting and amazing things, and they talk endlessly on that really thin, much smaller box they hold up to their ear. "If I tried," an ASD minor leaguer would think, "to do these things, I would get yelled at!"

One can imagine how our minor leaguers would continue, "Those major leaguers get to do all the cool things, like feed dishes, pots, spoons, forks, and knives, to a big, white, mysterious, and sometimes very noisy, monster in their kitchen..." This is likely how life appears to members of our ASD farm team members.

Now think about what it must feel like when an ASD minor leaguer tries to make the big white monster open its mouth and it won't! Just one more disappointment, in a long, frustrating line of them. This is just how they must feel. But then one day—*voilà*! After fiddling with it for a while, just one more time, success! The monster's mouth opens and there are all kinds of things to play with! Our minor leaguer makes a home run instead of a strike and feels proud, capable, and victorious!

Then, fresh off an RBI, he picks up something from inside the big white monster that slips from his hands and hits the floor with a pretty, tinkling sound. The same thing happens with yet another thing taken from the monster's innards! Cool! Wow! Then something else that's taken out drops and is followed by an altogether different, really loud, clanky sound and pieces of it go everywhere. Then, however, he hears the following directed at him,

"Oh no! What are you doing?! Get out of there! Oh Jeez!! You broke one of my crystal goblets. How could you? NO, NO, NO! You can't play in the dishwasher. Look out for the broken glass. You go in the other room! Now! I can't believe you broke one of the crystal goblets Mom and Dad gave me as a wedding present. Why can't you just stay out of things? You're such a little brat. What a mess you've made!"

Autistic children in this scenario know somehow they've been bad, that they've displeased those older and more powerful than they are. But they have no idea why. They were just exploring, but they're now bad, so now exploring must be bad too. They're confused, frustrated, and scared, and they've been sent away to cry over their confusion and frustration alone. Consequently, they feel unloved and unacceptable to their moms or other significant caregivers, and this makes them feel sullen. What precedes precisely sets the stage for an act of aggression on their part.

The world looks so different from the adult side of the fence. The child's behavior is unsafe and unacceptable from such a perspective. But in terms of the child's reality, what they did was appropriate, normal, creative, and victorious. Both perspectives are true, in that they tell the same story from a different point of view. So both need to be honored and respected. When ASD parents are centered in their 'I am,' they act from their own center, rather than react to outside stimuli. What follows is how this might look when a mom happens upon what is really a legitimate dishwasher exploration:

"Oh my, you opened the dishwasher. A glass got broken and there's glass on the floor; let me take you to the other room so you don't get hurt. You were pretty clever, weren't you, figuring out how to open the dishwasher? I can tell you were having fun. Maybe you were exploring or maybe you wanted to do dishes like I do. You're getting big and you can do many things now, and I'm glad you're learning new things. I want you to be safe. Dishwashers are for grown-ups and bigger kids, and though you're getting bigger you're not quite big enough yet to do the dishes by yourself; sometime I'll let you help me with them, though. Little kids need help with the dishwasher. Even if you want to do it by yourself, you may not. Do you see why? Glass got broken, and you could have gotten hurt. I'm glad you didn't get hurt this time. I want you to be safe because I love you. Why don't you go play in your room while I clean up the glass so no one gets hurt?"

In this scenario, ASD kids would exit the incident feeling good about themselves. They probably wouldn't get into a dishwasher alone again, and the parental or other caregiver bond would most likely have been strengthened. Does that mean that these bigger people in their lives don't feel angry or frustrated, or that they don't want to scold their children? Not at all!

First of all, parents feel whatever they feel and need to accept responsibility for it. In other words, if they act out of madness, it's because they're mad and not because someone else made them mad, *made* them *react* with madness. The parent in the above new-and-improved version of how to react to the dishwasher scenario chose to be proactive and not reactive, and therein lies the difference!

I've tried to keep things in perspective in the child-rearing methods I've used with Hayden, and this has led me to see that children are far more valuable than anything that's possessed; their job as children is to grow, learn, and explore. And in fact, they learn particularly well by making mistakes. I also see that they are apt to be clumsy, have poor judgment, and just not understand some things. From this perspective, I'm able to extend to all ASD kids the right to be human and err. And also from this perspective I'm able to avoid setting them up for negative behavior and poor self-esteem. Of utmost importance, I'm also able to refrain from handing them that silver-plated vehicle by which to punish me sometime down the line. The more consistently I relate to Hayden from my 'I am,' by staying in the 'Adult' and acting proactively—not reactively—the more predictable his world becomes for him. This reduces his stress level by providing a secure framework in which he can grow, one that's free of concern about needing to make me happy or, on the other hand, wanting to punish me.

If I were to make decisions based on whether or not Hayden would scream or be aggressive, then I would, effectively, give him control of my actions. It's important to note, though, that to some extent, every child exerts a measure of control over their parents' actions. If, for example, my toddler is napping but I discover I need to run to the grocery store in the middle of fixing supper because I forgot to buy onions, I would probably wait until he wakes up to go, or nab a neighbor to babysit. This is perfectly reasonable and healthy. If, on the other hand, I'm fixing supper and my four-year-old comes in and asks for a cookie that I don't feel would be good for him, but I give him one to avoid his screams, I've let my Child take control of me. The lesson to be learned here is this: Any time we make decisions based solely on someone else's possible reaction to them, we've given away our power. When dealing with children, this means we've placed authority in their hands. Though children may know, chances are they do not know what they really need, which is to know they're really and truly loved.

Young children want and need boundaries. Suppose you set out to climb Mt. Rainier. If scaling summits is your thing, this could be a really exciting experience. Suppose sometime in the middle of the hike your guide suddenly says, "Okay, now you're in charge. You decide which way to go up the rest of the mountain." Are you going to respond, "Okay! I'd love to go any way I want to up to the top of this mountain." Or will you say, "No, thanks! I want you to be in charge"? I think we all know the answer!

Young children want the freedom to explore life but within the framework of parental security. In a way, they want what they don't really want, and they don't want what they really want. They really want the love and support they feel when mom, dad or the nanny is present, especially when they venture out to explore the world. They want to test the world as an independent agent, while knowing there's an adult to run back to should things go awry. If trouble is encountered, they want to be soothed by this adult so they can launch themselves again, going further afield each time.

Children also need to find solid security in knowing mom and dad love them deeply enough to say, "No." Sure, they'll fuss when they meet up with a "No," especially if they think they can thus control whoever is saying it by doing so. But if my words are consistent, if I'm very clear and really mean it when I say either "Yes," or, "No," the child I'm setting boundaries for will feel free and secure enough to quit trying to run things, and instead do the job of being a kid, which includes growing, learning, exploring and creating.

I'm not talking about setting a myriad of rigid, unreasonable rules that are forever immutable. Such rules stifle the development of children. Instead, my rules need to be based on my wants and needs and my child's wants and needs in a way that is reasonable, appropriate, respectful, and personal.

As Hayden's life-teacher, I must help him express his feelings and then validate those feelings. I must give him a feeling of control over his life by presenting him with simple, appropriate choices. I must also help him experience a measure of predictability in his seemingly chaotic world by explaining as much as I can, and I must be as transparent as possible in doing so. All of these stress-reducers for Hayden are: simple; financially inexpensive, but energetically and emotionally very taxing; readily available, but frequently difficult to assess and sometimes seemingly impossible to carry out. But they are all worth it. The benefit of reducing stress translates into improved behavior, which in turn opens the door to mutual respect and loving interactions with one's child.

As I have said before, behavior is a language to be understood, not a disease to be eradicated. If I were to publish a treatise on our culture as it stands now, I would entitle it *"Behavior Is Our Language, Punishment Is Our Disease."* But in a more perfect world, the single most important language we can learn after the one we speak is behavior, the one we see and hear. It's universal, eloquent, and crystal clear if we open our eyes to it. Further, behavior is the kind of language that occurs in response to stimuli. If a behavior is repeated, it's likely that in some way or other it was reinforced.

If I don't like my child's behavior I can try to punish it away by saying, "Be quiet! I don't want to hear you! You are bad!" But this communicates disrespect and teaches violence, pain, humiliation and deprivation. Of course, when my child turns 10, 16, or 30, I may find myself wondering why we're not communicating, why he or she is belligerent and has low self-esteem, is using drugs, has problems in school, or is a perfectionist, critical, superior and unhappy.

Punishment may facilitate a desired behavior. Hitler demonstrated to the world the conscience-less (I changed this from conscious-less to conscience-less for greater impact...) behavior that blind obedience and control by fear and punishment is capable of producing. The flip side of the punishment coin is fear. Punishment cannot exist without fear and at some level, anger. Repressed anger is still anger.

The purpose of fear and anger is self- and species-preservation. Thousands of years ago, it was either wrestling with a mountain lion or running from it. Today it's likely we're dealing with a four-wheeled beast rather than a four-footed one. If someone pulls out in front of me when I have a green light, my body chemistry instantly changes, just as that caveman's did when he suddenly faced a menacing mountain lion. Like the National Guard, my blood is ready to serve; its pressure spikes when danger is imminent. But unlike the National Guard, my physical being responds instantaneously, each of my billions of cells simultaneously stopping the routine work of digestion, elimination, disease prevention and clean-up to rush hormones into my bloodstream. These raise my blood pressure and heart rate, and supply me with energy to slam on the brakes.

The amazing thing is that this all happens without my conscious mind thinking about it. In fact, by the time my mind arrives on the scene, the danger may have already dissipated, but the troops are still out in full force. My heart is pounding, my stomach feels like an empty chasm, my palms are clammy, and fear has evolved into anger.

Thus, anger is a secondary emotion. Though it never starts the self-preservation motor, it's the fuel that keeps it running. Fear, pain, sadness, or feelings of rejection start the motor, but anger quickly takes over at the wheel. It keeps the adrenalin flowing and provides me with the added strength and endurance I need to handle the problem before me, either by fight or by flight. The result? My normal bodily functions are pre-empted.

If I have a healthy relationship with anger—if I'm able to accept, acknowledge and express it—it will dissipate and my body will return to its critical routines. If I don't have a healthy relationship with anger—if I deny, repress, suppress, project, or inappropriately express it—my 'anger tank' will remain full, ready to fuel a launch into fight or flight at a moment's notice while my body's normal work goes undone.

You've probably heard of the man who was yelled at by his boss, who in turn went home and yelled at his wife, who then yelled at her child, who then kicked the dog. Most of us know someone who seems to be angry a lot of the time. Unfortunately, sooner or later that anger will express itself as aggression, violence, disease, depression, self-hatred, superiority, and a hypercritical attitude.

What does all this have to do with kids and autism? Plenty! Kids both on and off of the spectrum often have their self-preservation motors running at full-speed because there are so many *internal* and *external* stressors in their lives. Some examples of *external* stressors: parents who ignore their children's feelings as well as their neurological issues; widespread illiteracy of the language of behavior among our general population; parents who 'modify away' the behavior of their children rather than mining if for the true meaning behind their children's actions; the existence of social pressures on our children to conform to arbitrary norms set by our educational and cultural institutions; psychologically abusive language directed at our children; and the frequent threat of punishment or the punishment itself of our precious progeny.

Some classic *internal* stressors for children are: a sense of no control over their lives; no clear understanding of what's going on around them; the inability to express themselves;

and, especially for kids with physical and neurological issues, the pain and discomfort entailed by the limitations dealt them.

Furthermore, often there's a negative feedback mechanism at work, with ASD children in particular. Their behavior clearly expresses their stress, but our ignorant, therefore inappropriate, responses to their behavior only increase their stress, and so on, until their behavior (language) gets louder, more violent, and more destructive.

Autism, or just plain being a two-year-old, are blamed for negative behavior. But neither autism nor being a two-year-old are the cause. If we think of behavior as language, we realize that it can be spoken softly, and will be if it is heard. When it is not heard and our children feel ignored, the language of behavior can be spoken so loudly that it cannot be ignored.

Negative behaviors are usually expressions of anger, which follows fear, pain, sadness or rejection. And anger can be healthy and beneficial, at which times it is undeserving of its sordid reputation. The problem is not with anger or even rage *per se*, but the way these emotions are used, or rather, "ab-used." We've tried to tame anger by suppressing it, making it a sin, disallowing it, renaming it, pretending it doesn't exist, blaming it on someone else, and just ignoring it.

However, anger is not a beast, so it cannot be tamed. It is simply a tool that enables us to protect ourselves physically and tell us about ourselves spiritually. The fact that the anger tool has been misused and abused so much does not negate its health benefits. When we accept our children's anger, we are free to help them not misuse, or worse, abuse it.

Children in general, but particularly young children and ASD children, are frequently thrust into what feels to them like life and death situations of which the adults around them are unaware. Because of such lapses in parental awareness, such situations—which hold so much fear for our children—go unacknowledged. This in turn entails that these children rarely have the opportunity to express and thus dissipate their feelings in a healthy way.

Picture a quiet neighborhood on a fresh spring morning. Rita has come out to check her mail. Right next door, Anne, just before opening her front door, promises her three-year-old, Johnny, a walk around the block. When she steps into the sunlight, however, Anne sees Rita and suddenly remembers she had promised to tell her highlights of the neighborhood association meeting of several nights before. Anne glances back to check on Johnny, then rushes over to Rita's to discuss what transpired at the meeting. They wind up in Rita's front yard locked in intense conversation about several points of contention that had come up at the meeting.

Meantime, Johnny has lagged behind, feeling mopey and disappointed that his walk has been put on the back burner. He notices some dandelions—the first of the year—popping up between the roadbed and the curb and makes a bee-line for them. By the time Anne turns around to check on Johnny again, he's made his way across their lawn and sidewalk and has just negotiated the curb. He's in the street! Anne immediately assesses the danger her son is in and reacts with a healthy amount of fear; she runs to him, scoops him up in her arms, and hurries him off the street.

In the process of all this, both Anne and Johnny's fear-motors were ignited. But Johnny's fear-motor wasn't started up by fear of a car on the road! It was his mom's behavior that turned his fear motor on and revved it right up. From Anne's point of view, when she yelled at Johnny, grabbed him, then scolded him, and followed this, out of a tremendous sense of relief, with copious hugs and kisses for him, her fear-anger-expression-dissipation cycle quickly played itself out.

But meantime, what happened for Johnny? Though Anne initially promised Johnny a walk, she decided to talk to a neighbor for a spell first. To Johnny, who was waiting for the talking to stop, this was a pretty dull scenario. So naturally, off he went to look for something more interesting to do than listen to his mom's neighborly conversation. It just so happened that he saw some pretty flowers, and decided to set off to investigate. In fact, he was full of excitement and anticipation. But then, out of nowhere, Johnny heard the angry, frightened voice of his mommy and sensed that she was upset, that something was terribly wrong. Even though his world seemed fine, his angry mom rushed to him, swooped down, scooped him up, and then scolded him of all things! His translation: "Mommy is mad at me. Mommy doesn't love me."

In reality, though, Johnny did nothing wrong. He was exploring, which at his age was a GOD given responsibility! And he wanted to see those pretty flowers, which seemed to be growing out of concrete—how cool was that? But now, all he could think was that Mommy was really mad...except... she hugged and kissed him, when all was said and done.

It's not difficult to see how confused Johnny would be about this whole scenario. In addition, he had good reason to feel tremendously 'unfaired-against.' As he saw it, he was innocent and his mom was guilty on as many as seven counts!

She had:

1. Lied to him (she said they were going for a walk but she talked to Rita instead)
2. Ignored him (for almost the entire time she talked to Rita)
3. Yelled at him (as she panicked and ran for him).
4. Grabbed him roughly (as if he had done something wrong)
5. Acted like she was really scared (mommy is not supposed to be scared—his tacit rule)

6. Not let him get to the pretty things
7. Not loved him

At this point, let me remind you of the Toddler's Creed, because it played a significant part in the little drama I've just described: **If I want it, then it's mine, and you'll let me have it if you love me.**

With all of this in mind, Johnny's response was, I believe, predictable, even healthy for a toddler. He screamed his pain, anger and indictments against his mom when she approached him in panic and fear, but she didn't hear them. How could she? In the good old U.S. of A we've never been taught to heed our children's behavior, to accept their anger as healthy and valid, or to see things from their disadvantage point. Suppose Anne also said, in response to Johnny's angry blaming, the oft' heard, "Hush, everything's okay now." Well, from Johnny's point of view, his mom would have just scored two fresh indictments:

1. Telling him to shut up
2. Lying to him... again!

If we look at the fight or flight elements of this story, we see that Anne's body chemistry was on its way back to normal maintenance mode as soon as she rescued Johnny from the street. But Johnny's? His was running full throttle on unresolved anger because he was still in a terribly confused state when his mom called the 'all clear.' At that moment, in fact, Johnny was only a few baby steps away from a tantrum.

For Johnny, what happened was dead serious. Being unloved by his mom was tantamount to annihilation for him: if she didn't love him, she wouldn't take care of him. The only way he understands love in our little tale is by the way he loves, and remember, as a toddler, he loves when he gets what he wants, he hates when he doesn't. Just good old 'mud pie love' and 'mud pie hate,' which are normal and healthy even for a three-year-old.

It's helpful to keep in mind that at Johnny's developmental stage everything is based on what feels good. There's no logic, no reasoning. This is what makes toddlerhood a very serious and scary place. The sheer precariousness of it often precipitates the acting-out behaviors that are frequently associated with toddlers. If mommy is scared, her progeny's world is in big trouble.

Johnny, of course, doesn't understand the dangers of cars or know love exists even when he doesn't get his way. The adult in our scenario–Johnny's mom, Anne—knows the dangers of a toddler in the street, but has momentarily forgotten the limitations of her toddler's awareness. What's more, both parent and child see their reality as the only reality.

However, an adult's response to a toddler in the street, especially if a car is coming, is going to be fear-laden and possibly angry; that's a given. It's just an 'is-ness' of life. When the physical crisis is over, the adult can, if she is enlightened in this way, take time to see things from the child's perspective and validate the child's point of view. Let's look back at our scenario to the point at which Johnny's mom has called the all clear. For her, the crisis is over, but Johnny is still screaming. How would things go if Anne took a look at things from Johnny's point of view and helped him in his process back to normalcy? She would be right on target if she were to say something like the following:

"Johnny, maybe I scared you, yelling at you and grabbing you. Maybe you're mad at me. I'm sorry I scared you. I got scared you might get hurt and I wanted you to be safe, but I guess I acted pretty scary and I'm sorry. Maybe I was very boring talking to Rita when I promised you we'd go for a walk. You were having a good time going over to see the flowers on the street, but I got scared because cars go in the street and cars don't always see little kids. I ran yelling and grabbed you up and scared you and sounded mean and grouchy to you. You don't like me to be scared and you don't like me to be mean and grouchy because that scares you and makes you feel unloved. Sometimes I do get scared and sometimes I do get mean and grouchy-sounding, but I always love you. When I yell at you for being in the street by yourself, it's because I love you. When I'm scared you might get hurt and I sound mean and grouchy, I still love you. I'm sorry I scared you and yelled at you. Will you forgive me?"

If Johnny doesn't forgive his mom after she's said something akin to the above, the right thing for her to do is reaffirm her love for him anyway. She might do this by saying that he can stay mad at her if he wants to, but that she will always take care of him and love him. When all the feelings are dealt with and there's no residual pouting, she might offer to take him across the street and keep him safe while he checks out those pretty flowers.

If Anne does all of the above, she will have covered all her bases because she's accepted Johnny's indictments against her, validated his position and feelings, validated her own feelings and viewpoint, apologized for her alleged misdeeds, assured him of her love, figured out a safe way for him to look at those dandelions and even snuck in an experiential lesson about crossing the street, if she's really thinking! This should dissipate Johnny's anger so that he's not primed for a meltdown when the next incident occurs.

Do I actually talk to Hayden and other kids like this? **You bet!** Because of Hayden's autism, he processes logical information much like a two-year-old. That's why kids with autism and two-year-olds have reputations for temper tantrums, non-compliance and aggressive behaviors. When we see behavior as language, however, it becomes clear that angry behaviors occur because kids are angry, not because they have autism or are two years old. When kids feel frightened, hurt, sad, or rejected, they cover it with anger. By looking behind the anger for the primary feeling, and by hearing, validating, and addressing that feeling, we can eliminate the anger and its negative expression.

In doing so, we help our kids grow and learn to use their anger as a tool for protection and self-knowledge, not as a weapon for punishment and revenge. If we respond to behavior as if it's a language, this allows our children to use words (or outward signs), rather than rebellion and violence, to express their feelings.

I have purposely discussed behavior after the neurological aspects of autism because sensory issues must be understood and accounted for before success can be had at eliminating negative behaviors. When both kids and adults are in emotional pain or are confused, they're not often candidates for Oscars in good behavior!

Chapter 4
Tacit Rules, Revisited

As we have discussed previously, a tacit rule is an unspoken rule. We have tacit rules about many things, about how they should be. Furthermore, we judge and we approve or disapprove of others based on our tacit rules. Any time we decide how someone else should do something, we exercise one of our tacit rules.

When a couple marries, for example, each person brings his or her own set of tacit rules to the marriage table, as well as the tacit rules of their respective families. I remember the first April Denny and I were married. It was almost the "Ides" of April and our taxes had not yet been done! It never occurred to me that a wife would, even could, do taxes. Men did that, at least in my childhood home. But not so in Denny's. We each had a tacit rule about who should do the taxes, but it was not the same rule!

All families seem to have tacit rules that typically kids pick up quite young, seemingly by osmosis. But this is not the case for a family that includes an autistic child. A lot of negative behaviors and tie-ups in family life occur because autistic children do not understand, *cannot* understand, the tacit rules held by their family members. They have their own set of rules for everyone and every situation, and become extremely confused, frustrated, and angry when these rules are ignored. Meantime, everyone else in the family is frustrated, confused, and possibly angry that their family rules are ignored by the autistic family member.

Society also has clearly defined tacit rules. Anyone who has taken an autistic kid to a public event, for example, has probably experienced first-hand the feeling of being ostracized because they do not conform to or make their kids conform to social expectations. Hayden, now taller than I am, sucks his thumb when he's tired or sad. It is truly amazing how many people have rules about acceptable places for my grandson's thumb!

To understand what the family dynamics are when that family includes a child with autism, it's first important to note that the autistic child is absolutely the tacit rule sovereign of that family. Autistic sovereigns feel, perceive, and process very differently from the rest of their family. The bodies of autistic sovereigns don't work particularly well, so they often feel uncomfortable and may not have a clue about where their bodies actually are at any given time (remember, proprioceptive disturbances are common among those with autism).

The sovereign's world seems to be totally unpredictable and therefore chaotic, thus extremely threatening. And so, sovereigns do what any self-respecting person would do in such a situation—they try their best to make the world predictable, organized and secure by positing rules about how things should be. They base these rules on how things once were, or how they would like them to be, but then end up feeling extremely violated when the rules are not observed by the world and people around them.

From the non-autistic side of the fence, a child with autism may seem to exhibit bizarre behavior and be non-compliant as well as aggressive, while everyone else—their family members and society in general—feels frustrated, exasperated, embarrassed, and angry.

For our autistic kids, however, what happens on the other side of the fence is very disconcerting. No one complies with their rules, for one thing. Moreover, others seem to behave oddly and do things that are painful and threatening and don't even care. Autistic people seem to think they are the only sane people on the planet! What a terrifying feeling that must be! Autism can look pretty confusing from those in non-autistic shoes, but seems like nothing compared to how it looks from the dis-advantaged point of an autistic kid's orthotics-stuffed tennis!

Tacit rules are the result of an autistic child's attempt to understand and organize the world and provide some measure of security. But some of these tacit rules are just not reasonable. If we simply disregard these rules, though, this will lead to unending frustration and misunderstanding for everyone. It will also spawn a lot of negative behavior on the part of the autistic person.

One of Hayden's tacit rules is: "She shouldn't let me get hurt, and if she loves me, she won't." (*a lá* the Toddler's Creed.) This is not reasonable, of course, but Hayden is not reason-able, and his rules reflect this. Another example comes to mind. It is actually painful for Hayden when people near him cough, sneeze, and blow their noses. This is because of his extreme auditory sensitivity. As a result, he has a rule that I should not cough, sneeze, or blow my nose! If I loved him, he posits, I would not do any of these things.

Obviously, I don't observe Hayden's tacit rules. But knowing that he's going to be angry at me when I blow my nose means that I can understand, accept, and process his anger so that it dissipates. This is a far better outcome, for all concerned, than pouting, withdrawal, aggression, or violence on his part.

Hayden was three when I became aware of his rule that I'm not supposed to let him get hurt. He was swinging at the park, and for the first time ever, he was to have the responsibility of holding onto the swing by himself. We'd been working on this for quite some time and since these swings were relatively low and the ground below was soft and sandy, it seemed a good place for him to practice holding on all by himself.

Well, he didn't! He let go, fell off, and screamed bloody murder. When I picked him up, he refused to cuddle and be comforted. Further, he pushed me away and wouldn't even make eye contact, all atypical for him at the time. What was worse—his screams were absolutely hair-raising and continued for some time. After I realized he was more startled than hurt, I noticed he showed signs of retreating into the not there *autistic space he'd been in through most of his very young years. I went right to work to get him out of that place, but soon discovered that, strangely, he wasn't* not there. *He hadn't retreated, but he had decided to actively avoid me, as if he was mad at me!*

"Are you mad at me?" I asked. The twisting away and screaming had stopped and been replaced by angry, guttural sounds, typical of the behavior he exhibited when he was clearly angry. We had been having such a good time at the park and now, I had no idea what had happened, why he so was mad at me. I felt completely in the dark. So, I pitched a question 'out there' and an answer came back loud and clear: "You're not supposed to let him fall and get hurt." At the time, this seemed incredulous, yet I was quite aware by then that when I asked a question and received an answer in this way, I knew the response would be right on. So despite my incredulity, I queried, "Hayden, are you mad at me because you fell off the swing?"

"I'm not supposed to let you fall and get hurt, is that it?" I asked, amidst a volley of angry sounds coming from Hayden.

An incontrovertible "Yes!" came from Hayden in response.

There, in the park, I finally began to catch on that Hayden's definition of being loved was getting what he wanted: If I really loved him, I'd give him only what he wanted. What's more, I'd keep him safe and not let him get hurt.

I smiled inwardly at this very immature concept of love, and on the heels of this moment of clarity looked back at Hayden and asked myself how many times had this little child tried to teach me what love means to him.

Then I asked Hayden right out, "Does it seem to you that if I really, really loved you, I wouldn't let you fall and get hurt?"

Loud sounds fraught with anger were his definitive response– they told me that this was exactly what he meant!

"Do you want to be mad at me for letting you fall off the swing?" I asked. Most definitely he did, and so I sang a 'Mad Song' hand-tailored to the occasion;

> *You are mad at me,*
> *You are mad at me,*
> *I let you fall off the swing,*
> *And you are mad at me.*

I sang this several more times until the anger ceased. Then I changed it up a bit:

> *You are mad at me,*
> *You are mad at me,*
> *You were swinging and you let go and fell off,*
> *And you are mad at me.*

I sang it this way a few more times, then made yet another slight change:

> *You are mad at me,*
> *You are mad at me,*

You want love to never let you get hurt, but sometimes it does.
And you are mad at me.

After singing it a few times like this, I went to:

I love you,
I love you,
When you let go and fall off the swing and get mad at me,
I love you.

Then, I went with yet another variation:

I love you,
I love you,
When you are mad because you fall off the swing,
When you are sad because it seems like I don't love you,
I love you.

Hayden is now twenty-eight, and I'm no longer surprised when he's mad at me for anything that happens that he doesn't like. I sing a 'Mad Song' at myself (because in his mind I let it happen), until I think that all the madness is expressed. Then I validate for him that he has a rule that says "if she really, really, really loves me, she wouldn't let anything happen that I don't want to happen." Then I add that I can't control everything, so I can't give him absolutely everything he wants. I then tell him that no matter what, l always love him. I always end this progression with an 'I Love You' song.

Even to this day, Hayden still needs this processing to move beyond his anger. If I try to take a shortcut around Hayden's anger, it will, sooner rather than later, affect his behavior until we do process it.

Every now and then, even when Hayden has indicated clearly with his behavior that he's mad at me, I just can't for the life of me figure out why he's mad at me. My strategy is to thoroughly scrutinize the goings on of the day, looking for anything and everything that he might be mad about. Primarily, I try to determine if I have, unbeknownst to myself, done something on his list of my worst-ever alleged transgressions. He may mildly agree to one or even several of them as I put my queries to him. But if I hit on the one that is foremost on his mind, there will be nothing ambivalent about his reaction! When this happens, I know I'm well on my way to knowing what exactly has gone awry between us. If, however, I run out of ideas about why he's mad at me before I get that unequivocal sign I'm looking for, I simply validate that he's mad at me and that he knows why, but I don't.

What can further complicate matters at this point, though, is that Hayden has the overarching tacit rule that I'm always supposed to know why he's mad! Consequently, if I ask him if he's also mad because I can't figure out why he's mad, that always yields a "Yes!"

So, how do I rescue us from this maze of questions and "missed understandings"? I simply resort to one of the oldest tricks in my book. We sing a 'Mad Song' at me about my unconscious transgression. We always include in this particular 'Mad Song' that he has a rule that I'm supposed to know why he's mad, and that he's always mad at me when I don't know why he's mad.

Everyone knows the adage, "A stitch in time saves nine." At first, it's easy to ignore a tiny rip in a mostly hidden underarm seam of my blouse. But if I keep ignoring it, the seam will undoubtedly continue to unravel, until I'm left with an unsightly and embarrassing hole in my blouse.

Negative behaviors are a lot like ripped seams. Often these behaviors start out small and insignificant, almost imperceptible, and at first they're easy to ignore. I just absent-mindedly hope that they won't get any worse.

Unlike a hole in my blouse, however, a potentially negative behavior may start out being cute. But something that's cute in a twelve-month-old will definitely not be cute in a twelve-year-old! A tiny rip in a seam means there's a problem—a broken thread, most likely. Unless mended, the rip will grow larger. A facial expression, gesture or sound—seemingly small and insignificant—often expresses a feeling, which, if ignored or unheard, may result in a big explosion later on down the line. I have trained myself to be on the lookout for the little signs transmitted unknowingly by Hayden that say, for instance, "I'm frustrated," and deal with them before they morph into something destructive or aggressive.

Like any new concept, tacit rules may seem hard to grasp. But once you understand them and begin to hunt for them, you quickly get the hang of it. They can even become obvious, and deciphering them, almost automatic. The pay-off for your effort in identifying the tacit rules at work in any given situation is a decrease in negative behaviors.

I still hunt daily for tacit rules upheld by Hayden, and have since he was quite young. But he is affectionate, well-behaved, and communicative. He also loves going to concerts, restaurants, plays, parks, on trips—you name it! He is also severely autistic, incontinent, non-verbal, quite dramatically delayed in fine and gross motor skills, and clueless when it comes to safety, logic, sequence, cause-and-effect and the passage of time. I utilize the concept of tacit rules to compensate for what he lacks in all of these areas, and to ease his confusion and frustration.

I understand that Hayden lives by, and thinks in accordance with, unwritten, definitive rules about nearly everything. And I believe these rules are very important to him. Perhaps one of the reasons he shies away from new things is that there are no rules in place that govern them so they're frightening.

When I see any sign of withdrawal or agitation in Hayden, I immediately try to discern what has just happened from his physical point of view, literally right at his eye level. It is often possible for me to identify the feeling behind the withdrawal or agitation and process it on the spot, then quickly eliminate these unsettling feelings for him. I've come to learn that withdrawals are like time bombs. Now, finally, I can diffuse them. But if I don't attend to them, if they 'keep on tickin',' pretty soon I'll 'take a lickin'!'

Immediately after I sense that something's gone awry for Hayden, I calmly, as if talking about the weather, put into words what I see, feel, intuit about what's going on, then say something to Hayden like,

"You're stomping your foot; do you have a problem?"

or

"You put your hand in my face; maybe you're telling me you're mad at me?"

or

"You're turning away from me; thank you for telling me you're mad at me."

We've been following this protocol since his second year on this earth, so we're both aware of and comfortable with the fact that he is often mad at me!

In the beginning, it's important to ask your child about how they perceive themselves rather than tell your child what you think defines them. It's disrespectful and presumptuous to tell another person you've decided what their feelings are or what their behaviors mean, even if you're sure you're right. A person's feelings and behaviors belong to that person alone; no one has a right to define someone else. It is my belief that our children can often sense, at some level, when we deny their feelings, discount their observations, and tell them who we've decided they are.

It's important at this point to note that if a child behaves aggressively or violently towards anyone or anything, my work with that child's tacit rules is superseded by a very critical overt rule that I stick to unfailingly: aggression is not acceptable. My response to aggression is a very firm, but not emotionally charged, "Ouch! I don't like to be hit… but thank you for letting me know that you're mad at me." While saying this, I gently touch the child and make eye contact, if possible.

Aggression and violence are never acceptable, never! That message comes first. However, such behavior often amounts to an expression of a child's having been violated in some way. If I respond angrily with put-downs, threats, or retaliation, I will invite anger and retaliation in return, and the situation will escalate into an angry, possibly violent, lose-lose scenario. If, on the other hand, I respond neutrally, with something like with something like the above, I can avoid setting the stage for retaliation and begin to work on the source of the problem.

Violence, destructiveness and aggression are basically angry behaviors. When I encounter children who act out in this way, I suspect they're angry, but don't pronounce them as such. I watch them very closely to determine exactly what's going on for them, what the true motives are for their behavior. Allergies, pain, metabolic issues, and many other factors can precipitate negative behaviors.

It is also the case that there some children who lie along the ASD continuum that are so *hypo*-sensitive (*under* sensitive) to touch, for instance, that they want, and need, to slam, bang, crunch things just to feel something, anything. These kids may *appear* to behave in an inconsiderate, aggressive, violent manner. While they are capable of hurting others in this state, they are not expressing anger but merely acting out their own hypo-sensitivity. While their behavior is inappropriate and must be curtailed, it's important to recognize that their motive is not anger.

Spitting is usually an angry gesture in non-ASD school-age children, but ASD children may spit at someone who feels threatening to them, has perhaps invaded their personal space in some way. Though spitting is never a socially appropriate behavior, and ASD children need to learn alternative ways to communicate, chances are they didn't spit in anger.

Some children's bodies need to express excitement physically, and rocking is a common way of achieving this. Hayden rocks when he's excited, sometimes quite violently. It's not always socially appropriate, and may not be safe in a crowd, but generally rocking is a rather benign way of expressing excitement. It's another story altogether when excitement is expressed through the jaws! For ASD kids, biting—usually an angry behavior—is not triggered by anger, but by excitement. Again, it's not socially appropriate, but neither are scolding, punishing, or the admonition "Don't bite!" when directed towards ASD kids. Telling a child whose jaw is where excitement is expressed not to bite is tantamount to ordering a non-ASD person who's been ordered to stand directly facing the sun, eyes open, on a midsummer day, not to squint! Biting may be dangerous, inappropriate and ultimately intolerable, but it's not always motivated by anger, especially in ASD kids.

For me, working with tacit rules has been very effective in eliminating negative behavior because at the very outset I make Hayden aware of his behavior and give verbal expression to his feelings, which are based on his perception that his rules have been broken. Once this awareness is created and verbally expressed, Hayden's need to act out has been eliminated. If I assumed anger or any other feeling is present when it is not, Hayden would feel confused, unheard, and distrustful, and so would become more angry, turning my endeavor into a fiasco.

If I tell a child he's mad and he accepts it, I've made him dependent on me and my opinions of him. All children, not just ASD kids, need to listen to their own beings' internal messages, not to someone else, to learn who they are. Their behavior may, at any given time, be reactive in nature, which is to say, they may not be consciously aware of what their bodies are doing. When I name Hayden's behavior by describing it in a neutral way, such as, "You're pushing me," "You're stomping your feet," or "You're turning your back to me," this helps him become aware of the bodily cues he's expressing. Yet, I have not named his behavior in a judgmental way.

One very young child I worked with had been acting aggressively towards his mom in what seemed to her to be at random times. What I noticed when I observed their interactions, however, was that the aggression occurred when things didn't go the way the little boy had wanted them to. After several sessions, I noticed that the child would react to his mom with hits, pushes, and bites–but then would glance at me, catch my eye, then stop the aggressive behavior. His Mom soon saw this pattern for herself. Hooray! We'd moved the behavior from the unconscious to the conscious. That's exactly what we had wanted to do, because that's the point at which change can take place.

If a child hits me, I respond by saying something like,

"I don't like to be hit, but thank you for telling me maybe you're mad at me."

If the child says "No," but I intuit that the hitting was done in anger, I might say,

"When I want to hit, I'm usually mad."

or

350

"People are usually mad when they hit."

or

"Why did you hit me, then?"

or

"You seem angry to me."

If nothing else comes from the child, I will end my side of the conversation with,

"Well, hitting for any reason is not appropriate, but I love you. If you were mad, I still love you."

In the case above that *seemed* to involve random acts of aggression, the little boy may not have known that he'd been mad. Or he may have known he'd been mad, but may have been afraid of losing adult love (care and protection). Or he may have been afraid of his anger and then pictured himself as some horrible monster. Whatever it was, if his mother brought it out into the open in a calm, matter-of-fact way; if an admission that even she feels angry sometimes is added to the narrative (along with an affirmation of her love for him; an acceptance of his anger as normal; an **un**emotional statement that his hitting is not appropriate); if she were to do all of this, perhaps her little boy might then have the time he needed to mull it over, while feeling safe, respected, empowered and loved. Then, perhaps the next time, or the time after that, he would feel safe and aware enough of his anger that he would be able to acknowledge it himself.

Dr. John Gray, author of *Men Are from Mars, Women Are from Venus*,[1] wrote another wonderful book called

---

1. Gray, John. *Men Are from Mars, Women Are from Venus: A Practical Guide for Improving Communication and Getting What You Want in Your Relationships.* HarperCollins, 1992.

What You Feel, You Can Heal.[1] This is very much akin to the principle I've been talking about all along. But I would make a slight adjustment: if children can feel it, then they can deal with it. Above all, we must remember that **kids are people too!** If they can 'feel their feelings'—identify them and have them accepted as such by the significant adults in their lives—then they can, ultimately, deal with them.

There's a dangerous myth prevalent in our culture right now that posits, in essence, that expressed anger is a bad thing, in fact, that all anger, even suppressed or repressed anger, is bad. As I see it, however, anger is neither moral nor immoral, good or bad. It just *is*. It springs from a natural impulse born of feeling hurt, threatened, unloved, or rejected. Anger expressed appropriately is safe, emotionally healthy, facilitates communication, and can even aid in the growth of relationships. Anger expressed inappropriately can destroy property, relationships, self-esteem, pets, humans and life, and anything else that gets in its way.

Repressed anger often manifests as the fear-based denial of anger. It sometimes sets the stage for destructive behaviors that will rear their ugly heads in the future. It can also be instrumental in configuring life-long patterns in peoples' behavior, such as being judgmental, critical, superior and intolerant. It may even lead to severe physical symptoms. Macabre daydreams, violent nightmares, perfectionism, insomnia, paranoia, claims of religious superiority (such as those made by followers of any brand of religious orthodoxy), are even more examples of such patterns that have their roots in anger pushed under and never acknowledged.

Consider the following scenario, one that's repeated every moment in our culture. It's a parable about repression and

1. Gray, John. *What You Feel, You Can Heal: A Guide for Enriching Relationships.* 2nd ed., Heart Publishing, 1993.

dishonesty...Linda is only three years old when Baby James, her first sibling, arrives in the household. She is just not ready to give up her status as the (one and only) baby in the family. She just doesn't want to give up even a second of all the attention she's been receiving. During Jamie's first year, after months of seething with jealousy and resentment over him, Linda says to her mother,

"I hate Jamie!"

Horrified, Linda's mother responds,

"You do not! You love him! He's your brother! I love him, Daddy loves him, and you love him. Don't you ever say that again!" Although Linda never again says that she hates her little brother, she continues to hate him, and consequently, she develops feelings of guilt for doing so and they begin to fester.

Jamie and Linda fight like cats and dogs through their school years, until his freshman year and her senior year of high school. Even then, Linda is angry that he exists because she is afraid, as she has always been, that he is going to be loved and she is not. The hate that Linda carries in her heart has become so big as to be nearly overwhelming and it eventually transmutes into the following model of low self-esteem:

"I'm a terrible person. I have always hated Jamie, even once I knew I wasn't supposed to. But no matter how hard I try not to hate him, I still hate all the same. This must mean I'm a terribly bad person. Why should anyone love such a person as me?"

If, as a three-year-old, Linda's feelings of hatred towards Jamie had been accepted and validated, then maybe she would have been able to process them and move on, and perhaps not have had such animosity towards him throughout their entire childhood together. Suppose this unfortunately typical scenario of sibling rivalry had been handled differently by Linda's mother? Let's go back to the first time Linda pronounced her hatred of newborn Jamie and hit the reset button...

"Mommy, I hate Jamie!" says aggrieved big-sister Linda, only three years old herself. Linda's mommy, who is holding and feeding her new baby responds, "Thank you for sharing your feelings with me. You know, I love Jamie and I love you. Even if you hate him, he still needs his bottle. Would you like to help me give it to him? Yes? Okay, you help me and when he's done I'll hold you and we can talk, if you want to."

or,

"...No? Okay, then you play while I feed him. When I'm done then I'll hold you and we can talk if you want to."

or,

"Okay, Linda. Jamie's done eating and is asleep, so why don't you come sit in my lap and I'll rock you. You sure are a special girl. I'm so glad you're my girl. I love you. You are such a lovely and loving little girl. I know there must be a problem if you hate Jamie. Do you want to tell me about it?"

In this new and improved scenario, the mom would then listen to whatever Linda had to say, accepting and validating everything. If Linda does not open up but just sits quietly, the mom would continue to hold her and rock her and would eventually ask,

"Are you scared that I love Jamie and not you?"

Remember, Linda is only three, and as a toddler, has begun to explore the world. Yet she still needs a solid base of support from which to do this. If her newborn brother gets all the attention, all the privileges, where will that leave her? Yes, she can do much more for herself than she used to, but the very real fear for Linda is that she will lose the mother love she still needs and desires. Let's go back to our scenario to see how Linda's fear can be allayed.

"You know, Linda, Jamie is a baby and needs lots of care, just like you did when you were a baby. When you were a baby, I held you and took care of you, just like I do now with Jamie. I love Jamie, but I love you too, just like before. My love is very, very big! I have enough love for you and Jamie. You needn't be scared. I will always love you. You are special; no one will take your place. When you need special loving, come tell me, and I'll hold you."

"Here, now, Linda, put your ear on my chest and listen. You'll hear my heart say, 'I love you, love you, love you, love you.' It always says that, all the time. When you need to, you can get on my lap and listen. It's okay if you hate Jamie, but you must not hurt him or say mean things to him. You can always come and talk to me about it. I will always love you and Jamie."

"I won't take care of you the same because you are not the same. I loved you as a baby when you were a baby. Now you are bigger—you are three! I love you as a three-year-old needs to be loved; I care for you as a three-year-old needs to be cared for. Jamie is a baby so I care for him as a baby needs to be cared for. When he is three I will take care of him as a three-year-old needs to be cared for. I will always love you just as much as I did when you were a baby, but I won't treat you like a baby, because you aren't one. I love you however you are."

In real life, I speak to kids the same way the mom has spoken to Linda above. What's more, kids generally comprehend and respond accordingly. I'm not afraid of their feelings, so I address what they feel, say and mean on the spot.

There is no question that new babies get lots of attention, care, and time, which can make their siblings feel left out, unimportant, unloved in the moment. This is when you must recall that young children live in the moment, so they must un-love back in kind. There is certainly irony in this, but it is crucial to see that when our kids are their most unlovable is when they most need our love.

As I am fond of saying, this is all very simple, but not at all easy. It takes focused time, attention, and consistency. If watching who jilts whom on a soap opera, or who wins what on a game show, is more important than listening to and really hearing what your child may be saying at that moment instead, your child will get the message loud and clear. And believe me, it's not the message you want to send!

Remember also that our thumb-sucking, diaper-clad gurus give us many opportunities to practice forgiveness and acceptance! Back in the day, when I was puked, pooped, and peed on by Hayden; when my walls were re-decorated, books scrawled upon, crystal shattered, sleep interrupted, make-up smeared, and juice spilled, did I feel irritation, acknowledge to myself my desire to strangle someone, yet still respond in kindness, love, acceptance, and forgiveness? Yes, I did, and so can you! Those of us who have kids or work with kids, have innumerable opportunities to practice forgiveness, and provide them with environments full of loving kindness.

By the way, do you know why priests, monks and nuns must meditate for hours a day and for years on end in order to gain spirituality? They don't have kids!

* * *

Generally, parents love their children as much as they can. But this doesn't mean that every child feels loved. Thomas Harris, in his groundbreaking *I'm OK, You're OK*,[1] claims that every child feels unloved at times. I suspect this is true. We can help our children feel loved—therefore lovable–if we validate and affirm them; listen actively to them; give of ourselves, with time and attention; make them our priority; discipline instead of punish them; truly understand that they are children; and finally, recognize that they are not ours to

1. Harris, Thomas A. *I'm Ok, You're Ok: A Practical Guide to Transactional Analysis.* , 1969. Print.

356

possess or control. They have only been loaned to us so that they can be reared and we can grow spiritually.

If we *ask* our children if they are mad or have a problem, instead of *tell* them they are or do, this will help build their feelings of personal empowerment and responsibility, as well their sense of autonomy. It's kind of like knocking on a door—a courtesy. For example, even if I know a friend is home, unless we have a prior agreement to the contrary or there is reason to suspect an emergency, I will not enter until invited. If we ask our children if they are troubled or angry, we have essentially knocked on their (emotional) doors. If they're too scared to open up, we need to accept that and build the security that will enable then to freely and willingly invite us in to their private and closely guarded emotional space where we can talk with them about their feelings.

My Protocol for Tacit Rules

- Understand that your child has very specific rules about almost everything.
- When you see signs of withdrawal, agitation, aggression, or violence, immediately look at what has just happened involving your child—literally from your child's point of view.
- Calmly note the behavior you see; suggest a range of feelings your child might be feeling: anger, fear, whatever it may be.
- If your child acknowledges feeling a certain way, don't take it personally because it's not the kind of mad that caused, for instance, Aunt Matilda not to speak to Cousin Mabel for twenty years. It's 'mud-pie madness,' nothing serious that will stick. It means most likely something like, "You did something I didn't like," or, "You didn't let me do what I wanted to do." Being mad back at you will be the strongest action your child will engage in for whatever you've done. If you were to take this madness personally, however, if you were to let it 'get

your goat' (push your buttons), you would be, in effect, handing your little one a way to punish you on a big, shiny silver platter; and I guarantee that you would see that anger crop up again.

Instead, all you need to do is smile warmly, then casually say, "Thank you for telling me you're mad at me. I love you even when you're mad at me. I'm not afraid of your madness. I'm not controlled by your madness. I don't feel guilty for your madness. I don't want to know why you're mad. You're such a loving child, I know there must be a problem if you're mad." If a child is prone to violence, you may have reason to fear the accompanying behavior, but not the accompanying feeling of fear.

- You can now ask of your child, "Do you have a rule that says I'm not supposed to do x, y, and z and that if I really loved you, I wouldn't?"
- If you've discerned the correct tacit rule under which your child has been operating, you can say, "Thank you for sharing with me that you have a rule that says I'm not supposed to do x, y, and z. Do you still want to be mad at me?" If the answer is, "Yes!" it's time to sing a 'Mad Song' at yourself for doing x, y, and z, until your child is finished processing the incident. If, on the other hand, you can't figure out why the anger has come up, validate it all the same.
- Then sing the 'Mad Song' at yourself, and sing it once more because you're supposed to know why and you don't.
- When the madness is over, sing the 'I Love You Song' and call it a day. It's over! For now...

When I use tacit rules this way with Hayden, I'm able to totally diffuse his frustration and anger and re-establish communication between us no matter what the situation. No disrespect or violence perpetrated, and it can all take as little as five minutes.

Suppose your child says, "No," to the question, "Would you like to talk about your feeling of madness?" At this point,

I would suggest you say, "Thank you for telling me that you do not want to talk about your madness but want to be mad instead. You may go to your room and be mad." I count screaming, rocking and stomping as permissible mad behaviors. I, personally, do not allow throwing things or tearing things up.

*One day, when Hayden was four, he was in his room being mad and I could hear that he was throwing things around. Horrified, I stopped what I was doing, centered myself, and entered his room calmly. I said firmly and without anger, "Throwing things is not appropriate; I do not allow it in this house. But thank you for telling me you are **very** mad at me. I will not allow you to throw things, but I love you. We need to pick these things up. I will help you." As we picked up the things that he had thrown, I said,*

"I can tell you are very, very, very mad at me, and you want to punish me by throwing things. But throwing things is not appropriate. I don't choose to be punished, so you cannot punish me. It takes two people to punish—one person to try to punish, and another person to accept the punishing. You can throw toys without my permission, but you cannot punish me without my permission. I don't choose to be punished. I love you. You think love will give you whatever you want, but that's not love. Love gives you what you need. You need to learn toys are only for playing, not throwing. I love you." I then talked about his feeling mad and we sang the 'Mad Song' at me.

Aggression and violence are never appropriate or acceptable. I know I've said this before, but it always bears repeating. When children partake in this kind of action, as far as I'm concerned they forfeit their right to choose not to talk about feelings. That is, they then must talk about their feelings. Hayden threw things just a few more times after the first incident, then once more as a 'tween. After that, it never happened again.

I can imagine that Hayden might someday start to throw things again, maybe if for some reason I stop encouraging talk about feelings. Frustration and anger are emotions, but they also have physiological components that must undergo a healthy physical release from the body. We can express feelings for non-verbal children as if we were them, and vicariously release them from their bodies. When Hayden indicates that he wants to be mad rather than talk about feelings, he goes to his room, since it's the place I have designated for mad behavior. I usually smile and say,

"Have a good time screaming. See how loud you can scream. Why don't you see if you can scream louder than you've ever screamed before? Have lots of fun! I'll check on you later." Usually he then shuts the door, sits on his bed, and screams bloody murder, which makes it sound like he's totally out of control–but he's not. When all is quiet, I knock on the door, open it, poke my head in and say cheerily, "Hi! Are you done being mad?" If not, I leave him to finish his madness. If so, I'll say, "Boy, I can tell you are very, very mad at me. You know what? You have a very good 'madder.' I don't have to worry about your 'madder' not working. It's important to have a good 'madder,' and you have a very good one. Now you must learn to be in charge of your 'madder,' so it doesn't do things you don't want to do or be in charge of you. Do you want some hugs?" He always does.

We may then go on to talk about the madness or sing The Mad Song.' But without exception, these sessions end in a bonding reconciliation between us. Hayden doesn't pout, withdraw, or punish, nor is he aggressive or violent. If there is unacknowledged or unprocessed anger, it will make its final curtain call at bedtime; he'll turn away from me when we lie down for the 'Quiet Song.' If this happens, we will talk about it again, briefly.

Once in a great while Hayden will go to sleep still mad at me, but not often. When this happens, though, I know the anger will surface again either when he wakes up the next morning, or remembers it later that day, or when a similar situation triggers the memory of it, the way my carrying the babies and toddlers reminded him that I will no longer carry him. When the anger finally dissipates, as evidenced by his smiling, touching, reestablishing eye contact with me, I'm ready to conclude the session. I validate verbally for him that it seems like love should let him have or do anything he wants and not make him do anything he doesn't want to do. Invariably he smiles and claps his unequivocal "Yes!"

This brings us back to the Toddler's Creed, and to Hayden's feelings. With the anger accepted, expressed, and dissipated, then and only then is he capable of hearing, receiving, and accepting any information that contradicts his original feelings. If I have processed everything according to the steps above, I can then calmly state that information (e.g., that it's inappropriate to throw things). Invariably, he accepts it.

My love for Hayden does not entail complying with his Toddler's Creed—not at all. I am no super-grandma who can ensure he won't ever get hurt by giving him everything he wants! Loving Hayden means, at least in part, not being trapped by his tacit rules, even if it feels to him like love means my following them to the word.

Hayden cannot understand love except in infant terms: an infant's wants and needs are the same, and an infant will love whoever meets those needs. Just as I can easily pick up a two-month-old baby and carry him to the store, I can easily validate Hayden and lead him to a feeling of love when he doesn't get his way. Hayden at twenty-seven years old and far taller than I am, is years, pounds, and inches beyond what I can handle physically. But with words, calm but firm words, and with an understanding of the concept of tacit rules, I manage to live peaceably side-by-side with him.

One final observation before we leave the topic of tacit rules. Generally speaking, parents will have as many tacit rules for their children as their children have for them. And parents always think their rules are perfectly logical because they are, for the most part, accepted by not only other family members, but by the culture as a whole. However, from the side of the fence that ASD children stand on, their parent's rules make no sense and may even seem mean. So once these kids have learned how to 'get their parents' respective goats'—in revenge for these mean, crazy rules—these very same rules will become weapons with which they will then punish their parents.

Let's look at car seats as an example. From the point of view of parents, they represent the safety of their children. From the point of view of most children, however, car seats are restrictive, boring, and of course mean and stupid. They afford no wiggle room! What's more, once strapped into them, there's nothing for children to do, stuck as they are in the back seat away from mom and dad, and therefore feeling alone and forgotten.

Parents think they're giving a solid rationale when they explain to their fussy, fidgety children that the purpose of a car seat is to keep them safe. But first graders would understand such an explanation about as well as they would algebra! Safety for toddlers and children with neurological issues is an experience not a concept; they would in fact feel far safer in the front seat beside a parent, or even in a parental lap.

Furthermore, the concept of a car accident is abstract to toddlers. When such children are subjected to car seats, it feels to them that their parents are just being plain old mean, especially if the children in question have a lot of tactile somatic issues, as many children with neurological problems do. Every time such children are strapped into car seats, whoever does the strapping is simply seen by the strap-ee as mean and withholding of love. It also means that somewhere along the line, such parents are due for a punishment.

Perhaps it's your very own tacit rule that your children stay in their car seats. Even when you get out to pump gas, you stretch, while your kids probably remain strapped into their automotive straightjackets! But one day they'll figure out how to get out of the pesky things, and *voilà*, they'll be free! Wheeeee!!!!! You'll be startled and frightened, so will probably respond emotionally. And by doing so, you'll be giving your kinds a sure-fire way to punish you. In fact, you'll have handed it to him on a silver platter! You had a rule–previously unspoken or maybe even spoken—and you felt threatened when it was broken, just as your kids feel threatened when their rules are broken. And you responded angrily–just as your child responds angrily in similar situations.

I'm certainly not suggesting that car seats be done away with! Hayden continued to ride in his long after I learned about his rule stating I was just mean when I put him in his because it was restrictive and boring. But it's not about *sticking* to kids' tacit rules, but about honoring kids by accepting the feelings that lead them to make such rules. In general I don't keep Hayden's rules, and I don't feel guilty when I break them. I do my best to understand his rules and help him through the feeling of vulnerability that follows when they're broken so that he feels respected as a person. If I am successful, he won't need to act out his frustration with how the world is through inappropriate behaviors.

Chapter 5

Punishment

Understanding the concept of punishment is an invaluable tool for managing behavior in children. Now, before you head my way with molten tar and a sack full of feathers, or dial up Child Protective Services, let me assure you that I am not talking about parents or other adults inflicting pain, guilt, or condemnation on children. Quite the opposite—absolutely not! What I am addressing here is how and why children inflict pain, guilt, and embarrassment on their parents and other adults. Do I have your full attention now? Let's explore this together.

Have you ever felt guilty about an interaction you've had with your child? What were you guilty of? Well, there's a good chance you were guilty of violating the Law of Love. If this is true, you were experiencing authentic guilt. When I violate the Law of Love with Hayden, I no doubt have been too preoccupied, busy, lazy, tired, grumpy, or hurried to *hear and respond to him appropriately and lovingly*. When I violate the Law of Love chances are that I've behaved in a less than loving way, regardless of the reason why, and I am guilty, and I simply need to apologize.

But what about those times you haven't violated the Law of Love, but you've felt guilty anyway? Your little Susan, for example, wanted a cookie before supper and you said, "Sorry, kiddo. It'll just ruin your appetite!" Susan cried, screamed, and whined, because she really wanted that cookie.

Another example: Marcie, your sixth grader, expressed the desire to wear makeup to school, and you simply said, "No, you're just not old enough, honey." She cried, she begged, she told you that all the other girls have already gotten to. Then she accused you of being nothing but an old fogey!

In these scenarios, did Susan or Marcie ever say, "You don't love me!" Did they ever hit you, have a temper tantrum, pout, or deliberately disobey you? Did they whine incessantly? These are all expressions of what I refer to as behavior meant to *punish*. I would also claim that the rationale for punishment is to get even: A does something B doesn't like, so, B does something A doesn't like. This is of course the scheme for simple, primitive retributive justice, or in language that goes back millennia, "An eye for an eye, a tooth for a tooth." This concept of justice fuels many behaviors of both children and adults alike and has for time immemorial.

The way it seems to me is that for toddlers, there's an element of innocence in this kind of punishment, a sort of cosmic justice intended to even things out, but not to inflict pain, guilt, or embarrassment. Though it looks like toddlers know that what they are doing is forbidden, they act as if they feel no guilt. All of the guilt, or so our little ones believe, belongs to the person who broke one of their tacit rules. They're just evening the score, keeping their world in balance. There is no malice in it, so they believe.

I also believe that when toddlers have their tacit rules violated, they respond in a *generic* way that can be characterized as follows: "I'm mad because I didn't get my way." Consequently, when scolded for their vengeful behavior, toddlers feel that the anger directed against them is undeserved.

Evening the score, to their toddler minds, is not the same as misbehaving.

Most often, however, the whole scenario escalates. Whereas before it was a case of, "You did something I didn't like, so I'll do something you don't like," it becomes, "You're mad at me, so I'll be mad at you," or "You did something mean to me, so I'll do something mean to you."

Thus, the pattern sets in. Every repetition adds momentum, adds anger, adds injustice, until the child's behavior is out of control and maybe the adult's is too. In the meantime, the toddler involved is inaccurately labeled as a belligerent, uncooperative, non-compliant child who is likely to become destructive, aggressive, and violent. It's all part of the toddler punishment cycle, commonly and erroneously referred to as the Terrible Twos!

In reality, though, it starts out as the Tremendously Terrific Twos. TTT toddlers are just becoming aware of their separateness from the significant adults in their lives. They feel free and totally loveable, and behave as if they believe that it's their GOD-given responsibility to explore everything, taste everything, feel everything, try everything, do everything, experience everything. The world loves them and is loved by them; it is their oyster. They feel invincible so plunge in, ready to discover and conquer life.

What TTT toddlers often encounter from their parents, however, is, "No!" "Don't!" "Stop!" "That was bad–don't do that again!" And all too often, a few slaps are thrown in for good measure, which triggers a cycle of retaliation between toddlers and their parents where all parties are locked in place on a 'not-so-merry' merry-go-round. All become dizzy as the swirl of it all accelerates and the whole enterprise gains in intensity. Once the child's justice cycle is complete, the adult's justice cycle begins, and when the adult's justice cycle is complete, the cycle begins again for the child.

In the end, sadly, TTT children are conquered. Their parents are bigger, for one thing, and they have the power not only to hurt their children, but to withhold love and protection. It feels, to our TTT kids, that they've been caught in a life-or-death struggle. Probably, by their third birthday they will have conceded defeat and learned the following: It's my responsibility to be good and do what they say. And I must make them happy so they'll love me and not hurt me. I can't explore much. I can't taste much. I can't feel much. I can't try much. I can't do much. I can't experience much. I must be good, so that they will love me.

This is how we break the will of the toddlers in our lives. Though they most likely tested high in creativity to start, they test low in creativity by the time they enter kindergarten, even though they may have started off with left hemispheres undergoing miraculous, exponential growth, as they began to figure out the logic of the world, to understand cause and effect, and to find their places in society. But soon they realized, though, that they jolly well better fit themselves into the families and society's round holes, even if they are a square, triangular, or trapezoidal peg, a totally unique being.

Kids with autism never have the advantage of possessing a developed left hemisphere, which is why they retain the primitive, eye-for-an-eye concept of justice, and faithfully, as mandated by the Preamble to Constitution, attempt to adjudicate every struggle in accordance with simple retributive justice. If you think autism looks grim from your side of the fence, mercifully, you can't even comprehend what it looks from the other (autistic) side.

Punishment, as I understand it, is a two-sided coin, entailing a punisher and an acceptor of punishment; it is based on the assumption that someone is guilty and someone is innocent. In Transactional Analysis, for example, in order for punishment to occur someone must be in the Child Position and someone else must be in the Parent Position.

But suppose instead I stay centered in my spiritual nature, my 'I-am-ness,' as the adult. I neither accept punishment nor do I dole it out. I view behavior as language, and I respond to the message behind the behavior, rather than the behavior itself. Because I don't accept punishment or guilt, I feel no anger. I simply do not take part in my toddler's eye-for-an-eye, anger-for-anger form of justice.

With this in mind, let's look at the incident of Hayden's first foray into the dishwasher. I had been on the phone too long, whatever counted as too long for him, so I'd broken his tacit rule: "I'm not supposed to talk on the phone too long, and if I loved him, I wouldn't." It didn't matter, of course, that I had never agreed to conform to this rule.

Recall that Hayden lives by the Toddler's Creed, one corollary of which is: "If I want it, it's mine and if she loves me she'll give it to me." His translation for the dishwasher scenario is: "If I don't want her to talk on the phone she shouldn't." Now, this is a very right-hemisphere, feeling-centered stance, and though he was already five or six at the time, Hayden's left hemisphere was still in the cradle. From this perspective I was guilty because I had broken his tacit rule. I had done something he didn't want me to do, so I didn't love him. Since he has a right to be loved no matter what, I was the guilty party. Further, Hayden's sense of justice (eye for an eye), dictated that he must do something to not love me back. Consequently, he opened the dishwasher and played with its contents. At the time, this had seemed like a fair, even exchange to him.

But why had Hayden chosen the dishwasher? Because I had unwittingly set him up to do so! One day, as he was exploring and experiencing his world, the dishwasher happened to be in that world. And so, he had opened it. "Wow, what cool stuff's in there! Look at what I just did!" is probably something very close to what he had said to himself.

But when I found him playing with things in the dishwasher, images of sharp knives and broken glass dripping with blood came up for me, so I had responded emotionally with, "Hayden, no, you cannot play in the dishwasher. It's not safe! Dishwashers are not for kids!"

Now at the time, I didn't validate a single thing for Hayden. Sad but true, there had been no, "What a smart boy! You figured out how to open that tricky little catch and look inside!" I just hadn't caught on yet, and so I got myself caught up!

Hayden immediately filed my harried response under 'How to Get Grandma's Goat,' with the subtitle: 'Ways to Punish Grandma.' Then at a later time, namely, when I was on the phone too long as described just above, he attempted to punish me by playing in the dishwasher. When I came upon him doing just this, I took the bait and for all my trouble, was indeed punished. I said, with a great deal of irritation, "What are you doing playing in the dishwasher when I've told you..." Hayden's little hint of a smile, along with the very direct look he gave me, stopped me stone cold. I wondered what was going on. What was he saying to me with that look and smile? Then I knew "Ha-Ha! I got you! Now we're even!" is what he was saying. His face was full of it, so much so that words were unnecessary. I had been on the phone and he didn't like it, so he was mad; he was in the dishwasher and I didn't like it, so I was mad.

From Hayden's point of view, we were now even. Justice had been done. Mission accomplished! And I realized at the time that my scolding him would have just begun another cycle of his getting mad and then punishing me for it. How many times had he already successfully used the dishwasher as punishment? Several, I'm sure, as he had been into it a number of times previous to this one.

Of crucial importance for me in this incident, was that the point at which I recognized and accepted Hayden's behavior as a kind of language was the same point at which I had the power to break the cycle. I could have accomplished this by dealing with the feelings behind what he had done. If I had the ability to scroll back in time to this point, I would say to him something like, "Are you trying to punish me for talking on the phone too long by playing in the dishwasher?" He would no doubt have laughed and clapped and squealed his validation of what I had already known. Then, it would have been my chance to say, nonchalantly, "The dishwasher is not for play, but thank you for letting me know that you're mad at me. No, the dishwasher is not for play, but I love you. If you want to be mad, you can go to your room and be mad. When I'm done on the phone we can work on your madness if you want to. I love you when you're mad and I love you when you're not mad. I just love you!"

I don't remember if Hayden went to his room and had an all-out temper tantrum that first time with the dishwasher. What I do remember is that he tested me again about a week later, by getting into the dishwasher when I was on the phone. I said what I had to say to him, with a low-key, non-attached, unemotional tone and he never again got into the dishwasher.

Looking back, I believe that had I gotten off the phone when he was in the dishwasher, I would have in effect rewarded Hayden's inappropriate behavior by allowing it to get him what he wanted. I now know that any time we reward inappropriate behavior by giving children what they want, we inadvertently purchase—with an emotional credit card—a guarantee that the behavior will be repeated. I may get what I want in the moment—compliance—but the bill will always come. And the interest is exorbitant!

Why did Hayden stop this behavior altogether? Behavior always occurs for a reason, usually for the desired pay-off. With the first foray into the dishwasher, it was exploration, but he soon learned he could 'get my goat' by doing it, so he did it when he wanted to punish me. But, when I took back my personal power and did not let his behavior elicit a reaction from me, there was no longer any payoff for his deliberate disobedience. So it stopped.

If kids don't get what they want and feel unloved as a result, the way for them to save face is to punish their parents, to make us feel unloved too. When I let Hayden 'get my goat,' he will punish me by not loving me, his inappropriate behavior is rewarded, and this pattern will recur. This is exactly what a temper tantrum is. When Hayden used to have them, I imagined he was saying to himself something like,

"Maybe I can be obnoxious enough to force her to change her mind and prove that she loves me. If not, I can at least be obnoxious enough to 'get her goat,' get a rise out of her, embarrass her, inconvenience her, scare her, hurt her, and make her feel unloved back, or at least make her mad."

It is my contention that no one *has* to play this game. By accepting that this behavior is telling us something, then figuring out what that is, we can then validate the feeling(s) that triggered the unwanted behavior in the first place and therefore make the behavior, ultimately, a moot point.

If we understand the concept of punishment as I have put forth here, and accept behavior as language, this does not mean that negative behaviors must be accepted. On the contrary, quite the opposite is true. By looking *beyond negative behavior* to what it's saying and then responding to *that*, the lifeline to the negative behavior is cut off. What every kid really wants is to be respected, heard, and validated—to feel loved. If children can't have that, the only thing left for them is the empty solace of: "At least I 'got her goat' and made her feel unloved." In the end, though, their first choice is to have the love, that wonderful, glorious unconditional love.

Intuitively, children know they are created for love, to be the object of this very special affection. But at first, they misunderstand this love and feel that it should get them whatever they want in the moment. When they don't get what they want, they feel unloved. This, to their very young minds, is 'unjust' in a primitive sense of the word. Further, if they can't have love, they go for justice. But justice is an empty solution: it doesn't satisfy and it fosters insecurity. In the end, it all gets down to the basic tenet that children need to learn that they are not in control. A corollary to this is that they simply cannot have everything they want, and they cannot be hurtful or destructive just because they want to be.

On the other side of this coin is that children must be heard because their feelings are valid, and they are loved— completely, irrevocably—for who they are. Think of it this way: If children were to consistently receive the unconditional love that is their birthright, they would no longer need justice.

The more we validate the children in our lives— understand their behavior, acknowledge their problems, sense their feelings, accept them for who they are, express our love for them in words that demonstrate our respect for them—the less they will feel the need to resort to punishment through deliberate disobedience.

Chapter 6

Communication: A Deeper Understanding

A speech teacher once told me that 93% of all communication is nonverbal. If this is true, then Hayden gets an A+ in communication! The problem is not that our ASD children have no means of communication, but rather we as adults are illiterate in their language. That language is primarily behavioral in nature, though they often understand our verbal language and are always fluent in our nonverbal means of communication, such as body language.

When he was younger, I had reason to believe that Hayden also saw auras, which would have broadened his receptive communication skills in a most unusual way. I don't know if this is typical of children with autism or other neurological challenges, and if it just boils down to the ability to read body language and determine someone's mood extraordinarily quickly and accurately. What I do know is that the following seems to be true of communication in general:

- When we are with other people we communicate continuously, albeit sometimes unaware that we are often not communicating what we think we are.
- We often communicate what we don't mean to communicate and may not want to communicate.

- We sometimes may not even be aware that we are communicating, when in fact we are.

And that's only half the picture. We are also communication receiving communication, often not what was intended to be communicated, or is known or desired to be communicated, by other people.

These communication chasms often exist between those non-ASD people who are intelligent, verbal, mature, neurologically sound adults. Are you beginning to comprehend the astronomical scope of communication barriers that can develop between the above otherwise 'good communicator' and the ASD person who is non-verbal, socially oblivious, developmentally immature, neurologically challenged and emotionally keyed-up? I hope I've made my point!

Making sense of communication that originates from your special needs child is challenging, but possible and rewarding. Perhaps the most difficult part is breaking through the socio-cultural-educational barrier that focuses on oral language, sign language, and the use of pictures as the only acceptable means of communicating because that's what we adults understand. If we stick to these as our only means of getting through to and receiving communication from the ASD people in our lives, we are bound to have tremendous difficulty, because in so doing, we will modify away their behavior. But behavior is the native tongue, as it were, of our special needs people. If we do not acknowledge this, we doom ourselves and our special needs children to the dark, silent, and frustrating existence of failed communication.

Please understand that this is not a put-down of formal communication. However, I know that right now, today, without competence in any of the skills mentioned above, Hayden is able to communicate most of his feelings and some of his wants and needs, if and when I am open, receptive, and I listen actively to all of his behavior. It is not true that our children don't communicate but we do. Nor is it true that we could communicate if only they would learn speech or signing. We all communicate, parents and their special needs kids alike.

Without a doubt, our children read our behavior far better than we do theirs. And they understand our spoken language infinitely better than we think they do. If we see behavior as a kind of language, we can bridge the communication gap to our special needs children. Moreover, when we express feelings for them, as I do with the endless formulations of 'Mad Songs' I sing to Hayden, not only do we communicate that we understand, accept, and love them, but we relieve their communication stress. Furthermore, if we also use our words to talk to the ASD people in our lives with language as well, it makes them aware of our interest in them, our acceptance of them as intelligent, worthwhile human beings. It is said that solitary confinement is the most severe form of punishment. How often do our children—non-ASD and ASD alike—feel the loneliness of isolation at home, school, and in the community because no one bothers to talk to them? Not talking to children, regardless of how much or little they actually comprehend, communicates disinterest and non-acceptance. And worst of all, it devalues them. It is almost as if they are…invisible.

I've been to numerous appointments for Hayden with physicians who never spoke a single word to him, never acknowledged him as a person. I know how hurtful this is to him. After one such appointment, Hayden returned to the car, got in, and just sat there, very subdued, with a thumb in his mouth and his head hung low. He was the very picture of sadness and dejection.

"You seem awfully quiet," I remember saying. "Do you want to talk?" His pinky waved "Yes!", while his thumb stayed in his mouth.

"Was there a problem for you at Dr. Peterson's?"

His pinky waved, "Yes!"

"Did you like Dr. Peterson?"

Angry sounds meant a resounding, "No!"

"You didn't like Dr. Peterson...Are you mad at Dr. Peterson?" I asked.

More angry sounds...

"So you are mad at Dr. Peterson? Did it seem like he didn't respect you?"

Yet more angry sounds.

"He didn't talk to you or pay any attention to you and you felt unimportant?" Again, angry sounds.

"I'm sorry he didn't respect you. Would you like to be mad at Dr. Peterson?"

"Definitely!"

So we sang the 'Mad Song' at Dr. Peterson several times and Hayden grew more alert and animated, even started to laugh.

"It seemed to me, too," I said, "that he didn't respect you. I'm sorry he didn't respect you. I'm sorry for him that he didn't get to know what a neat kid you are. He doesn't have autism, but he does have a disability about loving, so you both have things you need to work on, just like I do and everybody else does. I'm sorry I took you to someone who didn't respect you. I promise you don't have to go back Doctor Grouchy. Will you forgive me for taking you?" He forgave me that time.

But sometimes, he doesn't! When that happen, I say to him, "Thank you for letting me know that you feel so bad about going to Doctor Grouchy that you can't forgive me for taking you to him. That's okay. I love you anyway...Are you mad at me?"

"Yes!" he would likely respond.

"Do you want to continue to be mad at me?"

"Of course!" he probably would let me know.

I'd then sing the 'Mad Song' at me for taking him to Doctor Grouchy and include something about how the doctor didn't respect Hayden. In fact, I'd probably need to sing the 'Mad Song' several times in such a situation.

If Hayden feels especially put down, maybe we'd have to sing about his wanting to punish me. The general idea is that I would continue to validate his feelings until he laughs and relates well again. Then I would sing the 'I Love You Song' until his self-esteem is reestablished. I may even need to apologize several times to Hayden for taking him to a Doctor Grouchy, but if I find I need to repeat all of the above, I would probably add the second time through that the doctor was recommended by someone and I had no idea that he would act as he did. I would also reiterate that to me, the doctor didn't seem respectful either.

Lastly, perhaps I would have to reassure Hayden once again that he wouldn't ever have to go back to this doctor. Most likely, Hayden will forgive me after I have offered such a thorough apology twice. Until now, at age twenty-seven, he's always forgiven me after a second apology. But if he were to say "No," again, my response would be a little different the third time around. It would go something like this:

"Thank you for sharing that you're still mad at me. Maybe you want to keep your madness for a while. You can keep it until you're a hundred if you want. I will love you anyway. I'll check with you later and see if it's making you feel yucky and you want to get rid of it." When Hayden no longer needs to be mad at me, I sing the 'I Love You Song' and it will be over. He reaches for his tape player and there wouldn't even be residual pouting or withdrawal. He'd be ready to listen to his music and get on with life.

All children appreciate when they're talked to and heard. There's a saying: "Talk is cheap." I would agree! Talking to our kids is one inexpensive, convenient, social activity we can engage in often throughout the day. If it doesn't appear to you that your children are listening, think again. They most likely are. Remember the case of Hayden in church?!

* * *

In the movie *A Beautiful Mind*,[1] John, the lead character, gives his wife a crystal for her birthday. He reminisces with her about a time when they had been together in an art gallery and she had exclaimed, in wonderment, that there were colors everywhere. She says in response that she didn't think he had been listening to her. His reply to this is so telling: "I always listen."

Our kids always listen. Our verbal communication with our kids needs to be authentic and clear, and it must be delivered in a calm manner if we want to minimize frustration for them and ourselves. If we feel one thing but do or say something else, our kids will know. For example, if I were to say "Yes" to something that I'm not really comfortable with in an attempt to avoid a scene, Hayden would definitely pick this up. In fact, he'd hear "Yes" with his ears and "No" with his intuition. And this would make him feel extremely uneasy.

Yet another example comes to mind. If I were to say "Yes" or "No" from a feeling of guilt in response to something that Hayden wanted to do or have, he'd pick up on that. Truth be told, he would in addition learn a way to punish or control me by using that guilt against me.

Another kind of situation has also occurred. If I were said "Yes" or "No" to something, and then not follow through, if I just did not stick to my word, Hayden would see right

---

1. Grazer, Brian, et al. *A Beautiful Mind*. Willowdale, Ont: Distributed by Universal Studios Canada, 2002.

380

through me and judge me as untrustworthy; he would then ignore me at a later time. A concrete example would be if I said "No" to something he wants to have or do, and he begins to scream and become aggressive or violent. Then, suppose that I concede and change my answer to "Yes," because of his horrible reaction to "No." On the one hand, Hayden would feel uneasy because he would sense the ambivalence in me and that makes his world feel insecure. On the other hand, however, he would feel some measure of control in his certainty that behavior that's violent or aggressive, such as screaming, is a way to get what he wants.

With children, I hold to one immutable rule: the only things I will give to a child who cries or screams in anger are, no more and no less, the following: validation, an attitude of detachment, and a calm countenance. If it were otherwise, if I were to give a child something they wanted in order to stop an outburst and end my embarrassment and inconvenience, my reward would quickly turn to ashes, because my child would then resort to this very behavior whenever he wants something.

Because kids with neurological issues are especially adept at tuning out incoming stimuli (think of the tremendous survival value this skill holds for them), it's helpful to get their full attention before giving verbal instructions. However, when it seems that you're being ignored, it may well be that your child is in the process of tuning out the whole world. This happens for ASD kids when they're exposed to a hugely overwhelming (for them) amount of sensory input, in which case, they completely shut down.

There are ways, however, to help ASD children avoid this kind of extreme sensory shut-down. Parents or life-guides—you can help your children practice selective attention so they can at least hear what you have to say. For example, use your child's name; speak clearly and firmly; perhaps even insert yourself into your child's field of vision; or use non-threatening touch that you know your child can tolerate. Encourage your child to focus on your voice. Some kids need one-step-at-a-time directions, not because they are non-compliant or stupid, but because they literally can only process one step at a time.

Although Hayden took his first step alone at four years old, a few more years passed before his walking became fully functional. The summer he was six, we started to visit parks. Because he had begun to develop the kind of wanderlust typical for that age, and had the balance to support it, he would just take off and walk away all on his own. Just imagine the panic I felt! But I quickly discovered that yelling for Hayden to come back was an exercise in complete and utter futility. For one thing, he probably was unable to hear me. But even if he did hear me, he wouldn't have responded with an about-face and a walk directly back to me. He certainly had the *physical* means to do this: he got out there, so I knew he could get back. What he lacked was the logical thought necessary to initiate this kind of behavior.

I know it seems easy: "All he has to do is *come back*, for goodness sake!" But that requires logic and a mind that can think sequentially: "I want to go back, so I need to stop my forward motion, then turn around; then I walk back."

No, you and I don't think this way consciously; we just process logic and sequential information rapidly. But kids with neurological impairments often lack such ability. Hayden, however, was able to learn, one-step-at-a-time, what I meant and what to do when I said, "Stop and come back." When I say one step at a time, though, I mean that literally.

First, Hayden learned "Stop!" This is how:

- I held his hand and we walked forward.
- I said "Stop."

- I stopped walking.
- I physically stopped Hayden from any further progress.
- We did this over and over and over again, until eventually, I could let go of his hand, say "stop," and Hayden stopped on his own.
- "Thank you! Now turn around," I said, and then taught him the next concept in this complex command.

Finally, and in similar fashion, I taught Hayden what to do when I said, "Turn around." When we got to "Hayden, come back," he would very willingly come back to where I was.

If this seems like a lot of work, let me tell you, it was! But isn't a 24/7 marathon on the run after a 'non-compliant' child a lot of work? And when we assume that a child cannot learn something, we cheat everyone, don't we? Some kids need one-step-at-a-time directions, as did Hayden. Others need directions to be frequently repeated. And still others may need quiet time to process a direction before being able to accomplish it. For the latter, repeated directions would only interrupt their processing so they would have to start over each time they heard the direction. Other kids can process directions quite easily. When I came to understand that there are different ways to process, this helped me evaluate what and how my child understands or does not understand, which made it so much easier to know how to help him.

Music is the language of the right hemisphere; putting things to music is often a very effective way to connect with all of our children, especially those on with ASD. the 'Mad Song' is a great example. Much of the physical therapy Hayden and I did at home when he was much younger we did to music. I frequently used 'The Farmer in the Dell' tune, but any tune you know or even make up will work, especially if it's one your child is already acquainted with.

Years ago, in order to help Hayden learn how to crawl, I would position myself over him on my hands and knees, and move his arms and legs along beneath me as we sang,

We crawl hands and knees.
We crawl hands and knees.
Hi ho the derry-oh,
We crawl hand and knees.

When it came time for him to focus on taking his first steps, I would serenade him with, "Walking, Walking, Walking, Walking," a catchy tune from Hap Palmer's Baby Song *video series[1]. Even now, with Hayden in his mid-twenties, I still use music to help him connect to things in his world. One of Hap Palmer's* Baby Songs *videos includes the number, 'Hurry Worry Blues,'[2] which tells the story of a father who gets caught up in utter chaos as he tries to get his three children off to school in the morning. One morning in our life, I was behind in our schedule and about to be late for an appointment; I felt very pressured but tried not to hurry. Hayden, in the meantime, was oblivious to my state of panic. He didn't seem to feel any pressure whatsoever! In fact, Hayden moved at the same rate he always does –KOS (Kind Of Slowly). When they were passing out the* hurry gene, *he must have been absent*

Hayden did, however, sense my irritation, my nervousness, so he was quiet, even somber, when we finally made it to the car. He knew I was upset, but had no idea why. I apologized for my grouchy, crabby mood and confessed that I was just trying to hurry so we wouldn't be late. I added that I was not mad at him and that he had done nothing wrong. This lightened him for up a bit, but shortly thereafter, the light went

---

1. Palmer, Hap. "Walking." *Peek-A-Boo*, 1990.
2. Palmer, Hap. "Hurry Up Blues." *Baby Songs- Silly Songs*, Anchor Bay, 2001.

out again. This made it clear he still did not fully comprehend my upset-ness.

As it so happened, Hayden and I had been through this kind of scenario many times before, and my explanations, pretty much identical to what I offered on the day in question, had never helped him understand that he was not at fault. This time, I realized I desperately needed a new strategy. Fortunately, one came to me as a brainstorm. It started with this question:

"Hayden, does it seem like I've got the hurry worry blues this morning?"

His face lit up with the satisfaction and excitement something long not understood brings when it's finally comprehended. Hayden laughed and squealed and rocked away. Then he gave me a huge hug. So I sang what I could remember of the Hurry, Worry Blues and he laughed and squealed all over again!

Hayden eventually reached the point when he no longer felt responsible for my feelings of anxiety, especially about our late arrivals at appointments. When he did, his tension simply melted away.

Now Hayden regards my incidents of the 'hurry worry blues' as one of my top-five personal issues! And now, when I feel hurried or want to hurry things up, and I can't get Hayden to move any faster than KOS, I'll share with him "I think I have the 'hurry worry blues,'" and we'll both laugh. This breaks the tension, which allows both of us to relax and get back to normal. In fact, whenever Hayden's subdued and I can't figure out why, I check my own frame of mind. More often than I like to admit, I'll realize that I'm in 'hurry-worry-blues' mode. Once I do, I know exactly what to do in order to reestablish normalcy for Hayden. Every coin has two sides, though! We have also come to acknowledge that sometimes Hayden gets the 'slow-poke blues!'

* * *

We must also always remember to acknowledge our children's activities:

"You put your pants on!"
"You're playing with your ball!"
"You brushed your teeth!"

Always compliment a job well done or a concerted effort made. In doing so, it is of course so important to understand that tasks that are simple for most of us may well be gargantuan for our special needs children. Anything is easy when you know how to do it, but hard when you don't. If children hear, "Oh, come on! It's easy!" when in fact it's hard for them, they'll think that either you don't understand them or that they're stupid, because here they are unable to do even the *easy* thing...

If you see your child having a difficult time doing something, remember that there's always room for validation, and no harm can come from it! So, you can validate what you see with something like:

"I can tell that's very hard for you, and you're really working on it. I'm proud of your hard work." Just saying this will make children more apt to try, try, and try again. They'll also feel that you understand what life is like for them.

Granting a desire verbally, if not in reality, is another way to validate your child. Hayden loves water in any form. In Washington State it shows up as rain, almost nonstop during the winter. I have a very clear memory of the days when Hayden use to get off the school bus and it would be raining cats, dogs and even a goat or two! At the same time, it was only in the forties, yet Hayden would just stand and stare at it. I came to know this meant he wanted to stay outside and play in it, splash in the puddles, and look up it, as it came down on him, and try to swallow some raindrops. Obviously, I couldn't let him play in mud puddles for hour on end, as he would have desired. But I could grant his desire in words with something like:

"It's really raining hard, isn't it? I can see you'd like to play it, wouldn't you?"

"Definitely!" was his immutable answer.

"You think it would be lots of fun to splash in the puddles and walk in the rain," I would acknowledge. "I know you like playing in the rain and sometimes when it's warm I let you do just that. But today it's too cold to play in the rain, even though you want to. So we'll have to go in the house, even if you don't want to. I can't let you play in the rain today because it might make you sick. But I love you!"

When Hayden was three, he finally learned how to crawl and truly enjoyed the freedom it afforded him. But then, of course, he discovered the cat box! Now, Hayden's greater-than-normal tactile sensitivity (manifested as a need to frequently touch things) in conjunction with what I thought of as a more-or-less normal need to have simple, down-time activities to engage in between home therapy sessions, led Denny and I to dream up Hayden's rice box and bean box. These were made from discarded plastic kiddie pools, one that we filled with rice and another with beans, all of which we purchased cheaply at the local big-box store. In this way, Hayden—who would step right in and sit among his beans or his rice—would be able to stimulate his sense of touch in at least two different ways. Consequently, it wasn't much of a stretch for Hayden to think that the kitty litter box was yet another such play station made up just for him!

For obvious reasons, it just wasn't possible to let Hayden play in the litter box, so I gave him the following house rule: "The cat box is only for the cats to do their duty in and play

387

in, if they want to." I got plenty of laughs with this rule, but as I had phrased it, it didn't single Hayden out the way "Hayden is not to play in the cat box," could have. Generally, an "Everybody Rule" is much less hurtful than a rule that singles out someone in particular.

Another one of my house rules is: couches are for sitting; and yet another: screaming out of madness belongs in a bedroom with the door shut. None of these rules refer to anyone in particular, that is, each is neutral with respect to reference. So it's understood they apply to everyone, even if they are directed (in my mind) toward one person in particular (!)

Several years ago, two young brothers I was taking to a ball game with Hayden started a raucous fight with each other in the back seat of my car. So I said, "Excuse me! What's happening in the back seat of this car?" The two boys looked at each other and one said, "We're having a fight! In our car, we're allowed to fight with each other."

"Oh. Well, then. I have a rule for this car. Everyone sits in his own seat with a seat-belt on; cars are meant for getting places safely. I also think a car ride is a good place and time for a talk or a story, some music, and a look outside at the pretty scenery." The ninja fighters stopped immediately and settled down quite nicely, thank you!

Frequently, house rules can be stated in the positive instead of the negative. "Don't jump on the couch!!" can be transposed, for example, into "Couches are for sitting." This type of direction works well for kids who are capable of some degree of cause-and-effect reasoning, but not for Hayden. If he were to jump on my couch I'd probably be ecstatic; unfortunately, jumping is still beyond him. But if he could jump and I saw him jumping on the couch, I would first validate with, "You're jumping on the couch," then add, "I don't like the couch to be jumped on. The trampoline is for jumping. Couches are for sitting."

Try as I might, though, I just couldn't find a positive statement about the cat box that held any meaning for Hayden. I tried, "The cat box is for the kitty cat to go potty in." But this was no deterrent to his playing in it–he was willing to share!

According to psychologists, the unconscious mind does not compute the negative, so if I were to say, "*Don't* jump on the couch" it would register as "*Jump* on the couch" to the unconscious mind. This is easily tested. Suppose I say to you, "Don't think about a purple cow." What do you suppose your mind will immediately think of? Well, a purple cow, right?

When I do workshops about autism, I tack a red circle made of poster board on the back wall. At the beginning of my talk, I say, "There are two important rules for this workshop. Number one: Do not make a circle with your thumb and index finger, as I am now showing you, and do not look at the red circle on the back wall." What do you think everybody does or at least wants to do immediately? The more we eliminate first-person directives and instructions phrased in the negative, the more happily compliant our children will be.

Suppose I come to your home for supper and the roast beef gravy is as lumpy as an old straw mattress. Then suppose you apologetically admit to it. Then after supper I say to you,

"Supper was very good, but the gravy was really lumpy."

How would you feel? Any different than if I said, "The gravy was very lumpy but supper was very good."

It's pretty clear that "but" softens what comes before it.

Similarly, If I say to a child, "I love you, but I don't have time to read you a story," the child will hear only that you don't have time, because the 'but' will have gone a long way towards negating your profession of love.

When I was first learning this communication skill I could never remember if the positive or negative statement should come first. So I would constantly repeat to myself, "The dinner was good, but the meat was dry," and "The meat was dry, but the dinner was good," to try to remember. Now that I'm a seasoned ASD life-guide, I know that it's the negative one, or the one the child doesn't want to hear,—"I'm not going to let you play outside in the rain," that goes first, because the positive "...but I love you" softens the negative that comes before.

I would venture to say that we have all been in grocery stores and heard toddlers scream while their parents exhort, in raised voices, "Stop that right now!" Now ask yourself, do the toddlers ever "stop right now"? Usually not, unless bribed with a treat. Whenever I witness a bribe of this sort occur, I have to work really hard to squelch my strong desire to protest, because I know I'm also about to witness a disaster!

How do I know this? Simple. Whenever you deliver to children a directive that you cannot or will not enforce, you teach them that they don't have to obey you. When you say to kids, "Stop crying now!" unless you're willing to gag them, you cannot enforce this demand, so you've effectively undermined your own parental authority.

No one wants their children to scream in stores. But if you just say, "Stop, now!" you will only, as per above, establish, at best, your lack of authority. And unfortunately, there's really only one way such a conversation can go. Children will scream even louder and parents will then do any or all of the following: yell, threaten, belittle, slap, or bribe some more. In the end, there will be two out-of-control, angry people in the store–one big, one small—instead of one.

Suppose parents threaten instead of bribe? There's an outside chance that this will stop a child's screams. Even so, both child and parent are still angry and hurt, so another outbreak is likely in the making. What if instead a parent says something like, "You're such a brat! I hate taking you anywhere!" This again will probably lead to another outburst from the child. Sadly, the same is true if a parent slaps the child in anger and embarrassment.

Frequently, once parents have exhausted most of the options above, there is a very high probability that they will finally resort to bribing their children. Though blissful quiet will ensue, both parents and children will be left with the sour taste of guilt and anger from the whole ghastly encounter. And this, of course, only sets the stage for more negative behavior to come. What's more, unwittingly—actually witlessly—parents do an excellent and extremely effective job of teaching their children the way to get what they want in a store: scream bloody murder and stage an all-out temper tantrum. This is true of all kids. And yes, it's especially true of ASD kids. Such children continue to experience limited logic and cause-and-effect reasoning long after the toddler years have come and gone. As a result, they keep formulating tacit rules that entail that things are supposed to be the way they were the 'first time', or the time they got what they wanted.

So, if you're not willing to gag your children to avoid the super-market-temper-tantrum but you need to get groceries all the same, what then? Give your child options rather than ultimatums that you can't enforce. My rule about Hayden's screaming, for example, is that he can scream whenever he wants (why not have this rule - its enforceable!), but only in designated places. At home, it's in his room; away from home, it's usually buckled in his seat in the car.

One Sunday at church, the front door of the building was open because it was warm out; but it was also raining. Hayden loves rain, as I've mentioned earlier, so he headed straight for it and out the door. He could only have been about five years old at the time and he was tantalized by what seemed like an excellent opportunity to indulge his love of mud-puddle play.

My first move, as I ran after him (kids can more really fast when they want something) was to validate by saying, "You'd like to play in the rain, and the door's open so it seems like you should be able to go out and play in the rain. But you have good clothes on, and you're to stay in church." I repeated this a number of times as I led him away from the door. However, he began to make his pre-scream sounds,

"Eh, eh, eh."

"I can tell you're mad," I said. "So if you want to scream, you may scream in the car. If you want to stay in the church, you'll have to choose not to scream."

"Eh, eh, eh," sounds continued and increased in volume. Then, Hayden began to scream.

My next move was to say, "If you want to scream, that's okay. You have the right to scream if you want to. But it's not appropriate to scream in church; nobody else wants to hear it. Have fun in the car when you scream, though! Scream as loud as you can. I'll check on you pretty soon." I then locked the car doors, went back inside the church, and stationed myself where I could see him.

I clearly recall the interesting epiphany I had that day. When people scream, it seemed to me, it's like they're actors— it's usually done for an audience. If there's no audience, then actors will not have much fun...

That was the only time I've ever put Hayden in the car to scream, though he's had that option a number of times. I'd need a calculator to keep a count of all the times he's gone to his room to scream. When he was very young, I carried him there. Once he became a walker, he took himself to his room for a good scream. Through all the tough toddler years, because he basically never got what he wanted at home via a cry or scream, it has not been an issue as he's grown up.

I certainly do remember when Hayden screamed at a Parent-to-Parent (P2P) potluck Christmas supper years ago. There was a piano in the foyer of the mini-mall where P2P had its office. Hayden really wanted to play that piano, but I chose not to stay in the entry way, and it felt unsafe for him to be there alone. So I brought him back into the office, and this triggered those tell-tale "Eh, eh, eh," noises, his prelude to a big scream.

Hayden was mad and I knew it, so though I felt a little embarrassed when I did it, I found a place to sit with Hayden and quietly sang the 'Mad Song' into his ear so we could process his anger. It worked! That was the closest he came to a scream in his car seat since the church incident. Present your children with options instead of ultimatums as a way to show respect for them as well as to others close by; meantime, your parental authority will be maintained.

As you might have guessed by now, I do believe in parental or adult authority. Let me rephrase that: I *strongly* believe in it. I do not believe in disrespect, physical abuse, or control through fear. I do believe that parents should be in charge, make decisions and call the shots. I also believe that all of this can be accomplished while parents and other adults respect the children in their lives.

When I'm with Hayden and any other kids who visit my house or go on road trips with us, I am very clearly the one in charge. But I do not yell, threaten, put down, demean or hit. I respect kids, ask for opinions and about preferences, give options, listen, and validate whenever possible. When I make the rules and the decisions, I expect to be obeyed; usually I am. When absolutely necessary, I use the 'One Minute Scolding,'[1] which I'll talk about in the upcoming chapter about discipline.

There are three concepts involved in communication that I want to say more about here. Although I've already spoken

---

1. Nelson, Gerald E. *The One-Minute Scolding: the Amazingly Effective Approach to Child Discipline.* Xlibris Corporation, 2009.

of them at great length throughout this book, they are perhaps the most important and most basic points I want to get across. As I see it, then, they deserve a bit more attention.

The picture in my mind is this: Appropriate behavior based on mutual respect is like a three-legged stool. When all three legs are solid, it is dependable and predictable, but if any one of the three legs is wobbly, the whole stool becomes precarious. I feel compelled to further develop this metaphor. The three legs of the parent's behavior stool are:

1. Communication skills: be impeccable in your language with your child.
2. Stay calm when you realize your child's out to 'get your goat'!
3. Validate your child whenever, wherever possible.

In order to be impeccable in your word you must say what you mean and mean what you say. This is of paramount importance when we communicate with any child, and even more so when we do so with a neurologically impaired little one.

For example, if you say "No!" to Johnny when he asks for candy, you must stick to that "No!" regardless of what he does. Be as impeccable with your child as you are with your boss or friends. When I am impeccable in my communication with Hayden his world becomes that much more stable, predictable, secure; this then gives him something substantial upon which to build his sense of what appropriate behavior consists of.

We've talked at length about the omission of action based on anger, guilt, blame, coercion, or embarrassment when we respond to our children. In other words, do not let your child 'push your buttons,' or 'get your goat,' because this will only set you up to be punished by them down the line. Always communicate with calmness, non-attachment, (as opposed to "detachment," which seems to connote total disinterest, or absence from consideration), and acceptance, for these relieve children of the terribly burdensome task of being responsible for the feelings of the important adults in their lives. In my case, when I communicate from a stance of non-attachment with Hayden, this eliminates the entire punishment cycle, and gives him the freedom to feel, think, explore, about who he is, without the risk of feeling unloved.

When we validate our children, they then can develop healthy self-images, positive self-esteem, and a deep sense of self-worth, because they are able to see all aspects of themselves reflected in an accepting way by the significant adults in their lives. When children are authentically validated, they no longer need to employ negative behaviors. When I communicate validation to Hayden, this allows him to feel love, acceptance, value, and the sense of a right to be here in this world. When we learn new ways to communicate, it's like learning a new language, which can make us feel overwhelmed and frustrated. It can similarly feel like a slow process, even as it feels possible. But the rewards of healthy communication are fun and empowering for both parent and child.

Chapter 7

Self-Esteem

The most extravagant, exciting, personal, exquisite, useful, durable, fulfilling gift we can give our children costs absolutely nothing—in dollars and cents—yet calls for everything we've got and more, in terms of time, energy, patience, understanding, openness, tolerance, sacrifice, prayer and love. This gift cannot be wrapped or unwrapped; it can only unfold from moment to moment, day by day, month after month, year upon year.

In addition, it 'fits' newborns and teenagers, as well as every age in between, and even beyond. And this gift will never tarnish, break, rust, mildew, get lost, wear out, be stolen or destroyed, dissolve, oxidize, or vaporize. It can empower, enliven, increase exponentially, be shared, rejuvenate and shine brighter as time goes on. This gift of self-image, which is comprised of the triad of self-worth, self-esteem and self-acceptance, cannot, in its totality, really be given in the traditional sense (remember, it cannot be wrapped or unwrapped). It can only be built over a period of time, specifically, a lifetime. The parts that can be given are the tools and our guidance in how to use them—the assembly directions!

Poor self-image has many faces. Some are socially inappropriate, some socially appropriate, and still others, socially admired. But all represent pain, shame, and guilt for the individual with a low self-image. Whether this person is surviving by drinking, drugging, abusing, stealing; or by perfectionism, charity, conformity; it all stems from the same source: feelings of being unloved, unwanted, unacceptable, and unimportant, to them self, their family, the world, and perhaps even their higher power. For example, it is, in our culture at least, more socially acceptable to be a perfectionistic workaholic than an abusing alcoholic. I think it is even safe to say that the former is revered and honored. But spiritually, the behaviors of both types of people—the extremely socially acceptable and the extremely socially unacceptable—stem from the same sources: the sense of being unloved and of little value, and the feelings of shame and self-hate.

I remember the first time I caught a glimpse of this in my own life. One day, after a friend and her children had spent the day at my house, I complained to Denny about her, and enumerated her shortcomings: she had not helped with lunch or clean-up, had done a poor job of managing her children's behavior, and had not respected our house rules. I think I told all of this to my therapist because I expected, maybe even wanted and needed, his validation of my righteous indignation; I believe I wanted him to sympathize with me.

But this was certainly a case not getting what I expected and wanted, because instead of a simpatico response, I got a wry comment regarding my judgmental, critical nature. I guess I didn't recognize my own anger, so I felt hurt criticized, misunderstood, and terribly unfaired-against. How could John say such a thing?

Children who grow up seldom feeling loved or loveable (I believe that every child feels this at times), end up seeing themselves as inferior, unlovable, undesirable, and inadequate. This often then leads them to spend their lives trying to earn love by being ultra-good, or the opposite, rebelling against anyone who doesn't love them the way they want to be loved. Poor self-image can contribute, as it turns out, to both negative behavior and over-achieving perfectionism. Very early in life, we all make an unconscious decision about ourselves, about our intrinsic worth and lovability. This is usually greatly influenced by the important people in their lives, together with life circumstances. For instance, children who bully, boast and brag are usually judgmental and condescending and more often than not see themselves as superior to others in every way. But this is just a way of covering up a poor self-image with bravado; yet, it is still a poor self-image.

On the other hand, those with positive self-esteem have healthy self-acceptance and a strong sense of self-worth. They commonly have no need to boast about themselves, criticize others, or feel inferior or superior to anyone. They recognize both the intrinsic value of everyone, as well as everyone's shadow side, including their own.

There are tools that can help us build self-esteem in our children, and there are others that will unwittingly undermine this effort. Let's look at some socially accepted saboteurs of our children's self-esteem. First, let's examine the following (very negative) practice: the use of 'you' messages that are often yelled, scolded, cause shame, consist of harsh critiques, boil down to name-calling, and are punishments, teases, and ridicules. These are all extremely effective ways of letting children know that they have little value. Parents and other adults often 'explain' such abusive behaviors by saying something like, "It's for their own good," or "They know I'm just kidding," or "I'm just having a little fun." But this kind of fun and kidding are so one-sided! It's never, ever good for children to be degraded.

What can we give our children to help them acquire a good foundation for building their positive self- image? The following are high on my list:

399

- Time
- Respect
- Attention
- Validation
- Active listening
- Understanding
- Compassion
- Empathy
- Affection, both physical and verbal: hugs, and terms of endearment
- Time for play and fun, not for the sake of competition, but just for fun
- Smiles
- Invitations to give their input on matters that affect them
- More affection
- Permission from non-verbal children to talk about them at appointments
- Requests to offer their opinion, and respect when they give it (which doesn't necessarily mean to act on it)
- Choices, whenever possible
- Let your first morning and last evening (as well as after school, after work, etc.) contacts be loving, fun and positive to set the tone for their feelings for the rest of the day. A gosling will form an attachment to whatever it first sees when it comes out of its shell, and will follow it around from that point on. In my mind, I see Hayden when he wakes up as a gosling coming out of his shell; I want to make sure the attitude he sees first is positive, pleasant, affirming, and loving because I want that to be with him all day.
- Affirmations of their strengths
- Notice of their efforts, even the clumsy ones…especially the clumsy ones!
- Acknowledgement of them as your teacher, as much as you're theirs
- Acceptance of their feelings without being controlled by them
- Explanations for what's happening, where you're going, with whom, and why

- Talk about everything and anything they want to know about
- Consistency
- Gentle guidance for appropriate behavior
- Acknowledgement for struggles, weaknesses and the humanness of all of this
- Laughter whenever possible
- Calmness, patience, reassurance
- Apologies when you goof and the explanation that no one's perfect; that everyone makes mistakes, even grownups
- Honesty
- When your child is within earshot, conversations with others about your child's strengths
- Permission to just be a kid
- Affection
- Even more affection
- Time to read to them
- Time to sing to/with them
- Time to talk matter-of-factly about autism, CP, Downs Syndrome, etc., whatever disability or condition they or others may have. They already know something is different, so if you try to shield them from it, you will give them the message that you are afraid or ashamed of it and them. And this will therefore make them feel fearful and ashamed of themselves.

My friend Pauline told me she'd finally arrived at the place where she could say, "I hate Down's Syndrome. I love Nathan." Kids need to feel they are separate from their disability. They can feel that way if we do and if we, in effect, model it for them. See them first as children, and they will see themselves first as children too. See them as their disability first, and they'll do that instead.

- Assumption of responsibility for some of the problems that come up for them, thereby relieving some of their burden. It isn't always their fault. There are two sides to everything, in the physical world at least. For example, if we try to hurry our children, they will probably want us to slow down. Try not to say, "Hurry up!" and instead say, "Maybe I'm going too fast for you." And, instead of, "You spilled your milk! Why can't you be more careful?" We could say "Maybe I put the milk too close to the edge of the table." Doing this helps relieve our kids of the terrible burden of incompetence. At the same time, it also has the effect of dethroning us and making us more accessible in their eyes, which is always a good thing.

- Empathy but not pity
- Compliments on their appearance. If you as a parents always focus on their disabilities, that's all you'll see after a while and they'll sense that. Then they'll focus on their disability as well. Remember Roger! If you notice his cute pug nose, beautiful silky hair, long eyelashes, winning smile, intense eyes and loving spirit, then he will see them, too.

What if the disability is mostly what you see? What if you just haven't been able to move beyond that? You have to start where you truly are in order to change things for the better when dealing with your children. Accept that you've learned to focus on the negative, and then you can consciously choose to re-educate yourself to look for the positive.

Years ago, I told John, my therapist, that if there were a picture composed of a million lights and one was out, it would probably be the only one I'd notice. My daughter told me a story from when she was young about an order I had given her to clean up her room. She said that she had in fact obeyed me, but that I scolded her nonetheless, and said her room was still a mess! When she had asked what was wrong, I had responded, "The bedspread is on upside down!" It was a kid's bedspread, age-appropriate, with her favorite cartoon character on it and a very definite right-up-orientation. Still, to not see all that she had done and only see the one little mistake she made—what a great example of focusing on the negative instead of the positive. And what a little crest-fallen little girl I had before me.

402

The questions I should have asked myself on this occasions with my daughter were: What about everything else she had done to clean up her room? What about all the things that were put away? But I simply did not see them. I had learned to notice only the negative.

If you have also learned to see only the negative, you can change. The reason I know this is that I have changed. Today, if I were to see a picture of a million lights and they were all on, except for one, I would notice the 999,999 lights that are on, marvel at that, and be unconcerned about the one that is not!

Early on in my journey through autism, a member of Hayden's team of professionals at one of Seattle's big hospitals asked me: "How do you manage to keep such a positive attitude?

"I just look for the positive aspect of everything and validate that." I responded.

"But what about things that have no positive aspect?" he queried, still unconvinced.

My response was, "I can find something positive in everything."

But this answer was met with skepticism by the doctor in question, who then asked. "What do you find positive about Hayden's unwillingness to hold onto something?" Hayden had extreme tactile sensitivity then and it was actually painful for him to hold something more than a few seconds.

"Plenty!" I answered, and went on to illustrate the positive way in which I could communicate with Hayden about this issue: "Look," I would say to Hayden, "you can drop things! You do a very good job with that. I'm proud of you. It's important to be able to hold on to things and to let go of them, and you've got half of it down perfectly. Now, all we have left to work on is how to hold on to something!"

Remember the Cookie Thief! We need to be able to accept, laugh about, relax with, and go to sleep in spite of our own goofs, shortcomings, and foibles. When we can, we'll more readily accept those of our children. In turn, they will—you guessed it—be able to accept, laugh about, relax with and go to sleep in spite of their own.

Chapter 8

Discipline

Several years ago I was asked by a first-time care-provider for Hayden, "What method of discipline do you use with Hayden?"

The question caught me totally off guard. For someone who could effortlessly talk all the legs off a centipede about Hayden and autism, I had an amazingly difficult time answering this question. As I searched my brain for something to say, I felt terribly confused, for one thing, and nearly overcome with misgivings about leaving Hayden with someone who would ask such a question. Lamely, I answered,

"I talk about feelings."

"Yes," she replied, "but what do you do for discipline?"

Feeling like a schoolgirl singled out to answer a simple, obvious question, I remained clueless, and even had a tinge of guilt, when I said,

"I guess I don't have a specific method of discipline."

"Do you use time out?" she asked, relentlessly. "No, I don't use time outs because Hayden doesn't understand cause and effect."

"Well, what do you do when he misbehaves?" she finally asked, coming right out with it.

"I don't expect him to misbehave and he usually doesn't, but if he does I talk about why."

405

"What if he has a problem with another child?" she asked as she continued her interrogation.

"If a child has a toy Hayden wants and he tries to take it, I say "Thank you, Hayden, for letting me know you want this toy, but Johnny had it first, so you'll have to wait your turn."

"What if there's a problem?" she asked, still unsatisfied with my answers.

"I'd talk about it" was all I could think of in the end.

By the close of this painful conversation, I felt wholly inadequate and incompetent because I didn't have a method of discipline in place for Hayden. At the same time, though, I wondered why I needed one. But one last question from the new caregiver cleared up my befuddlement:

"If there were to be a problem," she continued, "would you, say, take him away from the situation; like, to another room to play?"

I smiled and said, "Yes, of course," and thought to myself, "That's not discipline, that's common sense!"

People do not consider Hayden an undisciplined child. Quite the contrary, over and over I hear comments about how well-behaved he is. Yet, I couldn't not come up with a specific method of discipline for that caregiver. When I think back about it, I realize that even though I am cognizant of the fact that discipline is not the same as punishment, at a feeling level I perceive them as one and the same. This was why I heard the question as "What form of punishment do you use with Hayden?"

Several years have gone by since this incident with the caregiver, and here I am writing a book about my understanding of kids, autism, and the way I work with Hayden. Yet here I am again with the question of discipline. So I ask myself, "How do I discipline Hayden?" and I realize the question throws me back into a déjà vu. I still don't know how to answer, yet at least now I don't feel guilty, inadequate, or incompetent. Instead, the question seems inadequate, ambiguous and simplistic, and my authentic bottom line answer is really the same as it was so many years ago: The method of discipline I use with Hayden is my day-by-day, minute-by-minute relationship with him. That is the best, and the worst, definition of discipline I can give, rolled into one. It's the best, because that's exactly it: everything in this book is about discipline. And it's the worst, because it's so simplistic and ambiguous as to seem entirely unhelpful. Having acknowledged my definition and its shortcomings, I'm now ready to take a harder look at discipline.

You'll notice that discipline is the last item I have put on the map of my journey through autism. Far more often, people want to talk about discipline first. But talking about discipline before understanding kids and autism is like putting roads on a map before cities, mountains, streams, valleys, lakes, forests and plains have been noted. An arbitrarily drawn road might go through the middle of a lake, for instance, or across the most rugged mountain at its peak, and miss the population centers completely.

So it is with methods of discipline. They might be totally off course if they're considered first, before we take into account the neurological, psychological, emotional, and spiritual terrain of a child. Indeed, they might end up being impossible to implement, and could by-pass the child altogether. Once we have mapped the autism habitat, however, we are ready and able to consider a form of discipline that is relevant and effective.

Healthy discipline is not any of the following: to control by fear, to criticize, belittle, demean, scold, or punish. It's also not what I do when a child displeases me. It's not easy, convenient, controlling, rigid, or dogmatic. Nor is it an outlet for my frustration or anger or about rules and their enforcement. Furthermore, my discipline does not have as its goal a way to make perfect 'Stepford Children,'[1] nor is it away to break a child's will; or a way to treat children like pets, trophies, slaves, or a confusing mixture of all three.

No, healthy discipline is based on unconditional love, which is about listening and hearing; accepting and validating feelings; building up, praising, appreciating; openness, honesty, respect, and being respected; accountability and logical consequences, allowing a child to fall down and get up again without criticism or unnecessary interference.

Discipline is what happens in interaction with my child as I model the behaviors and attitudes I want to teach. It is fun...and infuriating; it needs to be consistent and carefully planned, but as flexible as a rubber band; it happens as part of life, in the moment; it's inconvenient, exasperating, and just plain hard work. It is also an exercise in creativity, adaptability and patience; it's about understanding and empathy; it's about a partnership with my child for his guidance, love, support, and self-actualization. It' s also about respecting my child as a full human being who has emotions, opinions, ideas, rights, responsibilities, strengths and weaknesses. Healthy discipline is about my getting out of the way and facilitating my child's growth.

We, as the guardians of children, exercise true discipline when we lead, teach, and model the behaviors we want to see them embody. If I want the child in my life to be respectful, kind, open, considerate, cooperative, honest, have integrity and show forgiveness, I need to model these behaviors at all times. Then, and only then, do I have the right to expect these behaviors from my child.

Children are like mirrors; they reflect back to us exactly what they perceive in us. If I, with my words, expound upon

---

1. Forbes, Bryan, et al. *The Stepford Wives.* Los Angeles, CA: Distributed by Columbia Pictures, 1975.

patience, but with my actions express impatience, then I will teach impatience and dishonesty and expose my own hypocrisy. If I promise that I will do something later, but later never arrives, I will teach a lack of integrity, how to placate, and dishonesty. If I profess love and behave harshly and critically, I will teach criticism. If I preach kindness and gentleness, but practice punishment and violence, I can expect aggression, violence, and distrust, either towards others or myself or both.

Again, if I criticize, belittle or condemn others for no reason, I will foster prejudice, teasing and humiliation, also for no reason. If my child hears me criticize my boss, my neighbor, or my spouse because they are different from me in some way, or have different viewpoints or beliefs, why am I then shocked and horrified when I witness my child humiliate another child who is different in some way? Our children behave in ways we teach them. The following poem, *Children Learn What They Live*, says it very well:

CHILDREN LEARN WHAT THEY LIVE
  If children live with criticism, they learn to condemn.
  If children live with hostility, they learn to fight.
  If children live with fear, they learn to be apprehensive.
  If children live with pity, they learn to feel sorry for themselves.
  If children live with ridicule, they learn to be shy.
  If children live with jealousy, they learn to feel envy.
  If children live with shame, they learn to feel guilty.
  If children live with encouragement, they learn confidence.
  If children live with tolerance, they learn patience.
  If children live with praise, they learn appreciation.
  If children live with acceptance, they learn to love.
  If children live with approval, they learn to like themselves.
  If children live with recognition, they learn it is good to have a goal.
  If children live with sharing, they learn generosity.

If children live with honesty, they learn truthfulness.
If children live with fairness, they learn justice.
If children live with kindness and consideration, they learn respect.
If children live with security, they learn to have faith in themselves and in those about them.
If children live with friendliness, they learn the world is a nice place in which to live.[1]

Dorothy Law Nolte

I have talked about the practice of validating our children throughout this book because of its utmost importance in helping them feel heard and respected. Truly validated children have positive self-esteem. Positive self-esteem is not egocentric, narcissistic, inconsiderate, rude, selfish, or unkind. It is healthy, a sign of normalcy. If children have healthy self-esteem, they accept others as equals, as valuable individuals to be treated with respect, consideration, and kindness, just as they have been treated. Fully validated children grow up to be truly validated adults who live in accordance with The Golden Rule, which is present in some form in every major religion. Validation of a child's feelings is positive discipline in action. Children who genuinely feel loved, respected, and accepted for who they are, will generally be respectful, cooperative and content.

Hayden is twenty-eight. Almost every time I ask him if he's mad at me, he'll say "Yes." Or, if I ask, "Does it seem like I don't love you?" he'll say, "Yes." Yet, he is affectionate, happy, obedient and well-behaved. When he sees me,

1. Excerpted from the book CHILDREN LEARN WHAT THEY LIVE
Copyright © 1998 by Dorothy Law Nolte and Rachel Harris
The poem "Children Learn What They Live"
Copyright © 1972 by Dorothy Law Nolte
Used by permission of Workman Publishing Co., Inc., New York
All Rights Reserved

his whole face lights up and he comes right to me and gives me a hug. He knows he is loved because he knows he can hate me, be mad at me, refuse to look at me, curse at me with his repertoire of obnoxious sounds, and even attempt to punish me. He knows he can do all of this, yet still be accepted, respected, and heard the same as when he shows he loves me.

Hayden also knows he will not necessarily get what he wants. He is free to feel unloved when things don't go his way, which makes him know he is loved, even when things don't go his way. It sounds like a paradox. It is. It is freedom, and freedom is a paradox because freedom isn't free. The price of freedom is responsibility.

If Hayden were not allowed the freedom to hate me and be mad at me, these negative feelings would be repressed, and eventually acted out in their counterpart negative behaviors, such as pouting, depression, and the refusal to be present and engaged. Because he is allowed the freedom to be mad at me, even to hate me, such feelings are free to express their messages.

When Hayden was quite young, he hit, pinched, scratched, and kicked me. He pulled my hair, kicked my car, threw various and sundry things around, got into my stuff, and screamed enough to blow the roof off of every house in the county! Through the years, I've been able to change these negative behaviors by making Hayden feel accepted; I've also encouraged him to express his feelings fully. And I have allowed him to express his negative behaviors in safe, somewhat contained ways.

Little children are totally honest, open, creative, and self-loving. But before we know it, these qualities are ridiculed, ignored, and punished away by adults who may preach honesty and openness, but live dishonestly and deceitfully. These adults may also give lip service to creativity, but bow to the god of conformity; they may extol the virtues of love, but live a life of control, criticism, and punishment and thereby set the stage for their children to conform to their adult world, whatever that is, and become what others want them to be instead.

Young children's feelings of anger, hate and un-lovedness are just based on whether or not they get what they want in the moment. When their parents respond with the punitive anger inherent in *shoulds* and *should-nots*, children learn to suppress, repress and deny their original feelings and desires. But the feelings do not magically disappear. They most certainly will resurface in some way sometime in the future. In fact, if parents respond childishly to their children—in hurt, fear, and guilt—their kids will learn that they have a weapon with which to punish and hurt the grownups in their lives, one that attaches to their parents, with a full guarantee of high returns and exorbitant interest. On the other hand, if parents instead remain centered in their 'I am-ness,' they would respond to their children calmly at all times with something like:

"Thank you for sharing your feelings with me. You are mad at me (or you hate me). Maybe you are mad at me because I won't let you play in the rain. I won't let you play in the rain, but I love you. Would you still like to be mad at me?" When we allow our children's feelings to be expressed, and we immediately accept and validate them, then it's over—no repression and no weapon of retaliation.

What children really need is to be heard and respected, and to know they are loved, even though they may not get everything they want. Young children are predominantly their feelings: they feel loved when their feelings are honored; they feel unloved, inferior, or bad when their feelings are ignored.

Children, especially very young children, feel unloved by their parents, even the best of parents, at times; this is normal, healthy and inevitable. It only becomes problematic when parents don't understand, acknowledge, or accept it. There are several reasons why young children may feel unloved by their parents:

- Babies and toddlers feel loved when they get what they want, when they want it, the way they want it. When they don't, they feel unloved; which amounts to a lot of the time. It has nothing to do with whether or not they are loved. It is a healthy stage of development. These are little people, feeling unloved and furious about not being loved, with no means of expressing themselves except by crying, screaming, and saying "No!" If they're ignored, scolded, ridiculed or punished when they cry, scream, or say, "No!," their un-loved-ness is proven to them, which makes them feel even more angry and full of the fear that they may not be cared for. This brings us to the second and third reasons for why young children often feel unloved.
- Not having their ideas, feelings, wants, and perceptions validated and respected.
- Being punished, ridiculed, shamed, and blamed.
- Life circumstances: sickness, accidents, acts of nature, emotional and or physical injury in the family or child, death in the family, new arrival in the family, stress at home or in a parent's job, parents fighting and yelling, divorce, poverty, or parents with poor self-esteem. The list goes on.
- Last, but certainly not least, young children are deeply intuitive and they are well aware of their birthright, which is unconditional love. That is to say, by their very nature, they are born to be loved.

When behavior problems arise, I use and recommend *The One Minute Scolding* (also printed under the title *Who's The Boss?*) by Dr. Gerald Nelson.[1] In this book, Dr. Nelson espouses

---

1. Nelson, Gerald E. *The One-Minute Scolding: the Amazingly Effective Approach to Child Discipline.* Xlibris Corporation, 2009.

his theory that the true meaning of discipline is learning. My goal when I discipline Hayden is to effectively teach him appropriate behavior; respect for himself, authority, others and their property; honesty; responsibility; and accountability. The concept of consequences, not that of punishment, is necessary for Hayden to have in order for him to learn.

For instance, when children first touch a hot stove, it hurts terribly, so they instinctively pull their hands away. Hopefully, learning takes place naturally, 'by consequences,' and they will never touch a hot stove again. Children do not like pain, yet it is their friend, sometimes their savior.

By keeping the perspective that the negative behavior Hayden exhibits is due to ignorance, fear, anger, or pain, I can focus on forgiving him; that is, loving and accepting him in and through his anger without becoming angry or retaliating. By doing so, I thereby free him of his anger, which greatly impacts his world.

When I engage in this kind of forgiveness, however, it does not mean I condone negative behaviors. I never do this. Never. Never. Never. Rather, this kind of forgiveness means that I do not return hurt for hurt, anger for anger, pain for pain. I do not hang on to the hurt, for example. Instead, I return understanding, acceptance, and love for pain, hurt and anger. This is the very model for redeeming love.

The One Minute Scolding[1] proposes an excellent method to use with children and their negative behaviors. It's based on acceptance and accountability rather than criticism and condemnation. Although a 'scolding' is the centerpiece of this method, it has none of the negative connotations we usually associate with that word.

Children do not like the one-minute-scolding because it calls them to accountability. According to this method,

1. Ibid.

414

when children engage in troublesome behavior, their parents have thirty seconds at the most to tell them how they feel about this behavior. Parents must speak in the first person present tense and deliver an 'I statement.' For example, while they look at their children and touch them gently, they are to say something like "I feel sad," "I feel angry," "I am so mad I would like to _____." Whatever is true, age-appropriate and fits the personality of the child addressed is permissible.

Then parents are to pause, breathe deeply a few times, hug their children, and say "You are wonderful and I love you. You are very smart. I know you can learn not to _____ (or to _____). I'm going to help you learn because I love you. Every time you _____ I'm going to scold you, because I love you. For children who are verbal, parents can add "Why am I scolding you? Because I love you!" The children I've worked with seem to have had, for the most part, little difficulty when I've told them I'm upset with them because this announcement has been accompanied with a hug and expressions of love and praise. Sometimes, kids will cry, push me away, and say "What are you doing?" or "Don't." They know they're guilty of breaking a rule, and they expect, think, feel they deserve punishment. In fact, they're anxious to get it over with. But they soon discover that there is no punishment, only love. They feel unworthy of love because they feel guilty. They may test and test. They want to know exactly how bad they must be in order to be punished. When they realize they are responsible for their behavior and that I will not tolerate it when it's negative, but neither will I respond in anger or punishment, their behavior changes, not because of fear, but because of love.

Now to a less esoteric, more practical definition of discipline:

- As the adult, I accept and love myself.
- I see life from my child's eye level.
- I validate his or her feelings.
- I share with them an 'I-statement' to let them know right away if they've done something that I feel is unacceptable.
- This statement is accompanied by hugs, smiles, and such additional statements as "I love you," "I'm proud of you," "I'm glad you're my child."
- I spend as much quality time as possible with the important children in my life, and do things they want to do.
- When I communicate with children, I respond from my adult not as a child or with 'should-statements.'
- When I deal with children, I do so from a position of personal integrity; my language and actions are consistent with each other.
- I recognize children as the important, valuable, intelligent human beings they are.
- When I make a mistake, I say "I'm sorry. I was wrong. Will you forgive me?"
- I act towards children with a consistently firm, loving, non-acceptance of negative behavior. For discipline, I use *The One Minute Scolding* or something like "I don't like _____, but thank you for telling me you're mad at me," both of which are effective ways of dealing with problem behaviors.
- It is never acceptable for a child to be aggressive, cruel, humiliating, or violent towards anyone or destructive with anything. Never.
- Aggressive children must be removed from other children and adults, not as a punishment, but as a consequence. Sometimes the attitude of the adult in charge (non-attachment versus anger) is the only difference between a consequence and a punishment.
- It is never appropriate to scold or punish a child who has made a mistake, been clumsy, or because of ignorance. If very young children throws blocks, for example, I will calmly tell them: "Blocks are for building. Throwing blocks is not safe; kids

who throw blocks can't play with blocks." If another block is thrown, I say calmly, matter-of-factly: "Blocks are for playing with. Throwing blocks is not safe. You threw blocks again so they have to be put away for now. May I help you put them away?

In general, I encourage kids to pick up after themselves. In the case above of children throwing blocks repeatedly, my focus is on the immediate consequence and the fact that I must stay true to my words: "Blocks thrown means blocks are put away."

Any time we allow ourselves to be side-tracked from our goal in order to become involved in a battle of wills as a diversionary tactic, we have lost, as have our children. Lost also are precious opportunities for growth and relationship building.

Unfortunately, my generation of mothers did their mothering when the current wisdom was that children needed to be punished in a very particular way—by breaking their wills. This was the definitive strategy of the day and was accepted as the proper, desirable, child-rearing practice. I'm sorry to say that this was at times my mind-set as a young mother.

Now, though, as an older "acting" mother—I am 73 years young—I strive to protect, nurture, and develop the wills of the children in my life. And I have come to see that breaking children's wills is tantamount to breaking their spirits, teaching them to seek and depend on external approval. My husband, Denny, weighed in on this issue with great wisdom when he said that breaking children's wills is teaching them to be dishonest.

I expect and usually receive appropriate behavior from children by modeling honesty, respect, acceptance, tolerance, dignity, understanding, and non-controlling love. They receive from me in return non-controlling love and respect for their feelings, ideas, dreams, and behaviors. I thereby 'discipline' them to set their wills towards honesty, respect, acceptance, tolerance, dignity, understanding, and non-controlling love of themselves and others.

Let's return to the case of children who throw blocks, in order to further clarify and refine. We were speaking of what to say when kids do this. My tactic has been to say something like "We will have to put the blocks away, since you threw one. I'm sorry we have to put the blocks away. But the rule about blocks is that they are for building. If you throw a block and it hits someone or something; that could hurt or break someone or something. I love you too much to let that happen, so I'm going to help you learn how to play appropriately with toys."

If children refuse to help clear the blocks after I've said this, and they pout or cry instead, I would then say, "Maybe you're mad at me for putting the blocks away?" A child's ensuing behavior—either screams, smiles, laughter, nodding—would indicate to me that I have guessed correctly with my question. If so, it's time to validate with something like "Thank you for sharing your madness at me." If the child in question is not *too* mad, I might say, "I might feel kind of sad too if I wanted to play with blocks and someone told me we had to put them away." Pause. My voice then softer, slower: "Maybe you're acting mad because you're feeling sad that the blocks have been put away. And maybe you don't want to feel sad—because it feels so yucky to feel sad—so you've chosen to act mad instead?"

At this point, it's common to see a child's countenance transform from mad back to the more basic feeling of sadness, which is honest, healthy, non-violent, and bonding; the latter, especially if you comfort them in their sadness. Anger, you see, is never a primary emotion. It's a cover-up for pain, sadness, fear or feelings of rejection. And all of these translate into, "I feel unloved. If you loved me, you wouldn't let me get hurt; if you loved me you wouldn't make me sad; if you loved me you wouldn't let me be afraid; if you loved me *you would let me do or have whatever I want.*" My goal is to go through the anger to the primary emotion behind it, to bring that emotion into the open, and finally, to affirm my love in the face of the child's pain, sadness, fear and feelings of rejection. Thus, my strategy replaces a negative situation with a positive, loving, bonding experience, while also eliminating the need for negative behavior.

It was not unusual for Hayden to have minor problems at school: maybe a kid said something mean to him or about him, or a teacher acted mean and grouchy to him. Eventually, he didn't get upset or act out about these situations because he knew he could come home, go to the 'Talk Chair,' get his feelings validated, and process the situation. Keep in mind, it was not necessarily the case that everything he indicated happened, *actually* happened. In other words, maybe no teacher was actually mean and grouchy towards him. However, if he said he was mad at a teacher, it was probably because she or he didn't let him do what he wanted to do, made him do something he didn't want to do, or sounded cross, which is what led him to feel this teacher was mean and grouchy, just as he often feels I am.

So, my first step in such scenarios (and of course even though he's not in school now, these sorts of things still pop up), was and still is to validate his feeling(s). Then we would sing the 'Mad Song' at the alleged offender, say Mrs. Jones, one of his teachers, for seeming mean and grouchy.

The next step would have been, in the case of Mrs. Jones, taking his school days as an example, to ask if Mrs. Jones had made him do something he didn't want to do; or if Mrs. Jones just sounded mean or mad. I also tried to relate to the feeling he had at the time, if possible, by 'remembering out loud' that I didn't like teachers to sound mean and grouchy, either. In addition, I always asked Hayden if he had been a brat. Sometimes he would indicate "Yes!" and start laughing. If this was the case, I would have validated that he must have had a problem if he had acted like a brat, because he is such a fine boy. Specifically, I would say, "I'm sorry you had a problem at school."

Now let us consider the option that his answer to my query about how he acted had been that he had not acted like a brat. If that was the case, I would have said something like,

"Maybe Mrs. Jones was tired, or didn't feel well, or was just having a bad day; maybe she sounded mean and grouchy just like you and I do when we're tired and don't feel well."

I would next have thanked him for sharing his feelings with me, then told him how much I loved him, and chances are that off he would have run to do his own thing. When he ran off, I knew that it was all over, truly over, and wouldn't affect his next day at school. In most cases, his teacher wasn't even aware that there had been a problem. I considered it at the time quite mature and emotionally healthy for a non-verbal, 18-year-old young man with severe autism, whose motor skills were that of a 1-year-old, to be able to manage his own behavior appropriately in the face of a misunderstanding at school, then come home and let me know he wanted to talk about it and process it with words.

You may be wondering how I can say that Hayden is nonverbal and can process things with words in the same breath. Remember that the key is that behavior is not just behavior. If you want a different approach to discipline with autistic kids and this intrigues you, how do you begin? Here is a beginner's to-do list.

- Understand and accept behavior as a kind of language. If you strongly believe that the behaviors of children are random, or that children are by nature rebellious, or that negative behavior is inherent in autism, this method of preventive discipline, however, will not serve you.

- Begin to look for the reasons behind behavior. Climb over to the children's side of the fence and see things from their point of view. If they don't come when you call, ask yourself the right question. "If I didn't come when I was called, what might I be thinking?" Or if they hit someone, ask yourself, "What might have been said or done that would have made me want to hit someone?"

- Become familiar—no, intimate—with, and accepting of, your children's sensory issues, the way they process language and reasons, and how they perceive the world. For example, suppose I had decided in the beginning that I simply wouldn't accept Hayden's rocking because most kids don't rock. Hayden's body, though, is hard-wired to rock. Therefore, I could have validated his feelings and declared prohibitions against rocking until the cows came home, but he still would have rocked. If I had expected him to see my logic, understand, it, and accept it because I had explained it, I would have been in for a rude awakening!

- Be aware, alert to, and accepting of your own feelings so you can be aware, alert to, and accepting of the feelings of the children in your life. If you are afraid of or uncomfortable with your own anger or fear, this will interfere with your ability to recognize and accept your child's anger and fear. If you had the misfortune of growing up in a dysfunctional family where feelings were not accepted, you can begin to affirm to yourself that all feelings are valid, but acting on some of those feelings is not appropriate. Consciously give yourself permission to feel whatever you feel. This may seem awkward and difficult, just as any new language is awkward and difficult to learn; it will get easier.

- Validate your children's feelings and your own. When you validate feelings, this doesn't mean you must agree with the premises upon which they are based. I can and often do validate that Hayden is mad at me because it seems to him I'm mean to him, even when I know I am not being mean to him. Recall that Hayden lives from the following: "If she loves me she'll let me do whatever I want. When she doesn't let me do whatever I want, she's being mean to me."

I know this is a constant in Hayden's behavior. I also know that whenever I make him do something he doesn't want to do, or I don't let him do something he wants to do, then he will feel 'unfaired-against' and unloved, it will seem to him that I'm being mean, and then he'll become mad at me. Still, I validate his anger because it is a real emotion that arises from his *belief* that I am mean, even when I *know* I'm not. However, if I have been mean and grouchy to Hayden, I need to acknowledge this and apologize for it.

- Allow children to express their feelings, or express feelings for them if they are non-verbal or unable to express themselves in other ways. I allow Hayden to scream his anger as loud and long as he wants to in a designated place. At home, his room is the designated place; away from home, his car-seat is the designated place. Also, when he expresses his anger, he's not allowed to be abusive or destructive. When he was young, Hayden often screamed for long stretches of time. It's now been decades since he's done that. I also express madness for Hayden via the 'Mad Song.'

Giving children something forbidden that they want to stop their whines, tantrums, or screams is a sure-fire lesson for them in, "How to get what you want by whining, throwing a tantrum, or screaming at the top of your lungs." Feelings need to be validated but not necessarily catered to. This warrants repeating: Feelings need to be validated, but not necessarily catered to.

- Parents are not responsible for their children's feelings, and children are not responsible for their parents' feelings. Parents do not need to make their kids feel loved or happy; indeed, they cannot. But they do need to love them and meet their needs to the best of their ability. Children are not here to make parents happy, but to be cared for by their parents. Happiness, in other words, is strictly an 'inside job.'

- We do our children a gross disservice by wanting, trying or needing to make them happy. The destructive thing about trying to make children happy is that it teaches them that happiness comes from without. But this is both counterproductive and a lie. Why? Because it dooms children to unhappiness for the simple reason that they don't really know where to find this happiness. If I try to make someone happy, all I will end up doing is setting up a negative symbiotic relationship: "I'll make you happy and you make me happy." But such a relationship cannot work. The most important thing to see here is that when children's needs are met, they will be happy.

- Consciously reduce the stress experienced by ASD children: help them express their feelings, give them choices whenever possible, and build stability and predictability into their lives.

- Also, become aware of your children's tacit rules. This is absolutely imperative because it will help you catch their frustration and process it before it erupts into destruction or aggression.

- Work at staying centered. Do not let yourself get hooked or let your child 'get your goat.' Also, don't let yourself be goaded into coming across as the resident disciplinarian or army sergeant by employing forceful expletives. These often end up coming across as dares. If I am out of control emotionally, it's practically a certainty that my child will either be out of control emotionally, or inwardly full of fear, pain, and self-hatred for making me mad. When we as ASD parents are centered and calm, we provide a calm center for our children to come back to, a place where there are no perpetual punishment cycles.

- Communicate clearly and specifically. What is an axiom, a "given" for you (that is, one of your tacit rules), may be illogical or even unintelligible to your child. In other words, if you tell some autistic children to stay in the yard, it might seem to them that you're speaking Greek! Your yard, surrounded by your fence, may well be a concrete concept for you, but very well may not be for them. It's possible that they may not know where their own bodies end, and here you are expecting them to know where your yard ends. A fence, if they have good motor skills, is just an obstacle to be surmounted in their search for boundaries.

However, the good news is that children with autism can learn to stay in their own yards. A fence is a well-defined, physical entity, which helps. So a good strategy for parents is to take their ASD children out and walk the fence line with them, telling them calmly as they walk along, "The rule is that we stay on this side of the fence; that side of the fence (parent points) is the Franklin's." They may walk their children up to the fence and say, "Fence says Stop." I think you get the idea—one way to have success with this is to make it into a game.

The next step can be, then, to let their children play in the yard while they stay and watch. If their children stop at the fence, they validate with something like: "You remembered 'Fence says Stop.' You're really smart!" However, if parents observe their children even so much as place afoot on the fence, they can say, calmly, "No fence... Fence says 'Stop'." Further, if their children's bodies in any way continue to touch the fence, parents can then say: "You have to go in the house because the rule is 'No fence'." This is not a punishment. It is a consequence. The difference is all in the attitude of the parent who says it. If parents are angry or emotional in any way through the process just described, their children will feel punished and compelled to balance justice. If the cessation of activity around the fence is clearly communicated as simply a consequence, the child involved may be angry about the rule and having to go in, but not angry that their parent has been angry with them. **Let the rule be the bad guy, not you for once!** If you are anger-free, this can happen, and worry not, children understand rules!

To further refine the rule, let's rephrase it this way: "We stay on this side of the fence, and the Franklins stay on that side of the fence, unless we're invited through the gate. Then I will take you." Children can be mad about the rule and at the county property assessor or whomever you give credit or blame to for property lines. Many autistic children can understand straightforward, generic rules and can experience straightforward consequences and learn from them. But if you, the adult, are angry, your anger must be matched by theirs in order for them to even the score.

"Time-outs" are often ineffective for kids in the autism spectrum. Why? Because, first of all, they are not straightforward consequences. Consequently, time-outs feel undeserved by kids so sentenced. Secondly, time-outs disregard the message that children's anger was meant to express. This leaves kids feeling unheard and angered-against. Thirdly, children who are over-stimulated may learn to act out when they want to get away from everyone. A child who acts aggressively needs to be away from other children whom they can hurt.

Children are actually quite forgiving, and tend not to hold grudges and pout once all the feelings relevant to any given situation are brought out into the open and dealt with. For instance, when I'm wrong, crabby, or otherwise inappropriate, when I've just plain goofed or forgotten, I tell Hayden, "I was wrong," or "I forgot," or "I behaved inappropriately and I'm sorry." Usually he'll laugh and clap when I own up to my own failures, because he already knows them. If he were to feel really hurt or unloved, he would make angry "eh, eh," noises.

It bears repeating that when I ask if he's mad about some mistake of mine, he usually indicates that he is. After all, he has a nest of tacit rules regarding my behavior: that I'm not supposed to be wrong, forget, be crabby, tired, etc. If I ask if he wants to be mad at me—and he usually does—I sing the 'Mad Song' until he's done being mad. If I am guilty, however, I ask his forgiveness, and he usually gives it readily. I will then add that I need to be more careful or understanding or whatever it is, and he claps and laughs his agreement. Either way, these strategies take negative situations and transform them into invaluable bonding opportunities for Hayden and I.

Once in a while, Hayden will indicate that he won't forgive me, and I understand I have hurt him deeply. So I'll say "Thank you for sharing with me that you're so mad at me and feel so hurt that you don't want to forgive me. Maybe you'll forgive me later and maybe you won't; it doesn't matter to me, because I just love you. I will love you forever even if you never forgive me. I just love you." After I say something like this, I typically end the conversation. Sooner or later, he'll come to me and hug me or reach for my hair if we're in the car, and I'll say "Thank you for the loving. Have you decided to forgive me?" So far—at age twenty-eight—he has always come back to me to clear the air. When he does, I thank him for his forgiveness, validate that in fact I did something that he felt very bad about, and I make a commitment to do my best to act in kind, loving, and considerate ways. He laughs and claps his agreement when I say this, and this tells me that the whole thing is over. These kinds of interactions with Hayden are basic to my method of discipline.

I should perhaps say that I consider this preventive discipline. A child who generally feels loved, valued, wanted, appreciated, heard, and respected will generally be loving, considerate, respectful and obedient and have few discipline problems.

Part IV
The Journey Expanded

When I let my mind wander and think about a utopian state, the inclusive community I see sits on many acres of rural land and has a large recreational, living, therapeutic, and teaching center—like a huge mall.

Also on the land are a developmental preschool, an elementary school, perhaps a middle school working in cooperation with the public schools, a nondenominational spiritual center, an auditorium with a stage, and a pond, small lake, or river. Much of the land is wooded and crisscrossed with inviting walking trails and respite stops especially suited for meditation. There are also orchards and an organic farm with livestock. These would provide supervised, gainful employment for adults who may well be dependable, yet incapable of thriving in hectic workplaces.

This farm, as my mind's eye sees it, at least partially sustains the community and at the same time provides companionship and recreation for its residents, as well as opportunities for them to take on and learn about responsibility. Along with the animals humanely and healthfully raised for human consumption, there would also be animals trained for providing support and therapy for their owners.

One component of the main complex would be an extensive recreation, therapy, exercise, social and community center, for professional observation and teaching. Not unlike a YMCA, it would be equipped with a water park, a dry play area, a grand amusement park, not to mention a sensory-motor-integration therapist's dreamland! A number of therapists will have contributed their expertise to create what is on the face of it an uber-play center that includes as many therapeutic activities as possible in the most inviting and enticing way imaginable.

For example, there could be a large ball pit with steps leading up on one side, but also a ladder and ramp for easier access from another level so that it can be utilized by kids along a spectrum of functionality. The play-therapy equipment would be color-coded, so that an activity aiding the vestibular system alone might be blue, and so on. The children who visit, based on their ability level, would assist in small ways in the care and maintenance of the facility, as a way of learning responsibility.

As I see it, the recreation center would also serve the greater community, so would be a place where people of all ages and abilities could interact in scenarios of play, work, teaching and learning. Young people with full functionality who live in the surrounding towns could earn membership to the recreational facilities by working there as lifeguards, companions, and custodians. And the whole place could serve as a therapy center for the surrounding community during school hours and as a youth and daycare center when school is out.

The library, which could be accessed from the recreation center, would offer computers to work on, study areas, literacy centers, as well as the traditional books, magazines, and resource materials. A wide array of musical instruments, recorded music, and recording equipment would be available to bring music, universally loved by children of all ages, to everyone who is able to visit the center.

The main complex would house 1-, 2-, 3- and 4-bedroom apartments to accommodate families living at the center temporarily while their children undergo evaluations, participate in learning experiences, and establish more appropriate behavioral patterns. Meantime, their parents could enroll in home-enhancement programs and receive emotional support, and much-needed rest and respite care.

Other apartments could be available for retired people who have a lot of love, expertise and wisdom to share in exchange for housing; they would be able to choose their volunteering schedules.

Of course, this center would provide healthy meals to accommodate all sensitivities and ethnic choices. Meals could be delivered to a family's apartment or could be taken in a dining hall. Family members would also have the opportunity to learn about specialty cooking if they are to continue offering special diets upon returning home.

Laundry and cleaning services would be available to family members in order to relieve them of some of the stressors of everyday life; they could then focus in a more relaxed and supported way on understanding, parenting, and otherwise helping their special-needs children. This is not a luxury: many of these children require one-on-one, 24/7 care. Classes on parenting, nutrition, the nature of disabilities, ways to create more appropriate play times, and group and individual therapy would also be available.

Traditional and nontraditional healers of all kinds— occupational, physical, music and dance, and neurodevelopmental therapists, communication and auditory training specialists, body and energy workers, those who administer Eastern modalities, etc.—would visit regularly to evaluate, treat, follow-up, and make recommendations for home-based programs. The center would even have a multi-place hyperbaric chamber.

This center of my making would serve as an education and training locus for professionals working with the ASD population. Assisted living and employment services would also be available for those aging on the spectrum.

Other special needs individuals would be welcomed too, including pregnant teens, for example, who would be encouraged to attend school to learn academic material they had missed, childcare, homemaking, and parenting skills. There would also be a therapeutic daycare center for adults who have had strokes or have Alzheimer's or Parkinson's; they would also have use of the neurodevelopmental programs used by ASD children. These disabled adults—while they are able—would lend their unique skills and wisdom to the community at large as resource people, companions, grandmothers and grandfathers, for kids who are there for evaluation and therapy.

In my mind's eye, this ideal, utopian center would be a non-profit facility, funded primarily through grants, volunteers, and in-kind donations and services. I would want it to serve as a model facility to be duplicated many times over throughout the land, where ever there is a need.

Think of it this way. At present, we have domed sports arenas with luxury accommodations for corporate fans. We also have elegant restaurants, beautiful homes, deluxe automobiles, designer clothes, trendy coifs, custom jewelry, sophisticated electronics, overflowing toy chest, and endless entertainment, all made and consumed in lavish devotion to the gods of materialism, conformity, narcissism, power, and addiction. These things are not wrong per se, but to our detriment they have become our masters. As it now stands, the needy and helpless of our society are ignored, and the beautiful, strong, rich, and famous are worshipped. This is a clear indication that we as a nation have gotten off track. Our children can be our leaders and role models for what I have just imagined, if we allow them to be.

Herbert Hoover said: "The moral fiber of a nation is demonstrated by the way it treats those in the dawn of life (the children), those in the evening of life (the aged), and those in the shadow of life (those who are sick and disabled)." If we blame government for ignoring the needs of the weak, it is incumbent upon us to remember that government is made up of individuals. When we as individuals care for, respect and honor the most helpless of our society in accord with the Golden Rule—which is followed by Hebrews, Christians, and Muslims alike—then governments will just have to follow suit.

Carolyn Hunsinger, 2016

Bibliography

Harris, Thomas A. *I'm Ok, You're Ok: A Practical Guide to Transactional Analysis.* , 1969. Print.

Castaneda, Carlos. *Journey to Ixtlan: The Lessons of Don Juan.* , 1972. Print.

Markovna, Nina. *Nina's Journey: A Memoir of Stalin's Russia & the Second World War.* Regnery Gateway, 1989.

McKean, Thomas A. *Soon Will Come the Light: a View from inside the Autism Puzzle.* 2nd ed., Future Horizons, 1994.

Raffi. "It Takes a Village." *Resisto Dancing – Songs of Compassionate Revolution*, Rounder Records, 1991.

Boone, Debby. "Me and My Blanket." *Hug-A-Long Songs*, J2 Communications, 1990.

Diagnostic and Statistical Manual of Mental Disorders: DSM-5. 5th ed. Washington, D.C.: American Psychiatric Association, 2013.

Individuals With Disabilities Education Improvement Act of 2004, 20 U.S. Code § 1400 (2004).

Fulford, Robert C. *Dr. Fulford's Touch of Life: The Healing Power of the Natural Life Force*. Gallery Books, 1997.

Grandin, Temple. *Thinking in Pictures: My Life with Autism*. Expanded ed., Vintage Books, 2006.

Levinson, Barry, et al. *Rain Man*. Santa Monica, CA: MGM Home Entertainment, 2004.

Metcalf, C. W., and Roma Felible. *Lighten Up: Survival Skills for People Under Pressure*. Basic Books, 1993.

Kaufman, Neil Barry. *Son-Rise*. Warner Comm. Co., 1976.

Simon, Peg. "The Road to HANDLE® Leads to Hope for Children with Neurodevelopmental Needs." Seattles Child, Aug. 2005.

Gray, John. *Men Are from Mars, Women Are from Venus: A Practical Guide for Improving Communication and Getting What You Want in Your Relationships*. HarperCollins, 1992.

Gray, John. *What You Feel, You Can Heal: A Guide for Enriching Relationships*. 2nd ed., Heart Publishing, 1993.

Grazer, Brian, et al. *A Beautiful Mind*. Willowdale, Ont: Distributed by Universal Studios Canada, 2002.

Palmer, Hap. "Walking." *Baby Songs Original*, Anchor Bay, 1985.

Palmer, Hap. "Hurry Up Blues." *Baby Songs- Silly Songs*, Anchor Bay, 2001.

Forbes, Bryan, et al. *The Stepford Wives*. Los Angeles, CA: Distributed by Columbia Pictures, 1975.

Made in the USA
Columbia, SC
28 March 2022